The Political Philosophy
of Alexander Hamilton

THE POLITICAL PHILOSOPHY OF THE
AMERICAN FOUNDERS
Garrett Ward Sheldon, Series Editor

Garrett Ward Sheldon, *The Political Philosophy of Thomas Jefferson*
Garrett Ward Sheldon, *The Political Philosophy of James Madison*
Lorraine Smith Pangle, *The Political Philosophy of Benjamin Franklin*
Jeffry H. Morrison, *The Political Philosophy of George Washington*
Jack Fruchtman Jr., *The Political Philosophy of Thomas Paine*
Michael P. Federici, *The Political Philosophy of Alexander Hamilton*

THE
POLITICAL PHILOSOPHY
OF
Alexander Hamilton

MICHAEL P. FEDERICI

The Johns Hopkins University Press
Baltimore

© 2012 The Johns Hopkins University Press
All rights reserved. Published 2012
Printed in the United States of America on acid-free paper
2   4   6   8   9   7   5   3   1

The Johns Hopkins University Press
2715 North Charles Street
Baltimore, Maryland 21218-4363
www.press.jhu.edu

Library of Congress Cataloging-in-Publication Data

Federici, Michael P.
The political philosophy of Alexander Hamilton / Michael P. Federici.
p. cm. — (The political philosophy of the American founders)
Includes bibliographical references and index.
ISBN 978-1-4214-0538-4 (hdbk. : alk. paper) — ISBN 1-4214-0538-5
(hdbk. : alk. paper) — ISBN 978-1-4214-0539-1 (pbk. : alk. paper) —
ISBN 1-4214-0539-3 (pbk. : alk. paper) — ISBN 978-1-4214-0660-2
(electronic) — ISBN 1-4214-0660-8 (electronic)
1. Hamilton, Alexander, 1757–1804—Political and social views.
2. Political science—Philosophy.   3. Political science—United
States—History—18th century.   I. Title.
JC211.H24F43 2012
320.092—dc23
2011046456

A catalog record for this book
is available from the British Library.

Special discounts are available for bulk purchases of this book.
For more information, please contact Special Sales at 410-516-6936
or specialsales@press.jhu.edu.

The Johns Hopkins University Press uses environmentally friendly book
materials, including recycled text paper that is composed of at
least 30 percent post-consumer waste, whenever possible.

CONTENTS

ACKNOWLEDGMENTS

AN AUTHOR WHO spends years on a book project has had the help of friends, new and old, and professionals, all of them instrumental in completion of the project. Phil Belfiore, vice president for academic affairs at Mercyhurst University, kindly lowered my teaching load so that it was possible for me to both teach and make progress on the book. In addition, without a sabbatical leave from my teaching duties I would not have had the time or energy to write a draft of the manuscript. During my sabbatical, I spent three months in Dungarvan, Ireland, writing nearly every day. My Irish friends, especially Tom Keith, provided respite from the chore of writing, and the beautiful countryside allowed me to regenerate each day and prepare for the task at hand. Earleen Glaser, Mercyhurst University archivist, helped me find suitable images of Hamilton for potential use on the book's cover. Gannon University graciously allowed me easy access to the twenty-seven volumes of Hamilton's papers, edited by Harold C. Syrett and Jacob E. Cooke, in the university's library.

During the long gestation of the book, I was assisted by editors at the Johns Hopkins University Press. Henry Tom guided me through the early stages of the process with the calm and professionalism that were the result of his decades of experience. He retired just as I finished the draft of the manuscript, and within a few months, he passed away. Working with such a talented and well-respected editor was a privilege. The project then passed to Suzanne Flinchbaugh, who helped me respond to a reader's criticisms and begin to fine tune the manuscript. The Press's peer reviewer was instrumental in keeping me true to my own principle of analyzing Hamilton without taking a stake in the centuries of debate about his legacy. Robert J. Brugger picked up the baton and has pushed me to the finish line. I am especially grateful to Anne Whitmore, a talented copy editor, who improved my prose with precision and humor. The series editor, Garrett Sheldon, provided an encouraging voice, as well as insight into the importance of religion in Hamilton's political ideas.

I am also indebted to my friends and colleagues who read parts of the manuscript or listened to my arguments with careful attention. Ryan Holston of Virginia Military Institute, Justin Garrison of Catholic University, and Jeff Polet of Hope College were especially helpful in this regard. Barry Shain made useful suggestions regarding historical sources. A conversation while walking with Don Livingston through Colonial Williamsburg reassured me that my reading of David Hume and his influence on Hamilton were on target. Jeffry Morrison encouraged me to pursue the project, and his book on George Washington in the same series was a useful guide. I am grateful to a group of historians who have, over the years, inspired me to deepen the historical dimension of my scholarship. Richard Gamble, Walter McDougall, John Lukacs, and Thomas Fleming are chief among these. While I have taken the suggestions of editors, readers, and friends to heart, the shortcomings of the book are my responsibility.

Finally, I thank my wife, Frances, and my daughters Libby and Amy. They were often the first to hear about new information I learned while conducting research. I knew I had pushed them a bit too far in my enthusiasm for the project when I suggested naming our female Boston terrier puppy "Hamilton" and was met with a resounding "Enough already with the Hamilton stuff!" It is my hope that one day my girls, as well as my students, will read the book and discover the remarkable contribution that Alexander Hamilton made to American political thought.

*The Political Philosophy
of Alexander Hamilton*

INTRODUCTION

HAMILTON'S SIGNIFICANCE

MAKING JUDGMENTS ABOUT historical figures is challenging, especially about someone like Alexander Hamilton, who was both ardently opposed and strongly supported in his own day and long after his death. Scholars have been debating Hamilton's legacy for more than two hundred years, and, because of these opposing enthusiasms, few have achieved a level of critical distance that allows for accurate and just analysis.[1] That his life and especially his political ideas continue to occupy the minds of scholars is a testament to the relevance of his political theory. In his day, Hamilton had a polarizing effect on American politics. It should not, then, be surprising that the same is true today. To cite just one example, a recent book by Thomas J. DiLorenzo, *Hamilton's Curse*,[2] aims to counter John Steele Gordon's earlier work, *Hamilton's Blessing*. The book titles play in opposite ways on a remark Hamilton made about national debt. As the titles suggest, one disparages Hamilton's views and policies, the other defends them. Both books trace recent economic policies and practices to Hamilton's political economy and political theory as a way of commenting on contemporary political issues. Rarely are scholarly or journalistic works on Hamilton's life or political ideas ambivalent.

It is easy to get pulled into the ongoing debates about Alexander Hamilton's place in American history and the validity of his ideas. These debates are often motivated by contemporary issues that relate, in one way or another, to Hamilton's political theory. No doubt, the reader will find that the analysis provided here includes judgments about Hamilton's contribution to American political and economic ideas, as well as his role in forming the early republic. Most of the analysis, however, is expository. It explains Hamilton's ideas without taking sides in the long-standing debate over his legacy. Consequently, readers of Jeffersonian inclination are likely to find the book too kind to Hamilton and readers of a Hamiltonian ilk are likely to conclude that it does not do him justice. Whatever conclusion one may draw about Hamilton or the analysis provided in this book, there is no doubt that he continues to be a central figure in debates over American identity, American economic and foreign policy, and the meaning of the American Constitution. It is in these central areas of American life that Hamilton's political theory is most salient and most interesting. It is because his politics and policies spoke, and speak, to such central issues that they were contentious in his day and continue to ignite controversy today.

One area of American politics that continues to demonstrate the influence of Hamilton's political theory and practice is constitutional law. *The Federalist*, the series of eighty-five papers written by Hamilton, James Madison, and John Jay, have been quoted in U.S. Supreme Court cases hundreds of times by a variety of judges.[3] The further removed from the time of the Constitution's writing the Court has been, the more it has used *The Federalist* for guidance in deciphering that document's meaning.[4] References to Hamilton's particular contributions to *The Federalist* in recent Supreme Court opinions are common. His remarks at the Constitutional Convention have also been cited by Supreme Court justices searching for the engendering intent of the Framers. For example, in her dissenting opinion in *Kelo v. City of New London, Connecticut* (2005), Justice Sandra Day O'Connor invoked the words of Hamilton to support her claim that the Takings Clause of the Fifth Amendment requires "public use" and "just compensation." She noted Hamilton's comment at the Constitutional Convention that "one of the 'great obj[ects] of Gov[ernment]'" was "'the security of Property.'"[5] Justice O'Connor might have quoted, with the same effect, Hamilton's *Federalist* 70 or 85, both of which express the responsibility of government to protect private property.

In *Hamdi v. Rumsfeld* (2004),[6] Justice Antonin Scalia quoted

Hamilton's *Federalist* 8 to clarify the Framers' understanding of liberty in times of war. He noted that Hamilton and the Framers were well aware of the temptation to suspend laws that protect liberty in circumstances that place security at risk. In a separate dissent in *Hamdi*, Justice Clarence Thomas quoted Hamilton's *Federalist* 23 to support his contention that national security is the first concern of the federal government, and he referenced Hamilton's *Federalist* 34 and *Federalist* 70 to support the argument that a strong executive is necessary to protect the nation. Quoting from Hamilton's *Federalist* 74 to support the sole organ theory, Thomas maintained that the presidency was designed to allow a single executive leader to conduct war.[7] In his dissenting opinion in *U.S. v. Lopez* (1995),[8] Justice Thomas cited Hamilton's *Federalist* 12, 21, and 36 to demonstrate that the Court's case law was out of sync with the Framers' original meaning of the word "commerce." Justice David Souter cited Hamilton's *Federalist* 80 in his *American Insurance Association v. Garamendi* (2003)[9] opinion, in which he argued that the president has the constitutional power to issue executive agreements with foreign corporations and that states may not interfere with such agreements.

Even when not acknowledged by Supreme Court justices, Hamilton's views have been apparent in Court opinions; examples include *Fletcher v. Peck* (1810) and *Dartmouth College v. Woodward* (1819), which pertained to the meaning of the Contract Clause, and *McCulloch v. Maryland* (1819), which sanctioned the incorporation of a national bank. Hamilton's influence on Chief Justice John Marshall, who presided over these cases, is well documented. Marshall's opinion in *Marbury v. Madison* (1803) is an important instance.[10] A recent book by James B. Staab, *The Political Thought of Justice Antonin Scalia: A Hamiltonian on the Supreme Court*, explores the philosophical similarities between Hamilton and Justice Scalia. Staab emphasizes the influence of Hamilton's political philosophy on Justice Scalia's view of executive power, including his support for a unitary executive that assertively exercises inherent and constitutional powers (both enumerated and implied).

The use of Hamilton's political ideas by Supreme Court justices is merely one indication of the relevance and practical importance of his political theory. More than two hundred years after his death, he remains one of the most influential American Founders.[11] His ideas are part of debates about public finance and public administration, especially the national debt and taxes, commerce, foreign relations, constitutional interpretation, executive power, political parties, and federalism. Few American statesmen can match Hamilton's intellectual potency, his breadth of knowledge, or his production of seminal policies. What makes such a claim even more remarkable is that Hamilton did not come to the American colonies until he was seventeen, in 1772, and he died prematurely, in 1804, at the age of forty-nine. In a bit more than three decades, Hamilton shaped American ideas and events in a profound way that makes knowledge of his political theory essential to understanding the development of the American republic, economy, constitution, politics, and national identity. His statesmanship and political theory have also influenced debates about the meaning of American democracy. He has come to represent a competing variety of constitutional government to the one associated with his bitter political rival Thomas Jefferson. Differentiating between Hamiltonian and Jeffersonian constitutionalism illuminates the theoretical divide between the two major schools of American democracy, which are engaged in an ongoing struggle to define the meaning of the American Revolution and the republic to which it gave birth.

HAMILTON AS POLITICAL THEORIST

There is a significant body of literature on many aspects of Hamilton's life but much less of it pertains to his political theory than to his biography, perhaps because Hamilton was not a "professional" political theorist or scholar in the way that Plato and Aristotle were political thinkers. He did not consciously write political philosophy as a dispassionate observer of political action; few political theorists ever do. Hamilton was drawn to the heat of war and politics, and he craved a role in them that suited his extraordinary talents and his penchant for organizational and administrative leadership. He was driven, in part, by the desire to prove himself worthy of a prominent place in the American ruling class, because his childhood was filled with tragedy and turmoil and left him without parents, disinherited, and, so he thought, stuck in a station far beneath his talents. His rise from these circumstances inspired him to support not privileged aristocracy or hereditary monarchy, though many said he did, but meritocracy or what some called "natural aristocracy."[12]

Some critics disparage Hamilton's contribution to political theory because they consider it the product of political necessity rather than philosophical reflection. Clinton Rossiter, a generally sympathetic critic, writes that Hamilton was "a shotgun political thinker who fired only under provocation and at scattered targets." It is, no doubt, true that Hamilton's political theory was inspired by the demands of crafting and promoting policies that he considered necessary for the development of the young republic. His *Federalist* essays are a case in point. They were created to accomplish a practical political objective, ratification of the Constitution in New York, and they were a reaction to arguments made by the anti-Federalists. Yet, does it follow, as Rossiter claims, that *The Federalist* is "a less satisfactory work in political thought than *Leviathan* or *The Social Contract*?"[13]

The primary purpose of political theory is to convey the truth of reality. While most great works of political theory reach a theoretical depth absent from *The Federalist*, not all such works considered to be among the classics of political theory, *Leviathan* and *The Social Contract* included, penetrate to the truth of reality. In fact, an argument can be made that *The Federalist* possesses greater theoretical clarity on the problem of human nature and government than Hobbes or Rousseau achieved. In short, Hamilton's political theory, as scattered and unsystematic as it may be, lacks the ahistorical abstractions that plague the works of Hobbes and Rousseau and give them, in places, more the texture of ideological fantasy or "second reality"[14] than of political philosophy. Though inspired by the political exigencies of his day, Hamilton's political theory has an enduring quality to it because, in responding to the transient affairs of politics, Hamilton addressed perennial problems of political life. It is true that Hamilton's political theory is not articulated in the typical manner one encounters in works of political theory, and there is no book written by Hamilton that encompasses the thrust of his political theory. *The Federalist* comes closest to a systematic work of political theory, and it is a coauthored compilation of newspaper articles that were published over the course of about a year. Apart from it, there is no work that serves as Hamilton's magnum opus and no book in which he consciously articulated his political theory, his writings fill several volumes. Consequently, scholars must mine his letters, speeches, newspaper articles, and public papers and reports to discover the various aspects of his political theory.

Another disparagement of Hamilton's political theory is that it is short on originality and little more than an integration of eighteenth-century intellectual currents galvanized by political exigency. Hamilton was not, like Plato, Hobbes, or Machiavelli, the founder of a new school of political thought. While some of his policies were bold and innovative, their underlying theoretical foundation was not particularly novel. What can be said about Hamilton's political theory is that it was a reconstitution of older ideas in new circumstances. He, like many of the American Founders, was searching for ways to make republican government comport with the ends of politics, a topic that he addressed in *Federalist* 9. His theoretical conception of how the American republic might avoid the failures of ancient republics represents more than mere nuances of republican theory; his theory of constitutional government was clearly distinct from that of Jefferson, Thomas Paine, Benjamin Franklin, or even James Madison.[15] The development of American constitutionalism and republican theory owes much to Hamilton, especially in the areas of executive power, judicial theory, and constitutional interpretation. He was not merely the political leader of the Federalists but their intellectual leader as well. His contribution to constitutional theory and republican government tends to be obscured by the common charge that he was in favor of hereditary forms of government.

Discerning scholars have been able to get beyond critics' vituperations and polemics to identify the substance of Hamilton's constitutional theory. The divide between contrasting traditions and theories of American constitutionalism examined by, among others, Irving Babbitt nearly a century ago and Claes G. Ryn three decades ago is marked by Hamilton's political theory on one side and Jefferson's on the other.[16] In particular, Hamilton developed an understanding of constitutional government based on a moral realism[17] that opposed the populist and often romantic sentiments that characterized the political theory of Jefferson and Paine. The general distinctions made by Babbitt and Ryn do not obscure important differences between Hamilton and other advocates of moral realism, like John Adams and Madison. Hamilton shared with Madison theoretical assumptions about human nature and democracy, but his preference for a strong and energetic executive and his broader theory of constitutional interpretation set his political theory apart from Madison's.[18] Likewise, his desire for a substantial and professional standing army contrasts with Madison's and Adams's skepticism about professional armies.

The American brand of constitutionalism, which synthesizes popular sovereignty, federalism, and aristocratic leadership, was the product of many minds. Hamilton played as prominent a role in this endeavor as any American Founder. That a system of government was devised that incorporated a democratic House of Representatives (that Hamilton ardently supported at the Constitutional Convention), an aristocratic Senate, a single independent executive without a term limit, and an unelected judiciary armed with judicial review was due in part to the necessity of compromise, but no one surpassed Hamilton in achieving a theoretical defense and justification of that system. For these reasons alone, Hamilton should be considered one of the leading American political thinkers.

In his proximity to and interest in political action, Hamilton was less like Hobbes and Rousseau and more like the statesmen-thinkers Cicero, Niccolò Machiavelli, and Edmund Burke, because his interest in political thought was inspired by the immediate concerns of political action and his specific role in American politics. This is not to depreciate Hamilton's political theory, nor to suggest that it ranks as high as that of Cicero, Machiavelli, and Burke, but to give it its proper texture. For him, political ideas were a necessary part of conducting politics; they were not an esoteric abstraction. He reflected on "how widely different the business of government is from the speculation of it" and the "energy of the imagination dealing in general propositions from that of *execution* in *detail*."[19] He deplored "mere speculatists,"[20] people who formulated their political ideas in abstraction, apart from the concreteness of historical experience and a realistic view of human nature. They are apt, he thought, to forge political ideas that are pernicious at worst and irrelevant at best because they fail to account for the historical particularities of the human condition. Hamilton wrote to William Smith, a member of Congress, in 1797, "Over-driven theory everywhere palsies the operations of our Government and renders all rational *practice* impossible."[21] Yet, he was equally wary of individuals, like Aaron Burr, who, having no general principles or theory, operated merely on self-interest and lust for power.[22] When Hamilton was forced by the circumstances of the 1800 presidential election to choose between Jefferson, the abstract idealist, and Burr, the self-serving opportunist, he chose Jefferson. In this case, as in many others, Hamilton saw the alternatives of politics to be the lesser of evils. Jefferson was preferable to Burr because, as misguided as his political theory might be, it nonetheless was directed toward the common good. He predicted that the realities of governing would force Jefferson to abandon, to some degree, his abstract doctrines and serve the public good as prudence required, but that Burr, by contrast, did not aspire to anything higher than self-aggrandizement. In this distinction, Hamilton may have judged Jefferson and Burr correctly, but he may also have underestimated the destructive capacity of misguided or humanitarian conceptions of the public good. Jefferson turned out to be far less idealistic in the conduct of presidential politics than he was as a speculative philosopher. In the hands of a later idealist, Woodrow Wilson, however, abstract theories were not tempered by the exigencies of governing but exacerbated by them.[23]

In deploring "mere speculatists," Hamilton may also have underestimated the value of philosophical insight and the importance of philosophical distinctions. He seems not to have considered the distinction between theories that illuminate reality and those that obscure it, but his own political theory implies and makes such distinctions. In short, Hamilton himself engaged in theoretical analysis while disparaging abstract philosophy and offering in its place experientially grounded ideas. This side of Hamilton's political philosophy is easily missed, because his criticism of abstract, and especially Jacobin, speculation tends to be so broad in scope that it disguises the fact that he was simultaneously offering alternative theory. Hamilton's political philosophy encompasses a different kind of theory, one that is firmly grounded in the very reality of experience that he used as the foundation for his political thinking. He engaged in theoretical speculation of a sort. For example, he distinguished between the "true politician" and the "political-empyric."[24] He did not consider the distinction to be philosophically speculative because it was, to his thinking, sufficiently grounded in historical experience, meaning that the concepts reflected personality types found in the historical record and in his first-hand political experience. His tendency, however, was to apply theoretical insights not to produce them. In a qualified sense Hamilton, like Machiavelli, was a pragmatist or a historicist, if by those terms is meant one who believes that the validity of ideas is determined by their verification in historical experience. This is not to say that Hamilton believed that history was the universal or the determinant to the point of obliterating free will. His political theory implies, as do Machiavelli's and Burke's, that universality is discovered in historical particularity. When he complains about theoretical speculators, he means that their ideas are insufficiently grounded and unverifiable in historical experience. They are, to use different terms, idealistic, romantic, and ahistorical.

In Hamilton's weaker moments he let political divisions obstruct the process of philosophical search. He was not closed-minded or ideological as much as he was distracted by political objectives that tended to push philosophical insight only as far as was warranted by the immediate political struggle. He had difficulty seeing beyond the immediate political exigencies. Hamilton's intellectual vista was usually confined by politics in a way that precluded metaphysical, epistemological, and ontological questions. He was interested primarily in the things of Caesar and far less in the things of God and the things of Apollo.[25] His political thinking shares common ground with but never ascends to the level of Cicero or Burke because it lacks both the range and the depth of theirs. This shortcoming is due partly to his premature death and partly to his tendency not to connect political and economic aspects of life to aesthetical or ethical considerations. Not surprisingly, given when he lived and the work he did, the political and economic were usually primary, other things were tangential. Cicero, by contrast, wrote about such topics as old age, beneficence, and *homonoia*; Burke wrote about the sublime and the beautiful. These topics are outside of Hamilton's theoretical range or are superficially considered, and consequently his conception of the good life does not encompass the depth of analysis found in thinkers like Cicero and Burke. He enjoyed music and the arts but they were not significantly integrated into his intellectual life, and his early death deprived him of the opportunity to meditate on old age and the sublime. He wrote about government and political economy and little else.

Hamilton's political theory was enriched and influenced by the events and issues of his day, and he was by no means immune from the compromising effects of partisan politics. His judgment regarding the prudence of placing and exercising power changed when the presidency passed from George Washington to John Adams and then to Jefferson. Few human beings avoid some degree of hypocrisy and inconsistency, and Hamilton is no exception, but he remained steadfast in what he considered the foundations and principles of politics. His inconsistency was in how he applied those principles to situations that affected the fortunes of his political party or his public life. When the reins of government rested in Washington's hands, with Hamilton by his side, power was safely vested and could be extended to its constitutional apex. When Washington handed the reins to Adams and he in turn to Jefferson, Hamilton was significantly less sanguine about power and tended to view its appropriate scope as closer to its constitutional nadir. The analysis provided in this book accounts for the influence of partisan prejudice and aims to penetrate beyond it in order to illuminate the core and meaning of Hamilton's political theory.

In most instances, Hamilton thought about political and economic ideas in the course of searching for ways to bring order to the early American republic that he worried was slipping toward disorder and anarchy. He was conservative in the sense that he regarded order as the first concern of politics and thought that the human condition was such that man's hold on order was always precarious. His imagination was not inspired by a progressive historicism that promised an end to the tension between order and disorder, good and evil, justice and injustice. Like Machiavelli, he believed that order was especially perilous when newly established. Anarchy and Jacobinism were constantly challenging the newly established order in the United States, requiring statesmen to keep vigilant watch for signs of demagogues ready to ignite popular passion against governmental order. The persistent, and he believed permanent, threat of tyranny led Hamilton in *Federalist* 1 to question "whether societies of men are really capable or not, of establishing good government from reflection and choice, or whether they are forever destined to depend, for their political constitutions, on accident and force."[26] He held high hopes for the establishment of the Constitution and for America's future, but in moments of despair he worried that the nation's history would be short-lived.

While Hamilton came to believe that American independence was necessary—according to some of his biographers it was the very opportunity by which he hoped to escape his meager and broken life and rise to the level of his talents and abilities—he feared that war would unbridle the worst parts of human nature. It was one thing to rise in rebellion and throw off the shackles of an oppressive tyranny and another to replace the conventional order with a just and viable system. Tearing down was easier than building up. Consequently, he was vigilant against disregard for civil and social authority that might lead to anarchy. To his way of thinking, order was not something that existed spontaneously from the natural goodness of human nature or from the mere architecture and organization of government; it had to be cultivated, especially by natural aristocrats and the prudent administration of government. Governments could not run by themselves. In extreme cases, order had to be imposed by the force of state power. In this regard, Hamilton's view was similar to Locke's, which noted the need for executive prerogative in circumstances that challenged the fundamental interests or existence of the society.[27] That Hamilton shared common ground with Locke does not mean that he was Lockean on all matters related to human nature and political order. Locke suggested that order was ahistorically derived from abstract principles of natural rights and from a government that was made viable by the consent of the governed, regardless of historical contingency. He also touted a right to revolution that was far too perfunctory for someone with Hamilton's reservations about the masses and insistence on the primacy of order. Beneath the thin veneer of societal order, Hamilton believed, lay the potential for chaos and disorder. To strip away the former was to give license to the latter. Anarchy was the tyranny of the mob, but it also ripened society for another type of tyranny, namely the rule of demagogues and tyrants.[28] It was largely on this theoretical ground that Hamilton opposed the French Revolution and instances of domestic upheaval like Shays's Rebellion, the Whiskey Rebellion, and Fries's Rebellion. Jefferson, whose philosophy shares far more theoretical ground with Locke than does Hamilton's, was inclined to support rebellions and revolutions.

Even though Hamilton quickly sided with the patriots after arriving in America, he was highly critical of patriot mobs and the Sons of Liberty because they took the law into their own hands in seeking vengeance against Loyalists. Washington was appointed by the Continental Congress and his army was funded and under the political control of Congress and state governments, but the Sons of Liberty existed outside the boundaries of the rule of law and constitutional restraints. Hamilton came to the defense of his King's College president, Dr. Myles Cooper, a Tory, when an angry armed mob tried to seize him, probably with the intention of tarring and feathering him. Hamilton addressed the crowd long enough to allow Cooper to escape. One account of the incident has Hamilton saying to the crowd that their behavior would, "disgrace and injure the glorious cause of liberty."[29] He was especially critical of Isaac Sears's raid on New York, in which a vigilante mob composed of Connecticut rebels kidnapped and jailed the Reverend Samuel Seabury, whom Hamilton had debated in print. Sears also tried but failed to capture James Rivington, a New York Tory printer of the *New-York Gazetteer* who later provided valuable military intelligence to George Washington during the War for Independence. Sears and the Sons of Liberty responded to criticism of their tactics published in the *Gazetteer* by destroying Rivington's presses and property. Hamilton was moved by the experience. At this early point in his American life, he made up his mind on several points that would become the foundation for his political theory. In a letter to John Jay he called Sears's raid an "evil" while admitting: "I am fully sensible how dangerous and pernicious Rivington's press has been, and how detestable the character of the man is in every respect." Yet he felt obligated to condemn the behavior of Sears and his men.[30] Hamilton's reasons reveal important aspects of his political thought in its embryonic state.

> In times of such commotion as the present, while the passions of men are worked up to an uncommon pitch there is great danger of fatal extremes. The same state of the passions which fits the multitude, who have not a sufficient stock of reason and knowledge to guide them, for opposition to tyranny and oppression, very naturally leads them to a contempt and disregard of all authority. The due medium is hardly to be found among the more intelligent, it is almost impossible among the unthinking populace. When the minds of these are loosened from their attachment to ancient establishments and courses, they seem to grow giddy and are apt more or less to run into anarchy. These principles, too true in themselves, and confirmed to me both by reading and my own experience, deserve extremely the attention of those, who have the direction of public affairs. In such tempestuous times, it requires the greatest skill in the political pilots to keep men steady and within proper bounds, on which account I am always more or less alarmed at every thing which is done of mere will and pleasure, without any proper authority. Irregularities I know are to be expected, but they are nevertheless dangerous and ought to be checked, by every prudent and moderate mean. From these general maxims, I disapprove of the irruption in question, as serving to cherish a spirit of disorder at a season when men are too prone to it of themselves.

He added that it was further evidence of the inclination to anarchy that citizens of one state felt at liberty to meddle in the affairs of another state. Connecticut's encroachment on New York would likely increase the existing animosities between them and between New York and New England, he said. It would also send the message that New Yorkers were "disaffected to the

American cause." In short, rather than uniting patriots, Sears's raid would likely divide them. What he most feared was the encouragement of an "ungoverned spirit" that would not only jeopardize the American cause but breed a type of citizen that would refuse to be governed under any circumstances.

These were not the thoughts of revolutionaries like Paine, Jefferson, or even Locke who tended to be somewhat idealistic about revolution. They are more akin to Edmund Burke.[31] Hamilton's ideas reveal a conservative prejudice for order and the role that "ancient establishments" play in its cultivation and preservation.[32] As he witnessed the birth of the American Revolution and the formation of its political institutions, Hamilton did not see, as Paine did, the coming of a new age in which the order of being was transformed. He was, rather, concerned with the enduring problem of orderly government of a society of individuals who were imperfectable because of their fallen nature. At a mere twenty years old, Hamilton stood this theoretical ground, and for the remainder of his life he never relinquished it. It is this side of his political thought that is most consistent with the ancient and Christian tradition of moral realism.

Most of the literature on Hamilton attempts to place him in a particular tradition or ideological category (e.g., nationalist, libertarian, conservative, classical liberal, classical republican, Whig). As will become apparent in the following pages, Hamilton's political theory does not lend itself to easy or clear classification. When it does fit into a category, it rarely fits neatly. No doubt, one reason Hamilton's various admirers, critics, and biographers have come to widely diverging conclusions about his political theory is its enigmatic quality. Hamilton's political theory can be explained without forcing him into categories that obscure or exaggerate it, yet classifying his political ideas is unavoidable, because the work of political theory requires distinctions, classifications, and definitions. In evaluating Hamilton's political theory, for example, it is necessary to more carefully scrutinize such concepts as nationalism, democracy, realism, empire, and capitalism than the existing literature does.

Too often Hamilton is placed in a commonly used category that is itself in need of distinction and differentiation—nationalist. It is easy to forget that the meaning of words can change over time.

Calling an American a "nationalist" today brings with it more than two hundred years of history that includes the rise of totalitarian nationalism and democratic imperialism, political phenomena unknown to Hamilton. If he is classified as a nationalist, it should be with carefully qualified attention to historical context and typological differentiation. Chapters 2 and 5 provide more detailed analysis of Hamilton's nationalism and place it in the context of his arguments for ratification of the Constitution and his theory of international relations.

The same qualifications should be applied to discussions of the "antidemocratic" nature of his political theory, which is discussed in chapters 3 and 4, and of his support for capitalism, discussed in chapter 6. Hamilton was generally in favor of free markets and private property, yet he did not hesitate to argue for some degree of governmental regulation of trade, commerce, and industry, including the development of taxes and the use of bounties. He generally opposed tariffs and any policies that interfered with the free exchange of goods between nations, and he adamantly opposed using trade sanctions as an instrument of foreign policy. His political economy is largely a synthesis of free market economics and mercantilism.

In foreign affairs, Hamilton was generally a realist but not of the amoral variety. National interest was the focus of his foreign policy views, but they incorporated conceptions of honor and respect for the law of nations, one of several features his political theory shares with Cicero. He was in favor of a standing army, not as an instrument of imperial expansion or militarism, but as a means of defending the fragile republic from the empires of Europe. In many cases, Hamilton had to overcome deep-seated cultural prejudices in others when trying to promote his view of the public good. Standing armies, for example, were generally regarded as instruments of monarchies and oppressive governments that needed to suppress their people. Republics, by contrast, were thought to be guided by popular sovereignty and to avoid the demands of imperial expansion and subjugation. Standing armies were not only inimical to republican liberty but they placed a tax burden on the people. Hamilton's support for a standing army was based on the practical exigencies of late-eighteenth-century America. The European empires of England,

France, and Spain were all present in North America and they all desired expansion of their territory. Conflicts with imperial powers and Indians were inevitable as American settlers advanced the geographical perimeter of the nation. Hamilton knew that these circumstances required a professionally trained and ready military force, but he was not blind to the danger that available military power posed to civilian political rule.

HAMILTON'S PERSONALITY AND CHARACTER

Hamilton's personality and temperament are not the focus of this book, but they naturally factor into assessment of his political ideas. Even from his early days in the West Indies, he seems to have been in a hurry, as if he knew that his life would end prematurely and he wished to squeeze as much accomplishment into it as possible. Although he suffered from a variety of physical ailments (e.g., yellow fever, malarial infection, rheumatic pains), he was rarely at rest. Shortly after he arrived in the American colonies, Hamilton petitioned John Witherspoon, the president of the College of New Jersey at Princeton, for permission to advance through his coursework as quickly as possible. He was eighteen years old at the time but, although a young man of tremendous intellectual ability, he was in a rush to advance his career. An extensive and deliberative course of study did not suit his temperament or his ambitious disposition; political ideas were important to him as part of the challenges of social and professional advancement, not principally as subjects for contemplation. He was not disposed to live the contemplative life; unlike Plato, he did not wish to forgo the life of politics to devote himself to the intellectual life. Throughout his life, however, Hamilton engaged in reading, writing, and contemplation. His remarkably strong work ethic allowed him to harmonize his practical life as a soldier, statesman, and attorney with his intellectual life. For example, while encamped with the army at Morristown, New Jersey, in 1779–80, he wrote his six-thousand-word "Letter on Currency."[33] Throughout the Revolutionary War, Hamilton used blank pages of a pay book to take notes on his readings of Malachy Postlethwayt, Cicero, Demosthenes, and Plutarch.[34]

Because of this style of intellectual life, his political ideas have to be teased out of his writings and one has to be aware that Hamilton was often writing not to explicate philosophical truth but to accomplish a political objective. At the same time, one must be careful not to read too much into Hamilton's motives. Much of his work can be taken at face value. In fact, his contributions to *The Federalist* are important pieces of political theory apart from what may be hidden meanings or political motives. They stand on their own as insights into a constitutional system that Hamilton may not have fully embraced but which he helped create and defend. In some respects, it could not have been any other way. The Constitution was the product of many minds, and many probably agreed with Franklin's statement at the conclusion of the Constitutional Convention: "I agree to this Constitution, with all its Faults . . . because I think a General Government necessary for us, and there is no *Form* of Government but what may be a Blessing to the People if well administered . . . I doubt too whether any Convention we can obtain, may be able to make a better Constitution."[35]

In a similar vein, Hamilton was reported by Madison to have expressed his full support for the Constitution with some qualification: "No man's ideas were more remote from the plan than his were known to be; but is it possible to deliberate between anarchy and Convulsion on one side, and the chance of good to be expected from the plan on the other."[36] Comments like this one tend to obscure Hamilton's political ideas and motives as well as create a seeming inconsistency between his political ideas and his political actions. Franklin could make such a statement without his affection for American or republican government being questioned by future generations. This trust in Franklin's patriotism exists even though he came late to support for independence. Franklin favored reconciliation with Britain and generally admired the British political system. Hamilton was quick to take up the American cause, but unlike Franklin, he was not a known advocate of the common man or opponent of aristocratic pretense. Franklin's roughish antics (e.g., wearing a coonskin hat at the French court), had an endearing effect on those Americans who resented the high culture of Europe. By contrast, Hamilton was an impeccable dresser and was comfortable in the company of the most lofty elites. Biographer Ron Chernow writes that Hamilton "aspired to the eighteenth-century aristocratic ideal of the versatile man conversant in every area of knowledge" and notes his observance of fashion, his use of a French tailor, and his attention to the appearance of his hair.[37] When serving as inspector general during the Adams administration, Hamilton went to great pains to design in intricate detail the uniforms for General Washington and other officers.[38] Although his financial lifestyle and his upbringing paled in comparison to those of Jefferson and Madison, Hamilton's deportment and sense of decorum were more refined than theirs. These traits, combined with his preference for a government that contained features of monarchy and aristocracy and his encouragement of entrepreneurs and financial investors, caused Hamilton to be viewed with suspicion by Americans who shared with Jefferson an affinity for the virtues of populist simplicity. Even in the scholarly literature on Hamilton, one finds a disapproving undercurrent for what is perceived as aristocratic pretense.

Hamilton accepted less than he desired when it came to the Constitution, but in most instances he was dogged in his pursuit of his political objectives. He won the day in promoting the assumption plan and the national bank in part because he outhustled his opponents; his industry and determination were beyond the capacity of his opponents. Fortitude did not ensure him victory in every instance; it often deepened the opposition's resolve to smear his reputation. In reflecting on this aspect of Hamilton's character, Jefferson wrote to Madison, "Hamilton is really a colossus to the antirepublican party. Without numbers, he is an host within himself."[39] Jefferson knew as well as anyone that Hamilton was a formidable opponent because of this combination of intellectual acumen and industry. In most cases while the two of them served in the Washington administration, the president chose Hamilton's view over Jefferson's. One telling example of the contrasting styles of Hamilton and Jefferson was their respective reactions to President Washington's request in 1793 for advice and information on the expanding war in Europe. Washington was out of town attending a family funeral and sent word to Secretary of State Jefferson to prepare a plan for conducting American neutrality. According to historian Forrest McDonald, on the president's return, Jefferson "greeted him with nothing more tangible than a stack of routine correspondence." By contrast, Hamilton

> moved as vigorously as Washington had. Without waiting for the president's orders, he had reacted to the news from Europe by inducing Jay to prepare a draft of a neutrality proclamation. He had also begun to sound out popular opinion regarding the war by writing to friends around the country, and had begun to sketch the first of a series of essays designed to convince the public of the importance of neutrality. When Washington arrived, he drew up a list of thirteen questions to guide cabinet discussions. Washington submitted those questions to the cabinet as his own.[40]

Hamilton's industry in reacting to the European war was typical of his conduct as treasury secretary; once appointed by Washington to the post, he hit the ground running and never looked back. Jefferson, by contrast, took months even to decide if he was going to accept Washington's appointment as secretary of state. When Jefferson arrived on the scene, he found that Hamilton had been shouldering many of the secretary of state's duties on top of his own. During the crisis with France in 1793, Hamilton, as was his wont, took to his pen in defense of Washington's neutrality proclamation. Writing as "Pacificus," Hamilton took the lead in making the case for neutrality. Jefferson, frustrated by Hamilton's seeming sway over Washington and American policy, complained to Madison, "[N]obody answers him," and pleaded, "[F]or God's sake . . . take up your pen, select the most striking heresies and cut him to pieces in the face of the public."[41] As Madison was to learn, taking on Hamilton was no small task. The secretary of the treasury was not only quick and prolific with his pen, but sharp in detail and argument. His rhetorical skills were enhanced by his work as an attorney in New York, where he was considered a master at oral argument and persuasion. Hamilton's operating speed seemed to require a gear that most of his contemporaries, including Madison and Jefferson, did not possess. The merit of his arguments should be judged not by their quantity or the rapidity of their production but by the soundness and theoretical clarity of their substance. While Hamilton could engage in polemics with the best of his age, at his best he was also as theoretically penetrating as any Founding Father.

INFLUENCES ON HAMILTON'S POLITICAL THOUGHT

A study of Hamilton's political theory must trace his intellectual genealogy, in order to provide some sense of its origins and pedigree. Contrary to the prevailing interpretation of Hamilton, which classifies him primarily as a modern Enlightenment thinker, I argue that his political theory incorporates Classical, Christian, and modern ideas. A variety of thinkers influenced him, both ones with whom he agreed and ones whose ideas he opposed. Hobbes, for example, was more of a foil for him than a support. Hamilton, like Hobbes, was sober minded in his political thought, but not in the same way, to the same degree, or for the same reasons. He was suspicious of Jacobin idealism and realistic about the human condition without engaging in Hobbesian or Machiavellian amoralism. At the Constitutional Convention, he argued that most human beings are governed by their passions, the primary ones being ambition and self-interest. If one paints with too broad a brush, it is easy to color Hamilton's political theory as "realism" while failing to differentiate between types of realism.

Many critics are guilty of impressionistic coloring of Hamilton's ideas. Being predisposed to idealistic conceptions of human nature, they recognize similar traits in the political theory of Machiavelli, Hobbes, and Hamilton, but they fail to identify important dissimilarities that separate Hamilton from amoral realists. Without more refined distinctions, the following passage and others like it seem to verify that Hamilton and Hobbes share a theoretical pedigree: "One great error is that we suppose mankind more honest than they are. Our prevailing passions are ambition and interest; and it will ever be the duty of a wise government to avail itself of those passions, in order to make them subservient to the public good—for these ever induce us to action."[42] Placed in the whole of Hamilton's corpus, this passage conveys skepticism about the ability of virtue alone to support the public good, but it does not eliminate the need for it, especially in the ruling class of natural aristocrats.

Hamilton's religiosity is complex and requires distinctions between his personal piety and his theoretical beliefs. In one sense he was not a particularly religious man, but his political theory was sufficiently imbued with the Christian realism of his age, also reflected in European thinkers like Burke and Americans like Madison and Adams, that it shaped his view of man and society. *Federalist* 9 is important in identifying the texture of Hamilton's political theory because it synthesizes different traditions. What role his religious faith played in the development of Hamilton's political theory is discussed in chapter 1.

What is particularly intriguing about Hamilton is that most commentators portray him as an advocate of centralized power, nationalism, and even monarchy. He is the source, some say, of the desire for an American commercial empire that would make the United States a global power. One work that asserts this thesis is Stephen F. Knott's, *Alexander Hamilton and the Persistence of Myth*. While the Constitution does not provide the national government with the power to transform the nation from a modest republic into a global empire, Hamilton's loose constitutional interpretivism—loose constructionism—was the instrument for such a transformation. The national bank controversy is given as evidence in support of this thesis. Such arguments regarding Hamilton's constitutional theory must be measured against his comments in *Federalist* 78 and 81 and lesser-known instances in which he commented on the meaning of the Constitution and on the interpretation of laws and treaties. *Federalist* 78 and 81 define the role of the federal judiciary as guardians and interpreters of the Constitution. Hamilton rejected the idea that judges should either make law or change the meaning of the Constitution through the use of interpretation. In *Federalist* 78, Hamilton stated that the judiciary has neither force nor will but merely judgment; it is the weakest of the three branches because it is least in a capacity to harm the people or the Constitution, and being the weakest branch needs to be insulated from the president and Congress. The danger comes when judicial power mixes with legislative or executive power. Hamilton's theory of constitutionalism and the role of courts in the conduct of constitutional politics will be discussed in more detail in chapter 4.

Hamilton's reputation as an advocate of monarchy and empire is in need of reconsideration. On some occasions when Hamilton could have pushed the new nation toward military oligarchy (instances when it was most vulnerable to it), he did the opposite. In 1783 he opposed efforts by Continental Army officers to organize a coup. In that same year he helped to protect the Confederate Congress from an angry group of soldiers in Pennsylvania who intended to march on Congress in Philadelphia. What Hamilton advocated was a mixed government that incorporated aspects of monarchy, aristocracy, and democracy. At the Constitutional Convention, he pushed to make the House of Representatives more democratic by insisting on direct election of representatives in the House and requiring that individuals not be permitted to hold more than one office at a time.[43] In one often-maligned plan presented at the Constitutional Convention, he proposed that members of the national judiciary, senators, and a national executive serve for life, "during good behavior," but the senators and the executive would be elected.

Hamilton's imagination was shaped by the history of Greece and Rome; invoking ancient political leaders, he consistently used the heroes of republican government to support his arguments and likened his political rivals to the enemies of ancient republics. He chose "Publius" as the pseudonym for the authors of *The Federalist*, a name taken from Publius Valerius, a Roman republican known for helping to overthrow a king in order to establish a republic.[44]

The problem in characterizing Hamilton's political thought seems to be that he has been mischaracterized time and time again, both by critics who are sympathetic to Jeffersonianism and who cast him in the light of a monarchist and by twentieth-century American nationalists who are sympathetic to Hamilton but consider him the father of American empire. Both interpretations explain history in a way that justifies their particular ideology and tends to mischaracterize their ideological opponents as being on the wrong side of history. I have tried to provide a balanced, nuanced view of Hamilton, one that may be messy but is more true to his political ideas and life than any ideologically driven view. My intent has not been to neatly fit Hamilton's political theory into a category but to give readers a sense of its complexity and uniqueness. When necessary I have created new categories by which to classify Hamilton's political theory, or at least to clarify the meaning of existing categories. I began the project without a stake in Hamilton's legacy apart from a desire to accurately portray his political ideas. With that in mind, I approached the project with an openness that, I hope, has taken the argument where the evidence leads and avoided stilted categories that obscure rather than illuminate.

While some aspects of Hamilton's thought support the thesis that he tried to create an American empire governed by an imperial president, contrary strains of his political thought suggest that a more balanced view of Hamilton is required. For example, the Hamilton of *The Federalist* is not easily reconciled with the Hamilton who served as secretary of the treasury. Such inconsistencies are common in individuals who are both statesmen and thinkers. The challenges of governing often run counter to their previously articulated theoretical pronouncements. It is interesting that Madison and Jefferson were small republicans in their rhetoric, especially when opposing the Federalists, but once in power they tended to reverse course and favor more consolidated power. It was Jefferson and Madison, after all, who presided over the creation of the military academy at West Point, the Louisiana Purchase, the War of 1812, and the reauthorization of the second national bank.

Another example that counters the stereotypical view of Hamilton as centralizing nationalist if not monarchist is that he sought a more modest role for America in the world, one that was proportionate to her power and interests. Writing as "Pacificus," he cautioned against a Franco-American alliance, and his promotion of American power was not to assert American influence on the world but to protect her from outside threats, a position more in line with modest republicanism. In the context of the debate over involvement in the French war, Hamilton crafted arguments against the imperial designs of France that penetrate to the core of the issue of ideological empire. He wrote as "Americanus" in "The Warning" (January 1797) that France

> betrayed a spirit of universal domination; an opinion that she has a right to be legislatrix of Nations; that they are all bound to submit to her mandates, to take from her their moral political and religious creeds; that her plastic and regenerating hand is to mould them into whatever shape she thinks fit & and that her interest is to be the sole measure of the rights of the rest of the world. The specious pretense of enlightening mankind and reforming their civil institutions, is the varnish to the real design of subjugating them.[45]

Passages like those quoted here represent the theoretical richness of Hamilton's ideas and writings. The task of this book is to use them to illustrate and trace the core and complexity of Hamilton's political theory.

CHAPTER 1

THE PERSONAL BACKGROUND OF
A POLITICAL THEORIST

Hamilton was the supreme double threat among the founding
fathers, at once thinker and doer, sparkling theoretician and
masterful executive.

—Ron Chernow, *Alexander Hamilton*

THE FOCUS OF THIS book is the political philosophy of Alexander Hamilton rather than his biography. Before examining his
political and economic ideas, however, a brief review of the central events and experiences in his life is warranted. It is also necessary to provide some description and commentary on Hamilton's
imagination, insofar as it influenced his political theory. Hamilton demonstrated over the years an attachment to a particular
and consistent view of human nature, political institutions, history, and economics that defined his political philosophy.

In one sense, Hamilton's life (1755–1804) is divided into two
parts, his childhood in the West Indies and his adult life in
America. The latter was in many respects an escape from the
former, as his fortunes changed dramatically once he left his
boyhood home (to which he never returned) and settled in
North America. From a young age Hamilton was acutely aware
that his circumstances were holding him back from the better
life that he sensed he deserved. He longed for the opportunity
to pull himself out of his meager life, and he identified war as
one possible instrument. In his first known letter, written to
his best childhood friend, Edward Stevens, son of a St. Croix
merchant, he acknowledged, "[M]y Ambition is prevalent that I

contemn the grov'ling and condition of a Clerk or the like, to which my Fortune &c. condemns me and would willingly risk my life tho' not my Character to exalt my Station." He ends the letter, "I wish there was a War."[1] That Hamilton was determined to go to great lengths to improve his life reveals a penchant for self-reliance but also an appreciation for meritocracy and "natural aristocracy," the idea that virtue and talent, not birth, define natural leaders in society. Hamilton never used his childhood circumstances as an excuse for his shortcomings. His tendency was, rather, to ignore his early life and get busy with the work at hand. His biographers universally note his unusual industry, including his prolific writings. At times his drive and ambition coincided with impatience and even a rash disregard for civility, moderation, and modesty. He could be known to attach a level of importance and immediacy to his endeavors that was out of proportion to their actual significance. Especially during the Adams and Jefferson presidencies, he struggled to find his place outside the center of power, and he exaggerated the shortcomings of opponents' policies and character. His relationship with Adams was volatile, in part, because they shared tendencies toward vanity and impetuosity. He was at his best while at the center of power, with Washington, who had a moderating effect on Hamilton's impetuous tendencies and an ennobling effect on his sense of gravitas and seemliness.

HAMILTON'S LIFE

Alexander Hamilton's childhood was filled with hardship and instability. In 1746, nine years before his birth, his mother, Rachael Faucette, bore a son, Peter, with her husband, Johann Michael Lavien. She left Lavien and her son a few years after Peter's birth, and in 1759 Lavien was granted a divorce that prohibited his ex-wife from remarrying. Rachael had left St. Croix, a Dutch colony, in 1750 and set out for a new life in St. Kitts, where she met Alexander Hamilton's father, James Hamilton. Rachel and James's relationship lasted for about fifteen years and included the birth of two sons, James and Alexander. Alexander was born on the island of Nevis in the British West Indies. His birth date is uncertain, but 1755 is the date accepted by recent Hamilton biographers. At the time Lavien was granted the divorce from Rachael, Alexander was about four years old. By the time he was ten, James Hamilton had abandoned Rachael and the two boys. In 1768, when Alexander was twelve, his mother died of a sudden illness. Her meager estate was awarded to her first son, Peter Lavien, leaving the Hamilton boys disinherited and destitute. Peter Lytton, a cousin of the Hamilton boys, was granted legal guardianship of them. He committed suicide in 1769, shortly after taking in James and Alexander. Lytton had not provided for the boys in his will, so once again they were destitute and homeless. In his biography of Alexander Hamilton, Ron Chernow describes the situation at this point in James's and Alexander's lives: "Their father had vanished, their mother had died, their cousin and supposed protector had committed bloody suicide, and their aunt, uncle, and grandmother had all died. James, sixteen, and Alexander, fourteen, were now left alone, largely friendless and penniless. At every step in their rootless, topsy-turvy existence, they had been surrounded by failed, broken, embittered people. Their short lives had been shadowed by a stupefying sequence of bankruptcies, marital separations, deaths, scandals, and disinheritance."[2] From this point in Hamilton's life, his fortunes were tied to his employment by two New York merchants, Nicholas Cruger and David Beekman. The Cruger family traded a variety of goods, including slaves, and was involved in credit markets, shipping, and warehousing.[3] No doubt Hamilton's penchant for both administrative detail and economic affairs was developed while working for Cruger and Beekman. This experience was formative in his understanding of trade, currency, credit, banking, and politics.

Much of Alexander Hamilton's adult life corresponds to the formation of the American republic. His journey to the American colonies in 1772 at the age of seventeen, on the eve of the American Revolution, began a storybook political life. With the support of a Presbyterian minister, Hugh Knox and the consent of his employer Nicholas Cruger, Hamilton was sent to North America to receive an education. Knox was Classically educated at the College of New Jersey at Princeton; according to Forrest McDonald, he played a significant role in shaping Hamilton's moral imagination. "Knox inspired Hamilton with a religious piety that lasted for some time, impressed upon him the dangers of drinking to excess, and taught him to abhor slavery as the wellspring of many other evils."[4] Hamilton's prejudice against excessive drinking would evidence itself in his creation of the whiskey tax and the quelling of the Whiskey Rebellion. He would join manumission societies and with his friend John Laurens support the creation of a Negro army regiment that would have as one of its objectives the emancipation of slaves who fought for American independence.

Hamilton attended a preparatory school in Elizabethtown (now Elizabeth), New Jersey, with the intent of enrolling at the College of New Jersey (now Princeton). This study was necessary for him to meet the rigorous requirements for entrance to the college. Hamilton had had little formal schooling and needed time to hone his academic skills. While a student at Elizabethtown Academy, he studied Classics and the Bible among other subjects. After completing nearly a year of study, he met with the College of New Jersey's president, John Witherspoon, who gave him an oral exam and deemed him worthy of entrance. Hamilton immediately requested that he be permitted to accelerate his studies. Witherspoon took the matter to the trustees, who refused to grant Hamilton's request. Consequently, he instead enrolled at King's College, which became Columbia University after the American Revolution. There he studied politics, law, and political economy, after a brief flirtation with medicine. He was devout in religious observance while at King's. Later, as a soldier, he was also seen on his knees in prayer. Biographer Broadus Mitchell notes that after these reports of his religious activity, "no more is heard of his spiritual observance until near his death."[5] Hamilton never finished his degree, because he became captivated by the events that soon gave rise to the American Revolution.

His involvement in American resistance to British policies included writing pamphlets (*A Full Vindication* 1774, *The Farmer Refuted* 1775, and *Remarks on the Quebec Bill* 1775) and giving speeches supporting the American cause against Great Britain. His revolutionary activity was not blind or unqualified. On at least two occasions while a student at King's College, Hamilton opposed mobs led by the Sons of Liberty. In these cases, the attempted abduction of Myles Cooper and Sears's Raid, Hamilton was concerned that vigilante justice was replacing the rule of law. Keenly sensitive to the consequences of anarchy and the collapse of order, he knew a vulgar mob when he saw it, and he understood that its animating spirit would have to be tamed or the colonial rebellion would lead to disorder and injustices that would be worse than the oppressive British rule. In Hamilton's mind, resistance to England was not license to flout the limits of law and civility. Opposition should be inspired by the spirit of the law; creating a just order was the paramount concern.

His prose and his rhetoric gained him the attention of patriot leaders, which enabled him to secure a position as an artillery captain in the Continental militia and then as George Washington's aide-de-camp. As an artillery captain, he fought in the Battle of Brooklyn and soon after at White Plains, in the Battle of Princeton; he crossed the Delaware with Washington and fought the Hessians at Trenton. In June of 1778 he fought in the Battle of Monmouth, distinguishing himself by ordering a retreating brigade to line up, fix their bayonets, and charge the enemy so that their artillery would not be captured. In the melee of this battle, he was injured when his horse was shot from under him.[6] Hamilton became one of Washington's most trusted advisors and his chief-of-staff. He was at the battles of Brandywine and Germantown and helped uncover Benedict Arnold's treason. Consistent with his pattern of extraordinary effort, during the winter of 1777–78 he incurred serious illness after running himself ragged up and down the East Coast adjusting troop movements in the attempt to quell the British advance.

In the fall of 1778 he wrote for the first time as "Publius," taking to task Maryland congressman Samuel Chase for using intelligence about the French fleet's arrival in Philadelphia for personal financial gain. Chase had conspired with business associates to corner the flour market, hoping to reap great profits. This admonishment of another patriot's behavior is further demonstration of Hamilton's sensitivity to vulgar and unseemly behavior in individuals, in this case, an attempt to capitalize on the circumstances of war. He was consistently concerned with not only his own honor but that of others who aspired to assume positions of leadership.

His work on Washington's staff gradually became largely administrative. He tired of the job and longed for an appointment to a military command of his own. After a dispute with Washington in February 1781, Hamilton resigned from Washington's staff, but he pestered the general for months and in July 1781 succeeded in securing command of a New York light-infantry battalion, near the end of the war. As a field commander at Yorktown in October of that year, he distinguished himself by leading his men in a bayonet charge to seize a British redoubt. Once the British force had been overwhelmed, Hamilton restrained his troops from bayoneting their captured opponents. He was, even in the heat of combat, insistent that force be limited by laws of civility and honor that he regarded as immutable.

Shortly after he left the military, at the end of 1781, he was appointed by Superintendent of Finance Robert Morris to the office of receiver of Continental taxes for the State of New York, in which position he served until becoming a member of the Confederate Congress. During his eight-month membership, in 1782–83, he advocated holding a constitutional convention. Anticipating the need for political reform in the aftermath of the war, he wrote essays, as "The Continentalist," addressing the problem of union of the states and the insufficient power of the Confederate Congress. While serving in the Congress, he advised Washington to undermine a budding conspiracy among army officers at Newburgh, New York, in protest of nonpayment to the army. He did, however, suggest to Washington that he first let the officers' protest put pressure on Congress, an example of Hamilton's sometimes imprudent bravado.

Hamilton became a successful attorney (admitted to the bar in 1782) who was known for charging fees that were so low that he was considered by many to be "indifferent to money-making."[7] He often defended Tories who were being prosecuted under the New York Trespass Act. In one such case, *Rutgers v. Waddington* (1784), he made what may have been the first defense of judicial review in America and demonstrated an inclination to interpret law broadly by encouraging judges to exercise wide discretion. He wrote, as "Phocion," to oppose measures that would, he thought, treat Loyalists unfairly and drive them and their wealth from the state. In addition to his law practice, over time he was a member of the New York State Assembly, a journalist, a speechwriter, and a founder of the Bank of New York and the *New York Evening Post*.

Hamilton attended the Annapolis Convention in 1786 as a New York delegate (for which he wrote the call for the meeting in Philadelphia that became the Constitutional Convention) and the Constitutional Convention in 1787. He organized the writing, with Madison and Jay, of what became *The Federalist* and wrote more than two-thirds of the eight-five essays; he was a leading and tireless advocate of ratification of the Constitution. At the Pough-keepsie Convention, he again displayed extraordinary stamina and oratorical prowess, helping to win, by the narrowest of margins, ratification of the Constitution by the state of New York.

Hamilton was the first secretary of the treasury of the United States. During his tenure (1789–95), he devised a successful plan (the assumption plan) to solve the debt crisis, a plan that would solidify the union and empower the national government. By assuming debts incurred by states during the American Revolution, the federal government would have need to create a system of taxation and a national bank. The national bank would make assumption of states' debts possible and would provide the national government an instrument for distributing currency and incurring debt without depending on foreign banks and governments. In 1791, in response to a request by Congress, he wrote his *Report on Manufactures*. The report advocated the development of industry with the assistance of government policies like bounties, tariffs, and subsidies. The aim of these policies was union, national security, and economic prosperity. Economic development and national self-sufficiency were necessary, in order to protect, and to a degree insulate, the United States from the imperial powers of Europe. As treasury secretary, Hamilton's duties were not limited to economic affairs. He was engaged routinely in diplomacy with foreign nations and he advised Washington on foreign affairs, among them compliance with the Treaty of Paris, British occupation of western lands and British conflicts with American settlers migrating west, relations with the Indian tribes, navigation of the Mississippi River, American neutrality in the Napoleonic Wars, the Jay Treaty, and the treatment of American merchants and cargo by warring nations.

In 1794, while still secretary of the treasury, he donned his army uniform again and led nearly twelve thousand troops to western Pennsylvania to put down the Whiskey Rebellion, an anti–excise tax uprising, and in 1799 he helped to organize a combined force of federal and state troops to subdue Fries's Rebellion, an anti–property tax protest. During John Adams's administration, at Washington's insistence, Hamilton would serve as inspector general, second in command of the army.

His many duties did not keep him from his writing. He penned nine essays as "Pacificus" and "Americanus" in defense of Washington's Neutrality Proclamation (1793), besting his former political ally James Madison, who responded to his essays, writing as Helvidius. Hamilton's argument in these esssays is considered the origin of the sole organ theory, asserting unilateral presidential powers in foreign affairs, which was subsequently articulated by Secretary of State John Marshall in a speech to Congress in 1800 and solidified into case law by the Supreme Court's 1936 decision in *U.S. v. Curtiss-Wright Export Corp.*

In 1790 Hamilton was granted an honorary degree from Dartmouth College and later from Harvard, Columbia, Princeton, and Brown. He was elected to the American Philosophical Society in 1791. In 1793 a New York school designed by the Reverend Samuel Kirkland to teach Indian and white children was named after Hamilton (Hamilton-Oneida Academy), and he served as a trustee. After his death, the school became Hamilton College. His affiliation with a school for Indians was no accident. Hamilton consistently supported peaceful relations with the various Indian tribes and he counseled Governor Clinton in New York and President Washington to reconcile with them. Hamilton considered Indians and blacks to be equal members of the human race. He devised a plan to abolish slavery, an institution he had known from childhood (his mother was a slaveholder). No doubt his view of slavery was one reason many southerners viewed him with suspicion if not disdain. Hamilton was interested in the arts as well as education. He attended the theatre and purchased works by Albrecht Dürer and Andrea Mantegna.[8]

Back when he was encamped at Morristown, New Jersey, in

the winter of 1779–80, Hamilton met and spent considerable time courting Eliza Schuyler, the daughter of General Philip Schuyler. A year later they were married, on December 14, 1780. The marriage greatly bolstered Hamilton's social position, as the Schuylers were a prominent and propertied New York family. In the following years, Philip Schuyler became an intimate political ally, and the two often worked in tandem to oppose the policies of New York governor George Clinton. Hamilton's growing family—he and Eliza had eight children—gave him the domestic stability he had lacked as a child, but it also created the need for an income beyond what politics provided. Consequently, Hamilton took up the law as a profession, yet he never strayed far from politics. His combative and bold style of politics led to nearly constant disputes. Perhaps the lowest point in his public life came when political opponents revealed his extramarital affair with Maria Reynolds. Intent on preserving his honor, Hamilton published a lengthy essay admitting to the affair but denouncing claims that he had engaged in unethical behavior as treasury secretary. Hamilton's political disputes would bring tribulation to his family, friends, and political allies. His eldest son, Philip, was killed in a duel, defending his father's honor. Two years later, on July 11, 1804, entangled in a web of insults uttered against Aaron Burr, then vice president of the United States, Hamilton himself ended up in the duel that would take his life.

From the time of his youth, Hamilton never doubted his own ability to direct economic, military, or political affairs, though he often doubted the ability of others. Like Machiavelli's prince, he aggressively courted fortune. "His inclination was always to control events rather than to permit them to control him." As John C. Miller states the point, "Hamilton's credo" was "that fortune smiled upon audacity."[9] Henry Cabot Lodge said of him that the "greater the odds the more defiantly and the more confidently he faced opposition."[10] Whether as a soldier fighting in battles like Monmouth and Yorktown or a statesman contemplating how to address the problems with the Articles of Confederation, Shays's Rebellion, the debt crisis, the economy, the Whiskey Rebellion, the French threat to America, or Fries's Rebellion, Hamilton rarely deviated from his advocacy of bold action. A recurring problem was that what seemed bold to Hamilton

was interpreted by others as arrogance, impulsiveness, reckless-
ness, or mere bravado.

It bears repeating that Hamilton was at his best when flanked
by the caution and gravitas of George Washington. Once he left
Washington's administration, and especially after the death of
the man he referred to as "his Excellency," Hamilton engaged in
often bitter partisan vituperation. Two striking examples of Hamilton's immoderate partisan rants are *The Public Conduct and
Character of John Adams, Esq., President of the United States* and
his letter to James A. Bayard, January 16, 1801. In both instances
Hamilton overestimated his opponents' vices and took a hyper-
bolic tone. In the first document, a letter to leaders of the Federalist Party that fell into Republican hands and was widely published, Hamilton surmised that "intrinsic defects" in Adams's
character made him "unfit" for the presidency, adding, "he is a
man of an imagination sublimated and eccentric; propitious neither to the regular display of sound judgment, nor to steady
perseverance in a systematic plan of conduct." To these vices
Hamilton appended "the unfortunate foibles of a vanity without
bounds, and a jealousy capable of discoloring every object."[11] In
the letter to Bayard, Hamilton declared that Jefferson's politics
were "tinctured with fanaticism," and charged "that he is too
much in earnest in his democracy, that he has been a mischievous
enemy to the principal measures of our past administration, that
he is crafty & persevering in his objects, that he is not scrupulous
about the means of success, nor very mindful of truth, and that
he is a contemptible hypocrite."[12] The experiences of politics
and war seemed unable to temper Hamilton's anxious thoughts
and actions once the counterweight of Washington's character
was gone.[13] A side of Hamilton was overly anxious about politics
and public policy to the point of corrupting his judgment, not
only about the character of his rivals, but also about the possibilities of politics itself. His vituperations against Adams may
have cost the president reelection and brought Jefferson and
Burr to power. The Federalists never recovered from this self-
inflicted wound, and Hamilton's influence, like that of his party,
faded into near oblivion.

Near the end of Washington's first term as president, Madison
and Jefferson arranged for Philip Freneau to become editor of

the *National Gazette,* to counterbalance the Federalist paper the *Gazette of the United States.* Freneau unleashed barrage after barrage of criticism of Hamilton and the Treasury Department. Hamilton did not sit idly by but, of course, took up his pen and fought back. John Jay, Chief Justice of the Supreme Court at the time, advised Hamilton to seek vindication by writing his memoirs once he left public office.[14] The thought of waiting perhaps decades to respond to his critics and facing the prospect of achieving vindication only after his death, assuming his memoirs were published posthumously, was more than Hamilton's impetuous nature could endure. Fits of impatient enthusiasm were evident throughout Hamilton's life. During the Battle of Monmouth, Hamilton interjected himself into a heated discussion between Generals Washington and Charles Lee. With the British advancing and the Americans in retreat, "Hamilton charged upon the scene at full gallop. Flourishing his sword, he exclaimed to Lee, 'I will stay here with you, my dear General, and die with you; let us all die here rather than retreat.'"[15] Cooler heads prevailed and Hamilton's life was spared. Writing in 1775 as *The Farmer Refuted,* Hamilton noted that there was "a certain enthusiasm in liberty, that makes human nature rise above itself, in acts of bravery and heroism."[16] His impatience and sensitivity to matters of honor and reputation reveal more about his heart than about his head. His was a spirited personality. In moments of cooler reflection, he was more apt to counsel, "passion must give way to reason,"[17] "beware of extremes!"[18] and "justice and moderation are the surest supports of every government."[19] The tension between Hamilton's heart and his head should not be construed as contradiction as much as indication that he was reflectively aware that "[m]an, after all, is but man."[20] Had he taken Jay's advice in 1792 and written his memoirs in the coolness of retirement, we would likely know just how aware he was of his tendency to let spiritedness govern his soul. Then again, since Aaron Burr's bullet ended his life in 1804, Hamilton might never have written his memoirs and we would know even less about his character and ideas than we do.

Hamilton's remarkable rise from obscurity to the heights of the ruling class occurred in his thirty-two years as an American. His story is one of a natural aristocrat's rise to power from humble beginnings. He had no family reputation to give him a boost; in fact, his less than proper origins were a source of embarrassment to him and discrimination against him. Hamilton was, as Richard Brookhiser notes, the quintessential self-made man. What seems to be lost on Hamilton's detractors is his desire and efforts "to give others the opportunity to become so [self-made]."[21] He was repeatedly vilified by his political opponents, who were led by Thomas Jefferson. Some of this opposition was Hamilton's own doing, inspired by his provocative writings. For someone who could rant with vigor, he was surprisingly sensitive to criticism, especially with regard to his character and his duties as secretary of the treasury.

Hamilton had an unsettled if not anxious quality about him that might reflect the instability of his childhood. He tended to throw himself wholeheartedly into endeavors and then reach a premature point of exhaustion or disinterest and move on to something else. He enrolled at King's College but never finished his degree, even though he was nearing the end of his studies; the turmoil of colonial resistance against England was too much of a distraction for him to stick to the task at hand. He joined the militia and eventually was offered a position on Washington's staff, but he left Washington's staff before the end of war because he desired combat glory. After achieving that wish at Yorktown, he left the military and prepared for a career as an attorney, serving briefly in the New York state legislature and the Continental Congress. He served with zeal as secretary of the treasury but left before the end of Washington's second term to return to his law practice. Hamilton maintained an interest in politics for the better part of his life, but he moved in and out of various posts. The allure of political power was irresistible to him and pulled him back into public affairs time and time again. There was an impatience to his character that is reflected in his political theory, an insistence that if things are done right, the situation will significantly improve. Hamilton was rarely content to sit back and watch events unfold. He was too spirited to passively and dispassionately allow others to exercise political power without his influence. Gilbert L. Lycan remarks, "Hamilton relished the excitement of battle. Though in his adulthood he was never eager for war, once it came he wanted to take a leading role in it."[22]

The story of Hamilton's death provides insight into his character and his mind. After his duel with Aaron Burr, Hamilton remained composed while many around him were reduced to tears and sorrow. He knew immediately after being shot that his wound was mortal. Although in great pain, as Burr's bullet had "penetrated his right side a little above the hip, torn through his liver and diaphragm, and lodged in his vertebrae," Hamilton was concerned about three things: the safety of Doctor Hosack, the physician in attendance at the duel, and of his second for the duel, Nathaniel Pendleton; his wife and family; and his soul. Hamilton had never intended to fire at Burr and was unaware that his pistol had discharged when he was shot. While in the small boat that returned the party to New York, Hamilton cautioned his friends to be careful of his pistol because it was cocked and ready to fire. When they arrived on shore, Hamilton asked that Elizabeth, his wife, who had no knowledge of the duel, be told of the situation. He insisted that she be given some hope that he might recover. He was taken to William Bayard's home, where Dr. Hosack continued to care for him. After other physicians were sent for and each confirmed Hosack's diagnosis that the wound was mortal, Hamilton asked for Benjamin Moore, the president of Columbia College and an Episcopal bishop, who had baptized the Hamiltons' son William. When the bishop arrived, Hamilton asked to receive holy communion but was refused for two reasons: he had never formally joined the church and Moore considered dueling a sin. Hamilton persisted, asking for the Reverend John M. Mason, a Presbyterian minister, who also refused to give Hamilton communion, as it was forbidden in his church except during Sunday services. Hamilton then asked for Moore to return, and when he did, Hamilton expressed his desire to join the church and then to receive communion. The bishop asked Hamilton to renounce dueling and to promise, if he recovered, never again to participate in it; Hamilton obliged. Asked to repent his sins and to affirm his faith in Jesus Christ, Hamilton did so, and also forgave Burr, after which he received holy communion. In the course of Hamilton's attempts to receive communion, his wife had arrived at his side and learned of his condition. He comforted her by saying, "Remember, Eliza, you are a Christian." His seven living children were brought to his bedside to say farewell to their father. The bishop remained for several more hours. Hamilton passed away in the early afternoon of the day after the duel.[23] One wonders if on his deathbed he remembered the words he had written after a deadly hurricane he experienced before coming to America: "thy fellow creatures pale and lifeless; their bodies mangled, their souls snatched into eternity, unexpecting! Alas! perhaps unprepared!" Unlike the victims of the hurricane, Hamilton expected his death, and he took the opportunity to prepare for it.[24]

Hamilton died with great courage, regard for honor, and selfless regard for those who were close to him, virtues he had exercised imperfectly earlier in his life. It is interesting that this is not generally remembered about him. Americans have been mesmerized by the fact that John Adams and Thomas Jefferson died just hours apart on July 4, 1826, the fiftieth anniversary of the Declaration of Independence. Jefferson, who died a few hours before Adams, asked from his deathbed, "Is it the Fourth?"[25] A few months before his death, with his legacy in mind, he requested in a letter to James Madison, "Take care of me when dead."[26] In a letter written just two weeks prior to his death, Jefferson reflected on the significance of the Declaration of Independence and noted that he was flattered by the fact that the document was "pregnant with our own, and the fate of the world."[27] Adams is described as regretful when among his last words he said, "Thomas Jefferson survives."[28] Unlike Adams and Jefferson, whose last thoughts seem to have been of glory, and in Adams's case bitterness, Hamilton died with the dignity exemplified by his mentor, Washington. In his final hours, Hamilton did what seems to have been impossible for him during his life, something neither Adams nor Jefferson did on their deathbeds— he let go of politics.

Stephen F. Knott speculates that as he died Hamilton "may well have wondered if the journey that began in Nevis had been worthwhile, and how, or if, his countrymen would remember him in the ages to come."[29] It appears, though, that the tenor of his final reflections was not regret or doubt but rather the contentment that comes from knowing that he was loved by wife and children, that his soul was prepared for the final judgment, and that whatever his future place in American history he had done what he could. He certainly did as much as any Founder to win independence, bring the Constitution into existence, and orchestrate domestic and foreign policies at a time when the republic was fragile and its future in doubt. That Hamilton's political opponents would not see his legacy in these terms Knott and others have made clear.

HAMILTON'S IMAGINATION

Hamilton's intuitive perception of reality and his character and personality are part of what gave life to his political ideas and what differentiated him from his contemporaries. His opposition to Thomas Jefferson, for example, stems from their respective and competing types of imagination. They viewed the human condition in significantly different ways, and their respective political theories reflect their underlying philosophical differences. Hamilton was an ethical dualist; he believed that there was a permanent tension in human nature between good and evil inclinations. Jefferson tended toward ethical monism, convinced that human beings were basically good by nature.

Irving Babbitt, who cofounded New Humanism near the end of the nineteenth century, identified two central strands of imagination in the American political tradition.[30] One, the "idyllic imagination," Babbitt saw as the derivative of Jean-Jacques Rousseau and Francis Bacon; the other, the "moral imagination," derived from Edmund Burke. The former type of imagination has been tied to Jefferson and Thomas Paine, who combined romantic and scientific naturalism in their political theories. Both considered a plebiscitary form of democracy to be the only legitimate type of government, and both possessed great faith in the ability of human reason and science to permanently improve the quality of human life, if not transform the human condition itself. It bears noting that the historical figures most admired by Jefferson were Isaac Newton, Francis Bacon, and John Locke, Enlightenment and scientific minds who tended to view reality in a mechanistic way. By contrast, Hamilton's favorite authors were Plutarch and Alexander Pope.

Babbitt's second type of imagination has been associated with

George Washington, John Marshall, and Hamilton. It identifies a magnanimous quality of character that stems from inner restraint and ethical self-control as the source of civilization and social harmony. Rejecting the idea that human nature is malleable, moral imagination is sober about the possibilities of politics. Unlike Jefferson and Paine, Hamilton was not enamored with the wisdom of the people or with plebiscitary forms of democracy. He, like Washington and Marshall insisted that government, with constitutional checks and restraints, was necessary to controling the will to power. These competing traditions are based on radically different and irreconcilable views of human nature, politics, and democracy. Placing Hamilton in a broad tradition, as Babbitt did, helps illuminate his political theory and shows why it has repeatedly been contrasted with Jefferson's and those of others who held Jacobin sympathies.

In differentiating between the political theories of Hamilton and Jefferson, one runs up against their respective degrees of abstraction and concreteness. Abstraction, in the sense used here, divorces political ideas from the concreteness of historical experience. Hamilton's political theory tends not to be the product of abstraction but the consequence of reflection on concrete historical circumstances that compelled him to search for practical answers to the political and economic problems of his day. The substance of his political theory tracks closely with the development of the early republic and includes constitutionalism, political economy, foreign affairs, and national defense. Had his own adopted nation not been in its economic and political infancy, it is unlikely that Hamilton would have focused his intellectual attention on the problems of a developing nation. His country's circumstances shaped his political theory. For example, Hamilton advocated bounties as a means to protect infant industries, but he opposed them as permanent protections to shield domestic producers from foreign competition. In terms of its pertinence to the exigencies of the times, Jefferson's political theory was no less relevant than Hamilton's, but it was not typically as concrete.

Hamilton's political theory can be called concrete not simple because it engaged the problems of the day but because it was a consequence of philosophical realism as well. A thinker can address the issues of the day but do so in an abstract manner. Hamilton's political theorizing took the human condition as it was and avoided conceptions of life that were premised on the ability of politics to change human nature. He rejected progressive notions of politics and grounded his political theory in historical and philosophical realism. Hamilton consulted history in analyzing human nature and determining what was possible in politics. Political, social, and economic changes, he believed, occurred within the parameters of a structure of reality that was defined by historical experience. Leaping outside or beyond the limits of this structure would require a transformation of the human condition that, at its extreme, would include the perfectability of man and society. Hamilton's philosophical anthropology denied the moral evolution of human nature. It was sober in its assessment of the human condition and politics.

Hamilton, it should be remembered, was first and foremost a statesman. His thinking about politics and economics was rarely done in the environment of dispassionate critical distance. That immediate political concerns were foremost on Hamilton's mind does not mean that he was incapable of theoretical analysis or insight. Political urgency and philosophical reflection existed interdependently in Hamilton's life. Political crisis and necessity engendered political thoughts; political thoughts and imagination colored his view of contemporary political life. Hamilton's statesmanship kept him from flights of esoteric speculation. Not all statesmen avoid such abstractions in their political thinking. It takes more than occupation in politics to avoid idealistic abstraction. Jefferson, who was engaged in American politics as a diplomat, member of the Continental Congress, governor of Virginia, secretary of state, vice president, and president, often engaged in romantic theorizing. In his case, the demands of political statesmanship were as likely to stir his idyllic imagination as to inspire realistic political thinking, one reason his political theory is inconsistent and contradictory in places. Hamilton's moral and political realism, by contrast, was the product of an imagination imbued with Christian and Classical realism regarding the human condition. This imagination did not preclude efforts to reform American politics; few Americans did more than Hamilton to change the nation's political and economic institutions. A common misconception holds that individuals of conservative, traditional, or anti-idealistic imagination are generally opposed to change and reform. It is often remarked that such people favor the status quo. Hamilton's statesmanship, like Edmund Burke's, is evidence that individuals of a realistic imagination can be willing and eager to reform society. Hamilton's reforms, however, were not efforts to change the order of being, (e.g., end war forever, end poverty forever, end tyranny forever); they were not inspired by "metastatic faith"[31] or gnostic impatience; they were remarkably prudent and eminently practical, whatever flaws they may have included.

There is, then, a distinction to be made between Jeffersonian and Hamiltonian reform. The difference is not a desire to change versus a desire to resist change and protect the status quo. Rather, the two approaches to politics differ in the quality of reform they espouse. One tends to sever the current generation from the past, even to revolutionary degrees, and promises an order unknown in history; the other searches for ways to change while maintaining continuity with the past. One sees politics as the instrument for ontological revolution; the other sees politics as the art of the possible. This distinction is not intended to suggest that Jefferson was in every instance a revolutionary idealist and Hamilton a sober realist. Both statesmen had moments of idealistic flight and moments of prudent realism. In general, however, Jefferson was apt to be idealistic about politics[32] and Hamilton to be realistic.

Hamilton possessed extraordinary rhetorical skill that demonstrated the extent of his learning and the substance of his political theory.[33] In the cause of American independence, ratification of the Constitution, the Jay Treaty, or Federalist political candidates, Hamilton proved a master debater who combined spirited argument with substantive depth. He could carry a speech for hours, speaking in fully formed and organized paragraphs. In later years he was compared favorably to Daniel Webster and Henry Clay as an orator.[34] Supreme Court justice Joseph Story paid Hamilton this compliment: "I have heard Samuel Dexter, John Marshall, and Chancellor Livingston say that Hamilton's reach of thought was so far beyond theirs that by his side they were schoolboys—rush tapers before the sun at noon day."[35] As an attorney, Hamilton displayed these same rhetorical talents, often invoking the great works and minds of the Western legal tradition by citing Cicero, Blackstone, Grotius, Vattel, Barbeyrac, and Burlamaqui, but always with the intent of winning the case at hand. Much of his writing takes the form of polemical tracts published to influence the outcome of public policy debates and to win public favor for his political party.

He was especially critical of John Adams and others whom he described as "far less able in the practice, than in the theory, of politics."[36] Had Hamilton and Adams been contemplative philosophers, they would have shared enough common ground to be part of the same school of thought, which is not to say that they always drew the same political conclusions from their common theoretical foundations.[37] They both admired the British political tradition, distrusted Jacobins and the French Revolution generally, and held a deep disdain for slavery. Their underlying views of human nature were, for the most part, identical. They shared much more political ground than Adams and Jefferson, but unlike the second and third presidents, they never reconciled their personal and political differences. As statesmen, Hamilton's and Adams's sensitive egos and contrary policy preferences led to a stormy and contentious relationship. While their political squabbles make for good biography, they can obscure a thorough understanding of Hamilton's political theory. Hamilton's differences with Jefferson (discussed in detail in chapter 7) were both personal and philosophical. Comparisons between aspects of their respective political theories show Hamilton's central ideas fundamentally at odds with Jefferson's political theory.

As much as Hamilton was a man of action, his philosophy was no doubt shaped by what he read. In his youth he was known to be "bookish"; while the specific content of his reading is not fully known, it is likely that ancient sources such as Plutarch's *Lives* were part of it.[38] Throughout his life, Hamilton measured the men of his times against the heroes and the contemptible figures of ancient Greece and Rome. He equated Aaron Burr with Catiline,[39] the Roman conspirator who attempted to overthrow the republic but was impeded by Cicero, and he found in Jefferson likeness to another enemy of republican government, Julius Caesar.[40] His library contained sources by Classical authors like Justinian, Xenophon, and Ovid. He quoted Shakespeare, Milton, and Pope;[41] he used Montesquieu as an authority and claimed in *Federalist* 9 that the French political theorist supported an extended republic as a way to reconcile monarchy and republican government. He read Machiavelli, Hobbes, and Hume as well as Adam Smith, and was familiar with Demosthenes, Cicero, Montaigne, and Rousseau. Malachy Postlethwayt, Aristotle, and Locke were objects of study for him,[42] and his political economy was influenced by James Steuart and Jacques Necker. King's College required the ability to read Greek and Latin, specifically "Cicero, Virgil's *Aeneid*, and the Greek Testament."[43] Hamilton's knowledge of Latin is most apparent in his law briefs, some of which are riddled with Latin phrases.

From an early age, Hamilton was an avid reader and he continued to pore over books as his life took its twists and turns. Chernow explains that Hamilton's autodidacticism never ceased.

> He preferred wits, satirists, philosophers, historians, and novelists from the British Isles: Jonathan Swift, Henry Fielding, Laurence Sterne, Oliver Goldsmith, Edward Gibbon, Lord Chesterfield, Sir Thomas Browne, Thomas Hobbes, Horace Walpole, and David Hume. Among his most prized possessions was an eight-volume set of *The Spectator* by Joseph Addison and Richard Steele; he frequently recommended these essays to young people to purify their writing style and inculcate virtue. He never stopped pondering the ancients, from Pliny to Cicero to his beloved Plutarch, and always had lots of literature in French on his creaking shelves: Voltaire and Montaigne's essays, Diderot's *Encyclopedia*, and Molière's plays.[44]

Hamilton's library at the time of his death held hundreds of books.[45]

HAMILTON AND RELIGION

In his youth, Hamilton was known to be an avid Christian. His friends at King's College noted his commitment to prayer and doctrine.[46] Some of his biographers suggest that as he aged his Christian faith was less apparent, until he seemed to return to it in the final years of his life, after his oldest son, Philip, was killed in a duel. When he connected his religious faith to politics, it was usually to invoke Providence and to solicit prayer on behalf of the nation and to condemn the irreligion of the French Revolution and its Jacobin disciples. During Jefferson's presidency, Hamilton proposed the creation of the Christian Constitutional Society to promote the Constitution and the Christian faith on which its success, he thought, depended. Hamilton was raised as an Anglican (an Episcopalian after independence) and never left that denomination or questioned its doctrines. He penned one of the most famous passages by an American writer connecting religion and politics when he drafted Washington's "Farewell Address," which reads in part:

> To all those dispositions which promote political happiness, Religion and Morality are essential props. In vain does that man claim the praise of patriotism who labors to subvert or undermine these great pillars of human happiness these firmest foundations of the duties of men and citizens. The mere politician equally with the pious man ought to respect and cherish them. A volume could not trace all their connections with private and public happiness. Let it simply be asked where is the security for property for reputation for life if the sense of moral and religious obligation deserts the oaths which are administered in Courts of justice? Nor ought we to flatter ourselves that morality can be separated from religion. Concede as much as may be asked to the effect of refined education in minds of peculiar structure—can we believe—can we in prudence suppose that national morality can be maintained in exclusion of religious principles? Does it not require the aid of a generally received and divinely authoritative Religion?[47]

As was common in his day, Hamilton made references to "Providence" and life beyond earthly existence in both personal and public life. When a teenager, as previously mentioned, he witnessed a violent hurricane, as a result of which he published a letter that reflected his understanding of the relationship between mundane life and a higher divine order, of the relationship between God and man. "Where now, oh! vile worm, is all thy boasted fortitude and resolution? What is become of thine arrogance and self sufficiency? . . . Despise thyself, and adore thy God . . . Succour the miserable and lay up a treasure in Heaven."[48] In drafting speeches for Washington, he commonly used language like "the Author of all good," "gratitude to heaven,"

"Providence," and "the hand of the divinity."[49] He suggested to Secretary of State Timothy Pickering in 1797 and again in 1798 that President Adams proclaim "a day of fasting humiliation and prayer."[50] On both occasions he had the Quasi-War with France in mind as the special subject of prayer. He believed in the utility of religion, as is evident in the "Farewell Address"; a day of prayer and humiliation, he wrote to Pickering, would be not only "proper" but "useful to impress our nation that there is a serious state of things—to strengthen religious ideas in a contest which in its progress may require that our people may consider themselves as the defenders of their Country against Atheism conquest & anarchy." A war with France would mean defending "our fire sides & our alters."[51] One of the reasons Hamilton looked with suspicion on the French Revolution and Jacobinism was their spiritual anarchy. Skeptical of Hamilton's religiosity in this instance, John C. Miller remarks that his calls for prayer seem "to have come to Hamilton from Machiavelli rather than from on high."[52]

The subject of Hamilton's religious faith has most famously been taken up by Douglass Adair and Martin Harvey in their essay, "Was Hamilton a Christian Statesman?" published in 1955. They note that religion has both a public and a private dimension and that public behavior, to some degree, reflects one's inner life. Using this duality of religious manifestation as the foundation for their argument, they conclude, with some qualification, that Hamilton was a Christian statesman at least at the end of his life. They make much of Hamilton's behavior and professions of faith in the days leading up to his duel with Aaron Burr. Adair and Harvey are convinced that Hamilton fully intended to throw away his first shot because he was opposed to dueling on religious grounds. Why, then, would Hamilton have agreed to the duel? Adair and Harvey claim that he experienced Christian guilt over his treatment of Burr and was therefore obligated, by the day's code of honor, to grant Burr the opportunity to regain his honor by firing a pistol at his rival. This final act of contrition may have been part of a conversion Hamilton had been experiencing at least since 1802. At that time he proposed to James A. Bayard that the Federalists create the Christian Constitutional Society and he objected to James Callender's publication of Jefferson's Sally Hemings scandal.[53] Ron Chernow has pointed out that Hamilton's charity toward Jefferson may have been motivated by his own humiliation regarding his extramarital affair with Maria Reynolds.[54] It is possible that Hamilton had learned something about the Golden Rule after his marital indiscretion. Whether this seeming change in attitude and behavior was part of a spiritual conversion is difficult to determine, but there is no doubt that Hamilton was more attentive to his Christian faith in the final years of his life.

Chernow agrees with Adair and Harvey that Hamilton was more openly interested in religion in the last few years of his life, but he suggests, like Miller, that at least in some instances he "was not honoring religion but exploiting it for political ends." Chernow had in mind Hamilton's plan for the Christian Constitutional Society when he expressed doubts about the sincerity of Hamilton's religiosity. Chernow admits that religion was central to Hamilton's political theory, that he regarded it as the foundation for law, order, and the character of political rulers. Perceiving these two sides to Hamilton's view of religion, Chernow wonders whether Hamilton "believed sincerely in religion" or found it "just politically convenient?" The problem involves separating personal faith and virtue from the theoretical understanding of religion and its relation to politics. With regard to the relationship between religion and politics, Hamilton was consistent throughout his life. He considered religion one of the great pillars of civilization and expressed disdain for individuals, such as Burr and Jefferson, and political ideologies, such as Jacobinism, that thought otherwise. With regard to his personal religious faith and virtue, Chernow writes:

> Like Washington, he never talked about Christ and took refuge in vague references to "providence" or "heaven." He did not seem to attend services with Eliza, who increasingly spoke the language of evangelical Christianity, and did not belong formally to a denomination, even though Eliza rented a pew at Trinity [Episcopal] Church. He showed no interest in liturgy, sectarian doctrine, or public prayer. The old discomfort with organized religion had not entirely vanished. On the other hand, Eliza was a woman of such deep piety that she would never have married someone who did not share her faith to some degree. Hamilton believed in a

happy afterlife for the virtuous that would offer "far more substantial bliss than can ever be found in this checkered, this ever varying, scene!"

Hamilton was overtly more religious after the death of his son Phillip. He prayed daily, read the Bible, claimed to be able to prove the existence of God, and made plans to build a chapel in a grove at his home, the Grange. Chernow acknowledges what is most important for understanding Hamilton's political theory: there is "no doubt of his overarching faith in a moral order."[55] Belief in a transcendent moral order is difficult to reconcile with the theories of Hobbes and to a lesser extent Jefferson, both of whom affirmed the existence of a moral order, but in terms of naturalism rather than a more traditional conception of the relationship between divine reality and human obligation. The distinction between a transcendent moral order and naturalism provides a dividing line between competing types of universality that makes it easier to see the commonality between Hamilton and Cicero and more difficult to classify Hamilton as a purely secular Enlightenment or modern thinker.

Forrest McDonald's assessment of Hamilton's religiosity falls somewhere between Adair and Harvey's and Chernow's. McDonald asserts that Hamilton's "youthful faith never entirely departed him" and was reinvigorated in response to the atheism of Jacobinism and the French Revolution.[56] The death of his son Philip inspired a period of deep spiritual reflection, he points out, as one might expect from such an existentially wrenching experience. Not all individuals are predisposed to search for spiritual guidance in the wake of personal tragedy, but Hamilton was inclined to renew his faith because it was so deeply ingrained in him and, McDonald suggests, had not been so much abandoned by him as pushed aside by the frantic pace and weight of his public duties. Even this portrayal ignores the fact that Hamilton was usually aware, even in his most active times, of what Cicero called moral duty. In other words, moral concerns were not segregated into a part of his life called "religion" or "faith" that had no bearing on his public conduct. For Hamilton, the life of the soul, in terms of the disposition of character that some have called "virtue," was integrated into life in such a way that even outside the institutional or formal aspects of religion, the spiritual struggle that defines the core of the relationship between the human and the divine should be apparent in one's devotion to standards of conduct that embody magnanimity. It is difficult to imagine that the display of spiritual strength Hamilton exhibited on his deathbed was as a consequence of a relatively brief invigoration of religious piety, as if he were some kind of prodigal son. The behavior he exhibited at the end of his life more likely represents a lifelong commitment to living according to a higher law than mere self-interest or pleasure. Like any human being, Hamilton sometimes fell short of the virtue to which he aspired. His affair with Maria Reynolds, his 1800 letter demeaning the character of John Adams, and his lack of charity toward his political opponents, are examples of deficiencies in ethical character. On the whole, however, Hamilton displayed an abiding regard for virtuous behavior in both private and public life. That he did not formally join a particular church or was not generally inclined to regard religious dogma as central to the life of virtue does not preclude the conclusion that he was a man of religious sensibility. Ethical conscience aided by moral tradition provided Hamilton a spiritual guide that could account for the complexity of life's circumstances and the need to submit human will to a higher moral authority. Dogma was too close to metaphysical speculation for Hamilton, who considered the standard for right action to be historical experience.

$$\not\hspace{-0.3em}\gamma\!\!\!\!\gamma \quad \not\hspace{-0.3em}\curlyvee \quad \not\hspace{-0.3em}\epsilon\!\!\!\epsilon$$

CHAPTER 2

HAMILTON'S PHILOSOPHICAL ANTHROPOLOGY

> He was not, to be sure, a closet thinker, and distrusted men who
> were—especially if they preached the Jacobin heresy. For intellect
> divorced from tradition and experience, as for intellect divorced from
> conviction and morality, he had all the horror of Burke or Adams.
> —Clinton Rossiter, *Alexander Hamilton and the Constitution*

THE SEARCH FOR HUMAN nature's universal qualities and its
bearing on the individual and society has been called "philosophical anthropology." Alexander Hamilton's constitutional,
economic, and international relations theories developed in conjunction with his view of the human condition. When he entered
the realm of political action, he did not arrive equipped with a
rational, ahistorical ideology (e.g., social contract theory) with
which to navigate and interpret political affairs. He had certain
predispositions, consequences of his early life and education, but
they did not form a rigid ideological system. To the extent that
his political ideas aligned with any systematic way of thinking,
Hamilton can be identified with moral realism. This intuitive conception of life and its possibilities shaped both his political thinking and his political conduct. As it turned out, he held to this
philosophy consistently throughout his life with few deviations.

HAMILTON AND HUMAN NATURE

Moral realism takes human nature as it is found historically in
the "accumulated experience of ages" as Hamilton wrote.[1] It

denies human and social perfectability while acknowledging the reality of ethical conscience and will. Hamilton is reported to have said at the Constitutional Convention, "We must take man as we find him" and "The science of policy is the knowledge of human nature."[2] As found, humans are too selfish for the interests of the public good to rely solely on their patriotism and virtue. Consequently, people must be enticed by interest to serve ends above mere selfishness. Hamilton wrote, somewhat cynically reflecting the influence of David Hume, "Men are rather reasoning tha[n] reasonable animals for the most part governed by the impulse of passion."[3]

Hamilton did not push his realism to the point of amoralism. The selfish and depraved side of human character was not all there was to human nature, in his view. There was a transcendent moral order that incorporated the natural law and ethical duties. That human beings often failed to live up to these moral duties did not preclude their existence. Magnanimity was uncommon, but throughout history there had been rare individuals who possessed extraordinary character, "a few choice spirits, who may act from more worthy motives."[4] To support this point, Hamilton would cite examples from antiquity, which he had found in Plutarch and other sources; examples from his extensive experience with George Washington, who for Hamilton epitomized republican virtue; and the abiding love of Eliza, his devoted wife. Higher human motives were sufficiently present in human nature to make civilization, including constitutional government, possible. The actual conduct of individuals and the quality of the existing social conventions would determine the success or failure of particular constitutional societies. While human nature was fixed, human character was malleable. Hamilton believed that much could be done to change the basic maladies that stemmed from the human condition. Evil was a permanent part of existential, social, and political life, but the fallen nature of man did not negate the possibility of ordered liberty. Hamilton observed that societies, like individuals, varied in the degree to which they achieved order, liberty, justice, and happiness, and he believed that the degree to which a society realized these ends of politics depended on the quality of the leadership class more than any other factor. If endowed with republican virtue, political and social leaders could shape the institutions that steered citizens toward the public good.

As was typical of the founding generation, Hamilton frequently made reference to human nature as part of the evidence for his arguments. He was not inclined, as were some in his age, to Jacobin or idealistic abstraction. A sober realist in his assessment of human nature, he agreed with the older Classical and Christian views that human nature was dualistic, that good and evil were in permanent tension. Unlike the intellectual leaders of the radical Enlightenment, Hamilton did not believe that the human condition was determined by human agency. Given the limits imposed by the human condition, politics was the art of the possible. The possibilities of politics, then, depend on a candid assessment of human nature. "The true politician," Hamilton wrote, "takes human nature (and human society its aggregate) as he finds it, a compound of good and ill qualities, of good and ill tendencies, endued with powers and actuated by passions and propensities which blend enjoyment with suffering and make the causes of welfare the causes of misfortune."[5]

The imperfectability of man is at the core of Hamilton's political philosophy. Consequently, political institutions must account for the good and evil sides of human nature. Government must not only exist but also have sufficient power to control the lower inclinations of human will. Yet, government itself, as a human institution, being imperfectable needs checks and restraints. A delicate balance must be found between a government with so much power that it becomes tyrannical and one that is too weak to contend with the problems associated with existential, social, and political disorder. As Hamilton put it, writing as "The Continentalist" in 1781, "too much power leads to despotism, too little leads to anarchy, and both eventually to the ruin of the people."[6] Hamilton also recognized that human nature limited what political power could accomplish. Wise statesmen refrained from attempts to exceed the limits of human nature. A "true politician" with a realistic view of human nature

> will not attempt to warp or disturb it [human nature] from its natural direction—he will not attempt to promote its happiness by means to which it is not suited, he will not reject the employment

of the means which constitute its bliss because they necessarily involve alloy and danger; but he will seek to promote his action according to the byass of his nature, to lead him to the developpment of his energies according to the scope of his passions, and erecting the social organization on the basis, he will favour all those institutions and plans which tend to make men happy according to their natural bent, which multiply the sources of individual enjoyment and increase those of national resource and strength—taking care to infuse in each case all the ingredients which can be devised as preventives or correctives of the evil which is the eternal concomitant of temporal blessing.[7]

Hamilton's political and philosophical views connected him with Washington, Gouverneur Morris, and John Jay among other Federalists. Once settled into the Federalist political and social community, Hamilton found himself and his ideas to be at odds with the rival Jeffersonian views. Never one to back away from political confrontation, he repeatedly took up his pen and went to the rostrum to support his ideas and oppose those he found to be contrary to the public good. It is in these writings and speeches that his political theory is revealed and its underlying theoretical foundations are evident.

One distinguishing feature of Hamilton's philosophical anthropology is that he could tolerate stronger government than his political rival Jefferson or the idealist Thomas Paine because he was far more sober in his view of human nature. They placed a degree of trust in the wisdom of the common man that Hamilton thought fell short of the understanding of reality that a true politician should possess. He was far less democratic than they were because he believed that not everyone had an equal concern for or understanding of the public good and that the interests of the political and social elites were more likely to coincide with the commonweal than would those of the general population. Non-elites were provincial, parochial, and generally, by circumstances or natural inclination, less likely to transcend self-interest. Consequently, he thought that social hierarchy was necessary to ensure the best government, and he was more inclined toward an aristocracy than Jefferson or Paine. However, Hamilton believed in a "natural aristocracy." In the New York ratifying convention, he answered the charge that the Constitution created an aristocracy by stating, "[T]here are men who are rich, men who are poor, some who are wise, and others who are not . . . every distinguished man is an aristocrat."[8] This was Hamilton's formulation of natural aristocracy, rule not by wealth but by ability, a system we would now call a meritocracy. From his own humble beginnings, he knew that inequality could result from circumstance or from disparities in character and talent. His rise to America's ruling class from such origins made him especially sensitive to the existence of natural inequalities among people and aware that natural ability and virtue may be masked by the circumstance of birth. There must be mobility between classes because ability is not determined by the accident of birth.

While Hamilton asserted the need for social hierarchy, he strongly opposed hereditary forms of government. This part of his political thought tends to be obscured by the often-repeated canard that he was in favor of hereditary monarchy.[9] There is not a grain of support for hereditary government in the whole of Hamilton's writings. Moreover, there is a great deal in his writings and speeches that explicitly or implicitly rejects it as a legitimate or fitting form of government for the United States.

While he acknowledged the existence of natural inequality (i.e., inequalities based on talent and ability), Hamilton considered slavery an unjust convention precisely because it violated natural equality; he considered race an arbitrary standard by which to determine who was qualified for liberty. He consistently opposed slavery, regarding it as immoral. During the American Revolution he supported John Laurens's proposal to enlist slaves in the army and emancipate them in exchange for military service.[10] The contrast between Hamilton's view of and actions concerning slavery and Jefferson's conduct regarding it is noted by biographer, Ron Chernow, who remarks that Jefferson lived "a pampered life" that "rested on a foundation of slavery . . . However much Jefferson deplored the 'moral and political depravity' of slavery, his own slaves remained in bondage to his career and his incorrigibly spendthrift ways."[11] Whatever may be said about Hamilton's conception of democracy and the common people, he was far more likely than Jefferson to view blacks as his equal.

It is interesting that historians and commentators have characterized Hamilton's beliefs about human nature and his larger political theory in significantly different ways. Political scientist James B. Staab claims that, "of all the framers, Hamilton had perhaps the darkest view of human nature."[12] There are numerous passages in Hamilton's writings that lend support to this claim, but they do not represent the whole of his understanding of human nature. Fragmentary analysis can lead to a distorted portrayal of Hamilton's political theory because it takes part of his philosophy as if it were the whole. Because Hamilton was an ethical dualist, it is possible to find in his writings both laudatory and depreciating comments about human nature. The latter are more frequent because he was often arguing in opposition to idealistic and romantic attitudes toward human nature. To prove them wrong, he had to emphasize the lower side of human character. It also should be kept in mind that what one person considers dark another may regard as realistic and what one person considers enlightened another may regard as idealistic, naïve, or utopian. In other words, while idealists often discredit Hamilton's view of human nature, moral realists are likely to see it as accurate. Those who tend to regard the human condition idealistically are likely to perceive Hamilton's conception of human nature as bleak. Their characterizations of his political anthropology should be placed in the context of their own opinions. This suggestion is not meant to dismiss their views of Hamilton but to promote a deeper understanding of his political theory. Knowing how idealists react to Hamilton's moral realism can help identify central and defining aspects of his thought. These critics may be incorrect in their conclusions about his political ideas but keen in their identification of key features of his thought, drawing attention to aspects of his political philosophy that more sympathetic readers might gloss over because they are in general agreement with his sentiments.

Here are comments from several scholars with differing interpretations of Hamilton's philosophical anthropology: Economist Louis M. Hacker claims that Hamilton's theory of human nature "was in the older Christian tradition," because it characterized human nature in the light of original sin and the duality of good and evil potentialities.[13] By contrast, Gerald Stourzh, a historian, sees Hamilton as "caught in the cross fire of ancient and modern ways of thought."[14] Stourzh emphasizes the ancient and modern influences on Hamilton while diminishing the importance of Christian sources. Historian Darren Staloff, however, argues that "Hamilton's political principles were thoroughly modern," and he adds that Hamilton "was the Enlightenment fulfilled."[15] Henry F. May agrees that Hamilton was influenced by the Enlightenment but he places him as part of the "Skeptical Enlightenment," a far cry from the more radical territory of Enlightenment thinking occupied by Condorcet, Helvétius, Turgot, and Voltaire.[16] May's assessment of Hamilton avoids fragmentation and is, thus, richer in its portrayal of his view of human nature. As one might expect of a late-eighteenth-century American thinker, there are clear Enlightenment influences in Hamilton's political theory; yet there are also opposite tendencies that reject Enlightenment thinking and, as Hacker suggests, heark back to pre-Enlightenment traditions. At times Hamilton sounded much like the anti-Enlightenment thinker Edmund Burke. In a letter to Richard Harrison, for example, Hamilton closed by noting: "The triumphs of Vice are no new thing under the sun. And I fear, 'till the Millennium comes, in spite of all our boasted light and purification—hypocrisy and Treachery will continue to be the most successful commodities in the political Market. It seems to be the destined lot of Nations to mistake their foes for their friends; their flatterers for their faithful servants."[17]

Political scientist Michael J. Rosano acknowledges "key features of Christian and classical republican thought" in Hamilton's view of human nature, but, drawing on the work of political theorist Thomas Pangle, he emphasizes that it is "predominately and even radically liberal." Rosano focuses his attention on Hamilton's understandings of liberty, natural rights, nobility, fame, power, and greatness.[18] He also addresses the compatibility of Hamilton's political theory with that of the Declaration of Independence. After describing the liberal assumptions of Hamilton's *Federalist* i, Rosano observes that the Constitution was "perhaps a singular opportunity to establish a viable liberal republic in America, and thereby to vindicate Paine's proclamation in *Common Sense* that, as the American people: 'We have it in our power to begin the world over again.' "[19] The pairing of

Hamilton and Paine would seem incongruous if Rosano had given due attention to the part of Hamilton's political theory that connects him most closely to the Christian tradition and represents competition with the political theory of Paine and Jefferson, namely its ethical and historical dimensions. Paine's gnostic speculation about remaking the world is difficult to reconcile with Hamilton's sober philosophy of human nature and politics and especially his tendency to view the United States as historically constituted rather than the product of abstract rational speculation.

The difficulty with using categories like "modern" and "ancient" to describe a philosophy is that they leave the impression those historical epochs were characterized by a single monolithic way of thinking, yet there is, of course, wide variation in what may be called modern, ancient, or Christian philosophy. For example, the eighteenth-century political theories of Jean-Jacques Rousseau and Edmund Burke are modern but are based on fundamentally different conceptions of human nature and society. On the foundational problem of the human condition, one finds more commonality between Burke and Aristotle than Burke and Rousseau. Rosano's assessment illustrates the extent to which analysis can be inhibited by reliance on broad categories. He posits that "Hamilton's 'true politician,' in the vein if not the spirit of Machiavelli, avoids the classical and Christian politics of 'imaginary republics' by using political science as an 'effectual truth.'"[20] The reference to Machiavelli's *The Prince*, suggests that as a modern political theorist, Machiavelli was at odds with Plato's *Republic*, that Machiavelli was a realist who, like Hamilton, took human nature and politics as they were found and that Plato, by contrast, was idealistic in his conception of the best regime. Plato, however, does not represent the whole of ancient thought nor does his *Republic* represent the whole of his substantial body of political philosophy. One need look no further than his student Aristotle for a contrary view that is far from idealistic in its conception of regimes and human nature. In terms of their political theory, one could easily assert that Aristotle and Machiavelli share theoretical ground and have more in common than Plato and Aristotle. Even this suggestion obscures much of Plato's political thought, some aspects of which tend to be abstract and ahistorical, like his theory of the forms, while other dimensions are well grounded in historical experience, like his discussion of character types in the *Republic*.

In other words, to label Hamilton's political theory modern because it finds points of contact with Machiavellian realism, ignores the fact that Machiavelli's political theory is itself of a mixed theoretical pedigree; it shares with Christianity, for example, an appreciation for the sinful and fallen nature of man and shares with Augustine the notion that without government a violent disorder would reign and that even with it one can expect the *libido dominandi* to have significant influence. In this regard, Machiavelli is much closer to Augustine than he is to Locke, J. S. Mill, or many other moderns.[21]

Russell Kirk, in his work *The Conservative Mind: From Burke to Eliot*, included Hamilton in his list of prominent American conservatives that also includes John Adams, John Marshall, and Fisher Ames. Kirk considers these four Federalists among "the best exemplars of the anti-democratic, property-respecting, centralizing" brand of Federalism that marked conservatism's presence in the early republic.[22] Lyman Bryson would agree with Kirk, identifying Hamilton as "the leader of the conservatives in early American politics."[23] Biographer Clinton Rossiter called Hamilton "the American Hume" and added that he "was conservative and radical, traditionalist and revolutionary, reactionary and visionary, Tory and Whig all thrown into one."[24] While Rossiter's summary accounts for the complexity in Hamilton's political thought, it associates Hamilton with so many disparate philosophical and political views that he ends up looking formlessly abstract. John Lamberton Harper titled his book on Hamilton and American foreign policy, *American Machiavelli*, and says, "Hamilton's view of human nature, politics, and statecraft was strikingly similar to Machiavelli's."[25] Harper's argument is qualified and not as clear-cut as the title suggests, but he pushes Hamilton's political theory in the opposite direction of Rossiter by associating Hamilton too closely with a particular thinker. No doubt, Hamilton has elements of Machiavelli in his political thinking and his political conduct, but the thrust of his character and thought are not what is generally considered Machiavellian.

Many have labeled Hamilton a Tory and a monarchist. Some

of these assertions are closer to being vituperations than products of careful and evenhanded analysis. Hamilton was open to
the prudence of various regime types but he was not a monarchist and certainly not a Tory, as is demonstrated by his role in
the American Revolution and his undying support for popular
sovereignty. Historian of the Revolution Lance Banning classified Hamilton a "modern Whig" who was intent on creating an
American nation that possessed the attributes of eighteenth-
century England.[26] While this characterization comes closer to
describing Hamilton's politics, it misses the primary feature of
Hamilton's political theory: he was a republican and a constitutionalist. In *Main Currents in American Thought: The Colonial
Mind 1620–1800*, Vernon Parrington, who regarded Hamilton as
a Tory and monarchist, subtitled his section on Hamilton "The
Leviathan State" and there suggests that Hamilton was influenced by Hobbes, "whose absolute state was so congenial to his
[Hamilton's] temperament."[27] Writing in the context of colonial resistance to British policies Hamilton sounds Hobbesian in
"A Full Vindication" when he asserts that "[s]elfpreservation is
the first principle of our nature. When our lives and properties
are at stake, it would be foolish and unnatural to refrain from
such measures as might preserve them, because they would be
detrimental to others."[28] He also shared ground with Hobbes
by embracing consent as the basis for legitimate government.
Yet, a few months after "A Full Vindication," writing as "A Sin-
cere Friend to America" in "The Farmer Refuted," Hamilton
struck an anti-Hobbesian cord when he likened his opponent
Samuel Seabury, an Episcopal clergyman, to a disciple of Hobbes.
Hamilton refuted the Hobbesian acceptability of an amoral state
of nature because it left men free "from all restraint of *law* and
government," which is not how they are found historically. Hamilton rejected Hobbes's notion that all virtue is artificial and thus
due to the leviathan's social and political conventions. Such a
doctrine he found "absurd and impious" because it denied the
existence of an "intelligent superintending principle, who is the
governor, and will be the final judge of the universe."[29]

Hamilton was well aware that disorder and chaos were part of
human history, but he was unwilling to accept Hobbes's claim
that order was due merely to human artifice. For Hamilton, in-

dividuals were born into a world that was in tension between order and disorder. Hobbes put disorder and order into separate realms of existence, the state of nature and the state of civil society. Hamilton rejected Hobbes's amoral state of nature because he believed that "the deity . . . has constituted an eternal and immutable law, which is, indispensably, obligatory upon all mankind, prior to any human institution whatever."[30] Hobbes posited the existence of natural law, but his natural law has no social or moral duty attached to it as does Hamilton's. For Hobbes, there could be no injustice in the state of nature, because human laws did not exist to determine what justice was. Hamilton's conception of natural law, which draws on the natural law theory of several thinkers, including Emer de Vattel,[31] is more in line with a pre-Enlightenment view. His appeal to natural law in his revolutionary-era writings includes a quote from Blackstone stating that the natural law supersedes or informs all human obligations. "It is binding over all the globe, in all countries, and at all times. No human laws are of any validity, if contrary to this; and such of them as are valid, derive all their authority, mediately, or immediately, from this original."[32] Blackstone's description of the natural law is nearly identical to the one found in Cicero's *On the Commonwealth* and it shares a common pedigree with Richard Hooker's.[33] While Hobbes posited the existence of natural law, his version of it has no ties with transcendent reality. For Hobbes, reality was mechanistic and nature amoral. Such views cannot be reconciled easily, if at all, with Hamilton's understanding of transcendence or nature. Parrington's characterization of Hamilton is not only fragmentary but it forces his political theory into a classification that defies the wealth of evidence present in his writings and speeches.[34]

Karl-Friedrich Walling, a political scientist, recognizes the incompatibility of Hamilton's political theory and that of Hobbes. Walling interprets Hamilton's defense of natural rights and rejection of Hobbes as an endorsement of Lockean natural rights theory and Lockean notions of executive power. He suggests that Hamilton was, like Locke, a modern liberal-republican, especially when it came to matters of security and war. Rarely did Hamilton draw on one thinker or school of thought. That Locke was on his mind to some degree seems clear in particular instances, such as his understanding of prerogative powers. What he states about natural law, as has been suggested, could also have been inspired by Cicero or Hooker, two thinkers whose beliefs about human nature are much closer to Hamilton's than to Locke's.[35] The moral duty of natural law applies to nations as well as to individuals. Writing as "Pacificus," Hamilton argued, "Faith and Justice between nations are virtues of a nature sacred and unequivocal. They cannot be too strongly inculcated nor too highly respected. Their obligations are definite and positive their utility unquestionable: they relate to objects, which with probity and sincerity generally admit of being brought within clear and intelligible rules."[36]

No doubt, Hamilton's political theory is somewhat enigmatic and thus open to wide ranging interpretations. Yet, there is a consistency to his view of human nature in that it remains within the boundaries of the classical and Judaeo-Christian notion of ethical dualism reconstituted in modern circumstances and re-fracted through the political theory of David Hume and Montesquieu and of other influential modern thinkers, among them Blackstone, Hugo Grotius, Emmerich Vattel, and Samuel Pufendorf. Hamilton made such scant references to the principles of social contract theory that he cannot be cast as an advocate of that school of thought. Here and there he drops references to the people's "original right of self-defense,"[37] "natural rights," "natural law," and "consent of the governed," but such references are not systematically integrated into his larger political theory nor do they play a central part in his conception of human nature and politics. When his political theory is assessed from the perspective of his entire body of work, Hamilton defies clear classification, though he tended toward some traditions and schools of thought more than others. Social contract theory played a relatively minor role in the grand scope of Hamilton's political philosophy. It is most evident in his early writings, especially "A Full Vindication" and "The Farmer Refuted."

What is clear about Hamilton's view of human nature is that it avoided the extremes of Hobbesian[38] amoral realism and Rousseaustic romantic idealism. It was a composite of Classical, Christian, and modern ideas. He was much more sober about human nature than Thomas Paine and Jefferson but not as cynical as Machiavelli and Hobbes. His imagination was shaped by Plutarch's *Lives* and ancient mythology. Like Augustine, he believed that government was necessary because of the permanence of evil in human nature. In *Federalist* 15 he asked, "Why has government been instituted at all?" He answered, "Because the passions of men will not conform to the dictates of reason and justice, without constraint."[39] Politics for him was the art of the possible and never the attainment of some good without the risk of some evil. In arguing for the national bank, he noted both the risk of evil and the possibility of good:

> Great power, commerce and riches, or in other words great national prosperity, may in like manner be denominated evils; for they lead to insolence, an inordinate ambition, a vicious luxury, licentiousness of morals, and all those vices which corrupt government, enslave the people and precipitate the ruin of a nation. But no wise statesman will reject the good from an apprehension of the ill. The truth is in human affairs, there is no good, pure and unmixed; every advantage has two sides, and wisdom consists in availing ourselves of the good, and gua[r]ding as much as possible against the bad.[40]

Hamilton's perspective on the good and ills of power and government meshes with his view of human nature and is illustrated by his arguments for a national debt. Some commentators, in an effort to identify Hamilton as the source of the contemporary habit of excessive government spending, have cited his comment that a "national debt if it is not excessive will be to us a national blessing; it will be powerful cement of our Union."[41] What Hamilton's critics tend to ignore are his repeated warnings about national debt. He called "the progressive accumulation of Debt . . . the NATURAL DISEASE of all Governments" and warned that "it is not easy to conceive any thing more likely than this to lead to great & convulsive revolutions of Empire."[42] In arguing for the national bank he stated that the government's interest should be not to abuse public credit but to "husband and cherish it with the most guarded circumspection, as an inestimable treasure." Again alluding to the realities of human nature he added, "But what government ever uniformly consulted its true interests in opposition to the temptations of momentary exigencies? What nation was ever blessed with a constant succession of upright and wise administrators?" This view is not so much cynical as it is realistic. Taken in isolation, it might imply that Hamilton, like Hobbes and Locke, paid no mind to the quality of rulers' character. He does not discount the possibility of good government but cautions that, "careful and prudent administration" depends on the "keen, steady, and, as it were, magnetic sense, of their [administrators'] own interest, as proprietors, in the Directors of a Bank, pointing invariably to its true pole, the prosperity of the institution."[43] In this instance, Hamilton is certainly relying, in part, on self-interest to steer public officials in the direction of the public good. Such a notion is found in modern conceptions of politics (e.g., liberalism) as well as in the Classical thought of Aristotle.[44]

It is noteworthy that several commentators on Hamilton's view of human nature describe it as pessimistic, dark, or cynical. By way of background for this assessment, Chernow devotes a few paragraphs of his biography to describing the cultural circumstances of Hamilton's youth. Young Hamilton was exposed to a plethora of violence and inhumanity that included hangings, duels, murders, and slavery. The sugar economy of Nevis and the surrounding islands "made the tobacco and cotton plantations of the American south seem almost genteel by comparison." Chernow recounts the case of a Nevis slave owner who administered more than 650 lashes, combined, to two of his slaves (one a woman) and was acquitted of any wrongdoing by a local jury. Further accounts are followed by Chernow's conclusion that "Hamilton's vision" was darkened "for life, instilling an ineradicable pessimism about human nature that infused all his writing."[45] There is more than a touch of exaggeration in Chernow's analysis. He later states that "Hamilton was spurred by Hume's dark vision of human nature, which corresponded to his own" and refers to Hamilton's "pessimistic imagination." He quotes Hamilton's description in *Federalist* 6 of "this selfish, rapacious world," as evidence of "the darkness of Hamilton's upbringing."[46]

The use of the words "pessimistic" and "dark" is common enough in descriptions of Hamilton's attitude toward human nature and explains to a degree why some critics connect his political theory to Hobbes and Machiavelli. The appropriateness of this description, however, is dubious. Apart from what may be the case with Hamilton, a conception of human nature can be classified as pessimistic because it overestimates the evil inclinations in human will if in so doing it also underestimates the higher inclinations. Any case that a particular view of human nature is pessimistic, or optimistic for that matter, must demonstrate that the view does not comport with the facts of human experience. Hamilton's opinion can be considered pessimistic if, as Chernow suggests, it was indelibly shaped by a set of circumstances that does not represent the full range of human experience, that is, if it takes a part of reality and considers it the whole of reality. If Hamilton had taken his childhood experience as the whole of human experience, ignoring the vast and variegated experience of history, then a case could be made that his view of human nature is in some way incomplete, truncated, and experientially provincial. But he did not.

Chernow, in this instance, ignores evidence that he himself provides elsewhere, for example, that Hamilton's reading of Plutarch and others shaped his imagination and without a doubt led him to believe that human beings were capable of virtue as well as vice. That moderation and excess were both evident in human character and political affairs appears throughout Hamilton's writings and speeches. Hamilton's offending view may be that he did not think virtue equally present in all individuals, or at least sufficiently distributed to support democracy. Hamilton repeatedly referred to the standard of historical experience using phrases like, "the experience of all ages,"[47] and the accumulation of evidence suggests that his view of human nature was not skewed inordinately to the evil side of human nature. Did he, at times, depreciate the moral capacity of human beings beyond their actual level of virtue? Perhaps. He was surely blinded by political partisanship in assessing the policies and character of his enemies. The same, however, could be said of the idealistic Jefferson. On the whole, Hamilton's representation of human nature is neither pessimistic nor optimistic. He takes man as he finds him and is not blind to the depravity of human character. Yet, he was also tireless in his efforts, both intellectual and practical, to ameliorate, not human nature, but the human beings he led and governed. Such efforts might be regarded as pointless by someone who was overly cynical about the human condition. Also, it seems plausible that Hamilton's childhood experience with slavery, rather than making him pessimistic and cynical, helped to form his lifelong opposition to an institution that many around him (e.g., Washington, Jefferson, Madison) participated in and defended to some degree. Chernow makes this very point.[48] While Hamilton's opposition to slavery does not make him an idealist, it does indicate that he was cognizant of the failings of human beings but at the same time aware that human institutions and human beings can be reformed for the better.

It bears repeating that Hamilton's view of human nature should be distinguished from that of Machiavelli and Hobbes, who truly were cynical and dark in their conception of the human condition. Hobbes rejected the idea of a *summum bonum*, greatest good, in human endeavors[49] and reduced politics to the manipulation of power and interests. Only self-interest animates human behavior, he thought; there is nothing higher. The leviathan, the absolute sovereign, requires no virtue, only a monopoly of power. Machiavelli's prince is expected to use evil efficiently and for the public good without the support of virtue, assuming that expedience, glory, and the preservation of power (*virtù*) will be sufficient guides to prudence. Hamilton, by contrast, expected rulers to possess a sufficient degree of republican virtue, and he was steadfast in the belief that religion and morality were indispensable to good government. The charge that Hamilton was pessimistic about human nature may suggest more about his critics' view of human nature than his.

HAMILTON AND NATIONALISM

Hamilton's philosophical anthropology provides the theoretical context for understanding his conduct as a statesman. The connection between the philosophical foundations of his political theory and his specific policies or political opinions is illustrated in what his critics call his "nationalism." Care must be taken that classifying Hamilton as a nationalist does not disregard the thrust of his philosophical anthropology. Twentieth-century varieties of nationalism are based on underlying theoretical assumptions that would be at odds with Hamilton's ideas about human nature, history, and the moral order.

Scholars who make the claim that Hamilton was a nationalist rarely justify it on more than superficial grounds. They seem to assume that the point is self-evident. John C. Miller, for example, describes Hamilton's arguments in *Rutgers v. Waddington* as "a rousing plea for nationalism." Miller states that Hamilton's conception of nationalism failed to take hold, especially once the Jeffersonians rose to power, but he adds, "It remained for Andrew Jackson, Daniel Webster, and Abraham Lincoln to convey Hamilton's ideal of nationalism to the masses."[50] Chernow refers to Hamilton's "powerful vision of American nationalism," which he characterizes as "states subordinate to a strong central government and led by a vigorous executive branch."[51] What most commentators on Hamilton's political theory seem to mean by "nationalism" is that he favored a stronger national government, weaker state governments, and a strong union.

He was not a nationalist, however, if the term means that he subordinated all things to the nation and considered it the *summum bonum*. He was, rather, a cosmopolitan patriot who made sacrifices for his nation because he believed that those sacrifices were instrumental to the ends of political and social life.[52] That he favored a significantly stronger national government than the one that existed under the Articles of Confederation, and that after ratification of the 1787 Constitution he worked to maximize the federal government's power, does not mean that he was ideological about national power.

Hamilton's support for greater national power should be viewed in the context in which it was derived. Late-eighteenth-century America was, in many respects, the opposite of contemporary America. During the War for Independence and under the Articles of Confederation, the greatest threat to liberty, in Hamilton's opinion, was too little government, not too much government. At that time, to secure liberty it was necessary to create "a more perfect union," a national government that could provide for the security of the nation and promote the general welfare of its citizens. Security depended, Hamilton thought, not only on having a national government strong enough to fend off threats from foreign powers, but also on creating a union strong enough to avoid conflicts among the states. In *Federalist* 6, Hamilton argued that "a man must be far gone in Utopian speculations, who can seriously doubt that the subdivisions into which they [the states] might be thrown, would have frequent and violent contests with each other." The reason he thought that violence between the states would result from a weak confederacy illustrates his view of human nature. Men, he reminded his readers, "are ambitious, vindictive, and rapacious." He provided numerous historical examples to illustrate his point. He further questioned whether a particular form of government (e.g., monarchy or republic) could abate the tendencies in human nature to engage in violence in pursuit of power and wealth. Republics like Sparta, Athens, and Carthage "were as often engaged in wars, offensive and defensive, as the neighbouring monarchies of the same times . . . and Rome was never sated of carnage and conquest."[53] Hamilton believed that neither a particular form of government nor the geographic proximity of the American states to each other would save them from interstate conflict. Geographic proximity would make conflict between the states more likely, not less. Hamilton believed that political institutions could help alleviate disorder but that they could not eliminate the source of disorder and violence, the evil in human nature.

While Hamilton was not a nationalist in the modern sense of that term, he lacked an appreciation for the role that decentralized autonomous groups and associations play in the political and social order. He acknowledged in *Federalist* 17, "It is a known fact in human nature, that its affections are commonly weak in proportion to the distance or diffusiveness of the object. Upon the same principle . . . a man is more attached to his family than to his neighborhood, to his neighborhood than to the community at large." Yet Hamilton seemed somewhat blind to the contribution that local groups and associations made to civilization and order.[54] In his philosophy, order tended to emanate from the most centralized level of society; and when it began to unravel, it frayed from the least central, most local parts of society. The organic institutions of society provide a reservoir of cultural capital that makes constitutional government possible. There is a hint that Hamilton understood this in *Federalist* 84, but he never develops the implicit thought into a reasoned theory. Somewhat like Locke, he took for granted the existence of civilization and largely ignored the work that needed to be done to maintain the cultural foundations of constitutional government. This inattention to local communities lends support to the classification of Hamilton as a nationalist, although he certainly does not fit the characteristics of modern nationalism as it took shape in Jacobin France, Nazi Germany, or Fascist Italy. Further analysis of Hamilton's nationalism will be provided in chapter 5.

CHAPTER 3

THEORETICAL FOUNDATIONS OF CONSTITUTIONALISM

The doctrine of the perfectability of Man "Publius" set down as a preposterous fiction. His view of human nature presupposed that men in all ages and all places have been actuated by essentially the same desires and passions and that they would always continue to act in the same way. There was no possibility of an improvement in man's nature: the mold had been fixed for all time and the laws governing human behavior were as immutable as the laws of nature.

—John C. Miller, *Alexander Hamilton and the Growth of the New Nation*

AMONG THE CONTRIBUTIONS of Alexander Hamilton to American political thought is his multidimensional theory of constitutionalism, which includes now-standard American principles such as the separation of powers, federalism, checks and balances, representation, popular sovereignty, and judicial review. His political theory also characterized the aristocratic personality type and corresponding spirit that he thought were necessary for constitutional institutions to function in accordance with the ends of politics. Hamilton's philosophy recognizes the interdependence of political institutions, the importance of the character of leaders, and the need for effective administration of government. He insisted that these elements of constitutional politics had to be animated by a spirit of republican virtue that directed political power toward the public good, if republican government was to fulfill its purpose.[1] One factor that is not evident in his conception of constitutionalism is the role of cultural ethos, and specifically the place of the groups and associations intermediate between the government and people that Tocqueville regarded as vital to political health in nineteenth-century America. Of related interest is Hamilton's conception of federalism. While he advocated a federal structure of government, especially when writing *The Federalist*, he tended to favor national power and to disparage state and local autonomy in most other contexts.

THE CENTRALITY OF CHARACTER

Hamilton's formula for good government was predicated on the presence of individuals with aristocratic character, by his definition of natural aristocracy. John C. Miller notes that Hamilton's "ideal was government not by parties but by superior persons."[2] Civic virtue, the willingness and ability to subordinate self-interest to the common good, was central to Hamilton's political life and political theory. His constitutional theory relies on the presence of natural aristocrats and what he called "true politicians,"[3] people who possess a character that is conducive to the deliberative and administrative functions of constitutional politics. Such individuals, he believed, were necessary for constitution making and for the ensuing conduct of constitutional politics. Hamilton shared with ancient thinkers like Plato and Aristotle the belief that the pool of individuals with sufficient character to rule well was small. His best ruler was closer to Aristotle's *spoudaios*, Cicero's Scipio, and Machiavelli's prince than to Plato's philosopher king, because he held practical wisdom and experience in much higher regard than speculative knowledge and rational acumen. On the subject of the Jay Treaty and efforts by the House of Representatives to deny its funding, Hamilton wrote to Senator Rufus King, "Great evils may result unless good men play their card well & with promptitude and decision."[4] Without the disinterestedness,[5] discretion, and energy of "good men," constitutional institutions would lose their vitality and cease to foster happiness and the public good.

In a natural aristocracy, the most talented and deserving individuals rise to the leadership ranks from any class. During the debates at the New York ratifying convention, Hamilton responded thus to the charge that the Constitution favored the wealthy class: "Does the new government render a rich man more eligible than a poor one? No. It requires no such qualification . . . the tendency of the people's suffrages, will be to elevate merit even from obscurity." He admitted that, over time, as wealth accumulates in the few, "virtue will be in a greater degree considered as only a graceful appendage of wealth, and the tendency of things will be to depart from the republican standard." This development he found undesirable but a consequence of human nature.[6] It would be mitigated partly by having large legislative districts, which would help prevent factions and the wealthy from securing popular support for public office. In Hamilton's political theory, successful government relied on natural aristocrats and civic virtue exactly because he recognized the influence of lower inclinations: "It is as easy to change human nature, as to oppose the strong current of the selfish passions." Individuals of high character are needed because they "will gently divert the channel, and direct it, if possible, to the public good."[7]

Hamilton did not expect virtue to dominate politics. An ethical dualist, he believed that human beings were pulled by contrary inclinations to do good and to do evil, and he tended to follow David Hume in regarding the human condition in terms of competing passions. Hamilton distinguished between "the bad passions of human nature" and the "virtuous passions."[8] Which type of passion prevailed depended on reason, habit, custom, and "the deliberate sense of the community" or "the general spirit of the people and of the government."[9] Another Humean influence on Hamilton was his depreciation of reason. Reason, Hume asserted, "is, and ought only to be the slave of the passions."[10] Hume did not mean that lower passion should dominate reason but that reason was by itself incapable of directing societies to the good because it, like human nature itself, was flawed; just as passions were divided into higher and lower, so too was reason. Hamilton, recognized that reason was informed by experience and he disparaged speculative reason that ignored experience, a variety of reason prevalent in Jacobinism. He implied that reason must be subordinate to experience and virtuous passions if it is to convey truth. Speculative reason engendered factiousness, and Hamilton believed that factiousness, whether the product of reason or passion, could skew perception of historical experience and reality.

Hamilton's conceptions of leadership and of reason had implications for his understanding of republican government, including the role of the people in the function of government. In *Federalist* 71, he noted that republican government is based on the people's will, but not in an unqualified sense. Unlike Thomas Paine and Thomas Jefferson, Hamilton believed that popular will was not infallible, any more than was a monarch's will.[11] This difference is the primary reason Hamilton maintained an open mind regarding monarchy while Paine and Jefferson were closed to it on principle. For Hamilton, like Hume, human beings did not "always reason right"[12] about the public good. Reason is clouded by the bad passions, appetites that are inimical to justice, happiness, and order. Madison operated from a similar premise when, in *Federalist* 10, he argued that the public views must be "refined and enlarged" "by passing them through the medium of a chosen body of citizens, whose wisdom may best discern the true interest of their country, and whose patriotism and love of justice, will be least likely to sacrifice it to temporary or partial considerations." Filtering of the public will is necessary, Madison asserted, because "the reason of man" is "fallible," because it can be controlled by "self-love."[13]

Hamilton struck a similar note when, writing as "Camillus," he averred that the "true Patriot . . . never fears to sacrifice popularity to what he believes to be the cause of <public> good."[14] Momentary passion is rarely consistent with justice and the common good. Reflection, deliberation, and magnanimity are required to overcome the allure of immediate appetite. In his *Letters from Phocion*, Hamilton remarked, "Nothing is more common than for a free people, in times of heat and violence, to gratify momentary passions, by letting into the government, principles and precedents which afterwards prove fatal to themselves."[15] In this instance he was commenting that, in the aftermath of the American Revolution, New Yorkers were treating Loyalists and Tories unfairly. Lower passion, he felt, was leading some Americans to "suffer a departure from the rules of general and equal justice, or from the true principles of universal liberty," rules and principles that were the product of historical experience. Hamilton's defense of Loyalists and Tories in the press and in the courtroom was one of several instances when he sacrificed popularity for what he perceived as a greater good, a habit of conduct that contributed, as much as any factor, to the perception that he was unrepublican.

By what standard or evidence did Hamilton claim that momentary passion and democratic impulse were not the measure of the public good? On what basis did he claim that true politicians were capable of rising above the ephemeral and merely self-interested aspects of politics to follow the moderate path? His understanding of leadership and its relationship to justice and liberty was derived from his knowledge of historical experience and from a historically grounded view of human nature. He typically used historical examples to illustrate his points, implying that the weight of human experience was far greater than the popular passion of the moment or the speculative constructions of abstract theorists. In *Federalist* 6 he called experience "the least fallible guide of human opinions":[16] patterns of human behavior over centuries of time provide evidence against which can be measured the pressing issues of the day.

In the case of New York's postwar restrictions on Loyalists and Tories, Hamilton compared contemporary circumstances to similar historical examples. He cited the example of the English Whigs, who, after the Revolution of 1688, "from an overweening dread of popery and the Pretender," imprudently extended the length of Parliament from three to seven years in order to rest power more securely and more exclusively in their own hands. He also cited an example of the opposite behavior, when Queen Elizabeth, who had been returned to the throne from prison, "dismissed her resentment" and "retained many of the opposite party in her councils."[17] Hamilton implies that the queen's magnanimity cooled partisan animosity and created a more harmonious environment in which to restore order. He found her behavior as worthy of emulation as the seventeenth-century Whigs' behavior was cautionary. Each was animated by a spirit that promoted or eroded the quest for ordered liberty. One also detects the influence of Marcus Aurelius and the Christian tradition in Hamilton's willingness to forgive his opponents.

Hamilton often juxtaposed practical wisdom based on historical experience to abstract ideological doctrines. In *The Warning*, he argued that "revolutionary France" was attempting "to dogmatize mankind out of its reason; as if she expected to work a change in the faculties as well as in the habits and opinions of men."[18] The abiding habits and opinions of men Burke called "just prejudice"; they embodied the wisdom of the ages and were present in traditions and customs. Hamilton's political theory, like Burke's, was laced with the texture of historical experience. History, not abstract rationality or democratic impulse, provided a sense of universality. Hamilton sometimes conceived of universality in the form of customary and legal norms, like the law of nations or natural law. Such laws were binding on individuals of all nations because they embodied the wisdom of experience across time and political boundaries.[19] Consequently, in 1790, when Hamilton was faced with a request by the British government to march troops across American soil from Detroit to the Mississippi River, he used a combination of international law, national interest, and prudence to gauge the best course of action.[20] He considered several contingencies, including the likelihood that if Washington denied the right of passage, the British would move their troops without permission. Hamilton's advice to Washington in this case was typical; he outlined in a cabinet paper the arguments and principles of various legal authorities (e.g., Barbeyrac, Grotius, Vatel, Puffendorf) regarding right of passage, weighed the strategic and political interests of Great Britain, France, and Spain, and considered the interests and military capabilities of the United States. He did not force an opinion or policy on the president but laid out several options based on various scenarios and their likely implications for American interests. Nowhere in this cabinet paper is there even a hint of ideological calculation.

Not surprisingly, Hamilton repeatedly ridiculed "dangerous metaphysics"[21] and theoretical speculation precisely because he thought that they gave too much weight to a rationality that was divorced from historical experience. A "political empiric" "attempt[ed] to travel out of human nature and introduce institutions and projects for which man is not fitted."[22] For Hamilton, prudent statesmanship required knowledge and a realistic understanding of human nature, and history was the educational font of wise leaders. He considered idealists and Jacobins prone to devising policies and constitutions unfit for historical man, because these people did not accept the permanence of what the twentieth-century philosopher Eric Voegelin called "metaxic reality," the unchanging structure of reality that encompasses human nature and its higher and lower capacities. Hamilton's political theory does not reach the philosophical density or depth of Voegelin's philosophy of history, but they share an intuitive and theoretical suspicion of ideological abstraction. Hamilton's imagination was formed by a historical concreteness that that insisted on a sober and realistic assessment of politics. Reforms, policies, and revolutions that required a transformation of human nature for success he regarded as doomed to fail. Hume asserted, in his "Idea of a Perfect Commonwealth," that "[a]ll plans of government, which suppose great reformation in the manners of mankind, are plainly imaginary."[23]

Hamilton not only followed Hume in depreciating reason and discounting human perfectability, but he was also influenced by Hume's view of experience and custom. Hume called custom "the great guide of human life." He wrote: "It is that principle alone which renders our experience useful to us, and makes us expect, for the future, a similar train of events with those which have appeared in the past. Without the influence of custom, we should be entirely ignorant of every matter of fact beyond what is immediately present to the memory and senses. We should never know how to adjust means to ends, or to employ our natural powers in the production of any effect. There would be an end at once of all action, as well as of the chief part of specu-lation."[24] Like Hume, Hamilton believed that historical experi-ence provided patterns of human behavior that illuminated the meaning of human nature and from which statesmen could craft laws and policies that would stand a reasonable chance of serv-ing justice, the needs of order, and happiness.

HAMILTON'S THEORY OF DEMOCRACY

Because he believed that republics, like individuals, needed to avoid governing themselves by the passion of the moment, Hamilton was especially opposed to pure democracy. He saw it as giving license to momentary passion by creating a state of historical amnesia and chimerical dreaming in which the wisdom of historical experience can be lost or distorted. Without legislative representatives and the apparatus of constitutional government, a momentary lower passion is apt to overwhelm the dictates of reason and virtuous passion. For reason to prevail, it must be prejudiced by "ancient institutions"[25] that embody the wisdom of experience and the habits of mind and character that represent the product of trial and error. Hamilton invoked the "test of experience"[26] as the measure of the validity of policies and institutional arrangements.

Hamilton, like almost all of the American Framers, was not a democrat. To them, "democracy" meant direct or pure democracy, a system of government without representatives, in which the people literally ruled themselves by simple majority vote. Hamilton explained his opposition to democracy while defending the proposed constitution to the ratifying convention of New York.

> It has been observed that a pure democracy, if it were practicable, would be the most perfect government. Experience has proved, that no position in politics is more false than this. The ancient democracies, in which the people themselves deliberated, never possessed one feature of good government. Their very character was tyranny; their figure deformity: When they assembled, the field of debate presented an ungovernable mob, not only incapable of deliberation, but prepared for every enormity. In these assemblies, the enemies of the people brought forward their plans of ambition systematically. They were opposed by their enemies of another party; and it became a matter of contingency, whether the people subjected themselves to be led blindly by one tyrant or by another.[27]

He believed that democratic impulse should be checked and that foremost among possible checks was the deliberative temperament of true politicians functioning within the confines of constitutional structures. Hamilton's notes from the New York Ratifying Convention attempted to clarify the meaning of democracy, aristocracy, and monarchy. He differentiated between "representative democracy," which he considered consistent with good government and "pure democracy," which was inconsistent with it. In both cases, sovereignty rested with the people, but in a representative democracy, the people ruled indirectly through their representatives. In a monarchy, sovereignty rested with one person for life, and in an aristocracy it rested with a few for life. Monarchy and aristocracy might include a hereditary component, but this characteristic was not required to classify a regime in either category. The American Constitution, he contended, included elements of monarchy, aristocracy, and democracy because it was a mixed government[28] in which "these three principles unite."[29] The union of rule by the one, the few, and the many was, Hamilton believed, what made "democracy" an acceptable form of government. Sovereignty rests in the people, but the transient popular will—the cause of political turmoil in the ancient world—is appropriately checked and restrained by the aristocratic and monarchical elements of the constitutional system. This conception of mixed government is not identical to that of ancients like Aristotle and Polybius[30] or moderns like Algernon Sidney and Montesquieu, but is a reconstituted version that accounts for the circumstances of eighteenth-century America. There were not, strictly speaking, classes of aristocrats or monarchs in America, as there were in Europe. The parts of the American government did not correspond to class interests, as they did in Polybius's conception of Roman government. The divisions in American government are not class-based, but one part is intended to be more inclined to permanence, to check the impulse of democracy. The apparatus of the Constitution can reflect the energy of rule by the one in the presidency, the magnanimity of rule by the few in the Senate and the federal judiciary, and the force of the popular will in the House of Representatives.

Contrary to what some might expect from Hamilton, he fought vigorously at the Constitutional Convention for a democratic house in Congress. He could support a democratic component in the constitutional framework and oppose democracy without being theoretically inconsistent because in the democratic house the popular will was ensconced within the Framers' mixed system of separated powers and checks and balances, while pure democracy was determinant and operated outside the confines of separated powers and checks and balances. In this regard, Hamilton's constitutionalism owes a great deal to Montesquieu, who was also suspicious but not dismissive of democracy.

HAMILTON ON LEADERSHIP IN POPULAR GOVERNMENT

A foundational element of Hamilton's theory of constitutional leadership is summarized in journalist Felix Morley's comment that Hamilton had great confidence "in the unfettered judgment of aristocrats" and "no faith whatsoever in the ability of the common man to understand even his own immediate political interest."[31] These convictions account for Hamilton's insistence on a strong national government led by natural aristocrats, some of whom would be unelected and hold power as long as their behavior served the public good. Strength, energy (by which he meant efficiency and prudence in the use of power), centralization of power, and permanence characterize Hamilton's formula for good government.[32] From the time he was a soldier fighting for American independence, Hamilton argued that American government needed to be much more centralized than it was under the Articles of Confederation. Not only was centralization necessary, but the central government needed to be strong and energetic, exercising its powers with great vigor and fortitude. To ensure such energy and vigor, it was necessary to insulate some public officials from the influence of popular pressure by making their offices life terms. For Hamilton, it was vital that the executive be elected for life and be independent of the legislature. In his various writings and speeches on constitutionalism, Hamilton provided for a variety of checks and restraints on the transient popular will, arguing that the constitutional framework must have a "permanent will"[33] that would be opposed to the temporary and fleeting popular will. At the Constitutional Convention, Robert Yates recorded Hamilton's saying, "Nothing but a permanent body can check the imprudence of democracy."[34]

Morley suggests that Hamilton did not see a need to check the will of the few political elites who held the reins of government, and that his political theory, while at polar opposites from

Rousseau, "led to the same institutional conclusion of strongly centralized government."[35] Morley sees Hamilton as using different theoretical means to reach the same institutional ends. His analysis pushes too far a point that has some merit; it thus tends to obscure rather than illuminate the meaning of Hamilton's political theory. In fact, Hamilton was explicit about the need to check governing elites. In his June 18 speech at the Constitutional Convention, he admitted that in industrializing nations classes are divided into the few and the many. Just like Madison in *Federalist* 10, Hamilton argued that the framers of constitutions must be wary of these societal divisions and their corresponding interests, which threaten to tear the society apart: "Give all power to the many, they will oppress the few. Give all power to the few, they will oppress the many." The remedy for clashing class interests was not to rest all power in the few, as some accuse Hamilton of proposing. Both classes "ought to have power, that each may defend itself agst. the other."[36] In Hamilton's plan, the senators and the president would serve for life but representatives in the lower house of the legislature would not. The people's influence would be present not only in the lower house but also in their selecting, either directly or indirectly, the president and members of the Senate. More importantly, the political elites, who represented various classes, would not only check each other but be checked by the rule of law; they would be bound to follow the Constitution, which would serve as the greatest impediment to interests inimical to the public good. If the executive or legislature failed to abide by the Constitution, federal judges would use judicial review to check them. In short, Hamilton's constitutionalism provided a voice for all classes of society, but it clearly placed less faith in the popular will than either the Virginia or New Jersey plans did. Moreover, because he wrapped his "proposal" in admiration for British monarchy, it was taken—then, as it tends to be now—as unrepublican. Whatever its virtues and flaws, Hamilton's plan was enough out of sync with the zeitgeist of the convention and the larger sentiment of the public that it was, in the judgment of most of the delegates, unsupportable. Nonetheless, important aspects of his plan are evident in the institutional structure and theoretical principles of the Constitution. Hamilton's plan provided for three branches of government with a bicameral legislature, one house of which was elected by the people. The executive was given veto power, the power to direct war, treaty-making power with the advice of the Senate, appointment power, the power to pardon, and the power to nominate ambassadors and other officials. Federal judges would serve for life "during good behavior."

It should be noted that Hamilton frequently criticized both American and foreign leaders for acting contrary to their own and their nation's interest. As Miller suggests, he "always allowed a wide margin for the operation of irrationality and folly: particularly in international relations was he prepared to admit the potency of such imponderables as prejudice, pride and long-standing resentments."[37] During the turmoil over the Jay Treaty, Hamilton wrote that the British Ministry were "as great fools, or as great rascals, as our Jacobins."[38] He was often critical of such political elites as his state's governor, George Clinton, President John Adams, President Thomas Jefferson, and Representative James Madison, to name a few of the more prominent leaders who incurred his scrutiny.

Morley is not the only analyst to connect Hamilton's political theory to Rousseau. Cecelia M. Kenyon suggests that Hamilton's conception of the public good was, like Rousseau's notion of the general will, "morally and politically prior to private, individual ends, with which it was occasionally if not frequently in conflict."[39] Kenyon's analysis, however, fails to recognize that there is a third option. Just because Hamilton may have subordinated private, individual ends to the public good does not mean that he shared with Rousseau an affinity for authoritarian government or a conception of the common good that precluded the legitimacy of individual rights and interests. Hamilton was not inclined to social contract theory. In his political life, he was more apt to consider interests and needs as national because he represented the national government in most of his positions as a statesman. Parochial state interests often seemed to him to be inhibiting the public good, which he saw from a national perspective. But Hamilton tried to harmonize various interests to serve the public good. For example, his *Report on Manufactures* encouraged manufacturing in order to diversify the economy and provide more domestic markets for agricultural producers. Like Rousseau's general will, Hamilton's conception of the public good was not particularly protective of local autonomy but it did not obliterate particular interests, as Keynon and Morley suggest. It is true as Kenyon charges, that for Hamilton the "national interest was the primary end of government";[40] but the statement should be qualified to read, "Hamilton's conception was that the national interest was the primary goal of the *national* government." Whether Hamilton paid sufficient attention to state and sectional interests remains a legitimate question.

Apart from its political outcome, Hamilton's constitutional plan is important because it reveals his political thinking at the time of the Constitutional Convention and helps us to assess the charge that he was unfriendly to republican government. Chernow, in his biography, characterizes the plan as "harebrained" and suggests that it was inspired by Hamilton's "pessimistic view of human nature." Hamilton was torn between his optimism regarding the nation's future and his pessimism regarding human nature and democracy. As Chernow observes, "He was so busy clamping checks and balances on potentially fickle citizens that he did not stop to consider the potential of the electorate . . . Too often, his political vision harked back to a past in which well-bred elites made decisions for less-educated citizens."[41] Nathaniel Hawthorne expressed a similar point when he chastised Hamilton for not having "sufficient faith in the capacity of the people for self-government."[42] Here is the charge repeated by Morley, Chernow, and many others that Hamilton depreciated the ability of the common people and, consequently, the virtues of democracy; it is often accompanied by the charge that Hamilton was a monarchist.

Jefferson was one of the first to charge Hamilton with being an enemy of republican government and an advocate of monarchy, even "a monarchy bottomed on corruption."[43] One gets the sense from reading Hamilton's critics that they have in mind a narrow and largely Rousseaustic, or at least participatory, conception of democracy when they classify his political ideas as inconsistent with popular forms of government. Their criticisms are sometimes mere vituperation motivated by politics or personal animosity. The more thoughtful critics, however, leave traces of their sympathies for direct or participatory democracy with which one can compare Hamilton's political theory and draw conclusions regarding their compatibility.

Chernow, for example, makes a curious comment that provides some insight into his, and perhaps others', assessment of Hamilton's view of democracy. Regarding the delegates' decision to keep the proceedings of the Constitutional Convention confidential, Chernow asks, "Why such undemocratic rules for a conclave crafting a new charter?"[44] Such a question would be expected if the setting were the twenty-first century, but it is odd and anachronistic when applied to late-eighteenth-century America. The process used to create the Constitution was remarkably open and "democratic" for its day. That the delegates felt compelled to keep their discussions from the public, in order to encourage open and spontaneous dialogue among themselves, is in no way inconsistent with democracy per se, only with direct or participatory democracy. To advocates of direct or participatory democracy it seems counter-intuitive to assume that any limits placed on the popular will could enhance democracy. Yet this is precisely what Hamilton believed. This belief does not make him an advocate of monarchy, aristocracy, or oligarchy; but it does mean that he advocated a different variety of democracy and republican government than did Rousseau, Jefferson, or Paine.

None of the Framers of the Constitution was an advocate of pure or direct democracy. Hamilton and the other Framers did not believe in the dictum of direct democracy, *vox populi, vox Dei*, the voice of the people is the voice of God. In fact, they considered direct democracy to be a form of tyranny, because it concentrates all power in the hands of the people, failing to provide adequate safeguards for liberty and numerical minorities. Madison's *Federalist* 10 is clear that democracy (by which he meant direct democracy) cannot provide a cure for the disease of faction. In no uncertain terms, Madison, reflecting the prevalent view of the Framers, rejected pure democracy as a legitimate regime type. Tyranny is defined by Madison in *Federalist* 47 as the concentration of power. Thus, because direct democracy concentrates all power in the people, it is tyranny. Madison contrasted republican government and direct democracy in order to prove that the former is a superior form of government and the one prudent for the United States.

Chernow does not explain what specifically he means by "the potential of the electorate," but he is clear that Hamilton failed to consider it. He is well aware of the following: that Hamilton opposed slavery and most restrictions on eligibility to vote, including those in New York prohibiting Loyalists from voting; that Hamilton wanted citizenship to be the only requirement for holding office in the national government; that he favored a popularly elected lower house and the direct or indirect election of the Senate and the president; that he fought to lower the residency requirement for holding office; and that he took his arguments for various policies to the people through the press and in public speeches. Not the least of these efforts to communicate with the people was *The Federalist*. Measured by the standards of representative or indirect democracy, the creation of the American Constitution was highly democratic and Hamilton's role in it was perfectly consistent with the principles of constitutional democracy.

Jefferson's view of the relationship between government and the governed has long been regarded with more favor by Hamilton's critics. Although somewhat inconsistent with his political theory, Jefferson's characterization of republican government is "government by its citizens in mass, acting directly and personally, according to rules established by the majority." His measure of devotion to republicanism is the degree and extent of "direct action of the citizens."[45] Jefferson's objections to the Constitution were precisely that it failed to sufficiently empower the direct will of the people.[46] Hamilton's view of the relationship between representatives and the people was much more like Madison's and Burke's: representatives should always act in accordance with the public good, but they should exercise independent judgment because raw popular will tends to be provincial and parochial, in Madison's language it is in need of refining and enlarging. It may be that many of Hamilton's critics reject both his view of human nature and its corresponding depreciation of direct or participatory democracy. Consequently, what may seem to some as a realistic view of human nature is classified by Hamilton's critics as dark and pessimistic, and what may seem to some as a prudent and realistic view of democracy is disparaged by others as thoughtless and condescending toward the people.

HAMILTON ON LEADERSHIP AND REPUBLICAN VIRTUE

The role of "republican virtue" in Hamilton's political theory has been questioned by a variety of critics. Hamilton tended to be quick to judge the fitness of individuals to lead. Few measured up to his standards. Those who lacked what he considered the requisite boldness to lead he disparaged as "old women," "womanish," or "midwives."[47] He judged men by their ability to subordinate self-interest and ideological passion to the common good and to conduct public affairs with energy and prudence. In other words, he expected leaders to have a sufficient degree of virtue.

One example of Hamilton defending virtue was his public chastisement of a member of Congress, Samuel Chase, during the Revolutionary War. Chase, who would later be the target of President Jefferson's efforts to impeach Supreme Court justices,[48] was suspected of using his position in the Congress during the Revolutionary War to his financial advantage. As was mentioned in chapter 1, Chase formed a company by which, it was thought, he hoped to corner the flour market in Philadelphia, knowing that the French fleet was soon to arrive, which would drive up demand and thus the price of flour. Hamilton, although in the throes of the war, took up his pen on three occasions over the course of a month, writing for the first time as "Publius," and took Chase to task. In one of these three letters, all published in the *New-York Journal*, Hamilton called Chase a "degenerate character" and suggested that his greed, if imitated by others, was capable of undermining American independence. Hamilton recognized that some degree of greed had to be tolerated, given human nature.

> But when a man, appointed to be the guardian of the State, and the depositary of the happiness and morals of the people—forgetful of the solemn relation, in which he stands—descends to the dishon-

est artifices of a mercantile projector, and sacrifices his conscience and his trust to pecuniary motives; there is no strain of abhorrence, of which the human mind is capable, nor punishment, the vengeance of the people can inflict, which may not be applied to him, with justice.[49]

Echoing Cicero's admonitions to his son in *On Duties*, Hamilton stated, "[Y]our avarice will be fatal to your ambition." Hamilton makes clear in these letters that virtue is instrumental to the ends of politics. Chief among the virtues required for statesmanship is disinterestedness, that is, setting aside of self-interest. In addition, "the sincerity of a man, and the politeness of a gentleman" are required in all transactions.[50] These attributes are what Cicero called "honorableness," and they are, Hamilton insists, the duty of individuals in all facets of life. In a like manner, he wrote in his *Letters from Phocion*, "[t]hat honesty is still the best policy; that justice and moderation are the surest supports of every government, are maxims, which however they may be called trite, [are] at all times true, though too seldom regarded, but rarely neglected with impunity."[51]

Hamilton's understanding of duty and honor is consistent with Cicero's conception of them as articulated in his *De Officiis* (*On Duties*). In the form of a letter to his son, Cicero explained that every part of life, personal and public requires compliance with duty. Knowledge of duty requires one to apply the law of nature to circumstances. To follow mere self-interest is to shirk one's duty, for to be honorable means to seek those things that are ends in themselves and not means; to cultivate wisdom, justice, greatness of spirit, and seemliness requires "modesty and restraint."[52] What inclined both Cicero and Hamilton to republican duty was their commitment to public life, public things, and most of all, to their respective republics themselves. They were both republicans who were dedicated in their statesmanship and political thinking to *res publica*. Cicero explained, "[W]hen you have surveyed everything with reason and spirit, of all fellowships none is more serious, and none dearer, than that of each of us with the republic. Parents are dear, and children, relatives and acquaintances are dear, but our country has on its own embraced all the affections of all of us."[53]

Cicero elaborated: While human beings are naturally inclined to self-preservation, they are social beings with duties to others as well. Duty extends to enemies in war, slaves, and foreigners. Cicero joined honorableness and benefit, saying that what is best for individuals and for the political community as a whole will produce a just outcome. Following duty does not, as Machiavelli suggests, in certain circumstances put one at a disadvantage but promotes one's true advantage, which is found in the honorable life. As Cicero succinctly states the point, "[W]hatever is honorable is beneficial." Honor requires a greatness of spirit that lifts individuals above immediate self-interest to a place where virtue and benefit are joined. Cunning, deceit, and cruelty are contrary to what is honorable. Although the use of such means may sometimes seem beneficial, it will undermine the greatness of spirit on which honor and duty depend. Moreover, "the good man will never, for the sake of a friend, act contrary to the republic, to a sworn oath, or to good faith."[54] Duty to the republic does not mean that individuals must forgo friendships, but honorable people will not undermine the integrity of the republic in order to benefit their friends.

A few examples from Hamilton's political thought and conduct illustrate the connection to Cicero's understanding of duty and honor. Like Cicero, Hamilton was quick to criticize public officials who used their position to advance their private interest. He felt a responsibility to uplift the plight of slaves, and he conducted the affairs of the Treasury Department with the utmost integrity, refusing in one instance to help his friend William Duer, who had squandered money speculating on government securities.

Hamilton's intervention on behalf of Myles Cooper and his condemnation of Sears's Raid suggest regard for honoring, even being merciful, to one's enemies. This attribute is also present in Hamilton's reaction to the 1778 prisoner exchange that he was asked to negotiate while encamped at Valley Forge. Hamilton was appalled that some members of Congress, although recognizing that prisoner exchange under the circumstances would not be advantageous to the Americans, were willing to negotiate as a ruse, knowing that when negotiations failed the British would be blamed. Hamilton called the behavior "shameful" as well as "bad policy." The consequence of "such frequent breaches of faith" is to "ruin our national character." The preservation of national character was necessary to uphold the honor of the government at home and abroad. Hamilton explained:

> The general notions of justice and humanity are implanted in almost every human breast; and ought not to be too freely shocked. In the present case, the passions of the country and army are on the side of an exchange; and a studied attempt to avoid it will disgust both, and serve to make the service odious. It will injure drafting and recruiting, discourage the militia & increase the discontents of the army. The prospects of hopeless captivity cannot but be very disagreeable to men constantly exposed to the chance of it. Those, whose lot it is to fall into it, will have little scruple to get rid of it by joining the enemy.[55]

Hamilton, like Cicero, declared that virtue, honor, and benefit coincide. Following the honorable path is not simply done for its own sake but also because it will benefit the nation. This is a clear departure from Machiavelli, who instructs that rulers must "seem to be compassionate, trustworthy, sympathetic, honest, [and] religious" because merely appearing to be virtuous is often more important than actually being virtuous.[56] Hamilton admitted that the suspect members of Congress might be correct in concluding that prisoner exchange was not in America's interest, but Hamilton was not guided, at least in this instance, by national interest alone. He remarks, "And I would ask, whether in a republican state and a republican army; such cruel policy as that of exposing those men who are foremost in defence of their country to the miseries of hopeless captivity, can succeed?" Hamilton declared that he had "so much of the milk of humanity" in him that he rejected "*Neronian* maxims" in favor of the old proverb that "honesty is the best policy." He added, "I can never expect any good from a systematic deviation from" this proverb, and he refused to follow the lead of some political leaders and disregard "national character, or the rules of good faith."[57]

His efforts to chastise Samuel Chase for profiteering during the war are consistent with Cicero's sense of honor in business transactions and statesmanship. His honorable treatment of captured British soldiers at Yorktown,[58] his defense of Tories after the war, and his support of a captured British major's request to be shot rather than hanged[59] all remind one of Cicero's admonitions regarding the "laws of war," specifically how enemies should be treated. In British Major John André, Hamilton saw honor and virtue. André had been captured when Benedict Arnold's treason was discovered. He was considered a spy and so was scheduled to be executed. Hamilton met with André several times, and he wrote to his friend John Laurens, "Never perhaps did any man suffer death with more justice, or deserve it less." Hamilton noted that André, immediately upon capture, had written a letter to Washington apologizing for his action and insisting the he was not knowingly part of Arnold's plot, intending only to meet an unknown person on neutral ground to receive intelligence. He assured Washington that he had not acted dishonorably. Hamilton described this behavior as "manly gratitude." André also asked that he be permitted to send a letter to his commanding general, Henry Clinton, who had been good to him, so that the execution would not "leave a sting in his mind." Clinton intervened on behalf of André and asked for his release as a personal favor, offering to exchange any prisoner for him. When André made his request for a professional execution, Washington denied it. His final request was that those present be "witness to the world, that I die like a brave man." Hamilton remarked, "There was something singularly interesting in the character and fortunes of André," including his "elegance of mind and manners," his "taste for the fine arts," and his "proficiency in poe<try,> music and painting." After a long and poetic description of André's virtues, Hamilton reflects, "I speak not of André's conduct in this affair as a Philosophe[r], but as a man of the world. The authorized maxims and practices of war are the satire of human nature."[60]

With few exceptions, Hamilton's insistence that enemies be treated with mercy did not extend to those he considered the most pernicious to civilization, Jacobins. While he had reservations about the Alien and Sedition Acts, he criticized President Adams for not using them to deport seditious Jacobins. André, by contrast, was a man of aristocratic character and temperament, and New York Loyalists possessed some of the same characteristics and were useful to the economy. Hamilton had a more difficult time finding redeeming qualities in his Jacobin rivals. He did demonstrate mercy to Edmond Genêt once he lost his position in the French diplomatic corps; but as long as Jacobins presented a threat to American order at home and security abroad, Hamilton found little ground on which to cooperate with them. His most immoderate moments in public life involved Jefferson, to whom he showed little mercy, forgiveness, or respect.

In his law practice, Hamilton was known to charge fees that were low, and with few exceptions, he represented only clients he believed to be innocent. Chernow describes an incident from his law career that illustrates his reputation for honor. A former soldier who had served under Hamilton's command asked for his legal services. Hamilton seemed puzzled by the request, because the soldier had, subsequent to the war's end, become an outspoken critic of Hamilton's politics. The soldier, however, responded, "I served in your company during the war and I know you will do me justice in spite of my rudeness." On another occasion, he refused to represent the executor of an estate who was being sued by an heir after the executor presented Hamilton with a pile of gold pieces before explaining his case. Hamilton advised the man to settle the dispute in accordance with justice.[61]

Most commentators on Hamilton do not acknowledge the degree to which his constitutional theory depends on quality of character, and some place him squarely outside the Classical and Christian traditions that center politics on virtue and moral character. Hamilton's view of character and virtue is not identical to either the Classical or Christian perspective—not monolithic doctrines, because both encompass a range of views—but his understanding can be considered a reconstitution of the older views that incorporates modern ideas. His view of human nature is especially indebted to David Hume's *A Treatise of Human Nature.* Some historians, among them Bernard Bailyn and Gordon Wood, tend to overstate Hamilton's and the American Framers' emphasis on lower human motives and the necessity of political institutions in their establishment of constitutional government and understate their reliance on virtue and moral character; they likewise overestimate the influence of liberalism on the formation of the American Constitution and underestimate the importance of Classical and especially Christian influences.[62]

Wood argues that, "instead of virtue and the natural sociability of people, Hamilton, Washington, and other Federalists saw only the ordinary individual's selfish pursuit of his own private interests and happiness. Social stability therefore required the harnessing of this self-interest."[63] Wood acknowledges that Hamilton recognized the virtue of disinterestedness in a few elites but claims that he believed it to be absent, for the most part, from the common people. The success of republican government in America, in Wood's interpretation of Hamilton's politics, would depend on the presence of disinterested leaders like Hamilton himself and their ability to administer government in such a way that the people's self-interest would be directed in such fashion as to elevate the nation.

There is an element of truth in Wood's characterization of Hamilton's political theory, but he focuses too much on self-interest and not enough on elevated character. Hamilton clearly thought that self-interest could be useful in promoting the public good but that it was insufficient for the direction of public or private affairs toward happiness, justice, and goodness. Hamilton's political theory assumes a blending of the lower and higher aspects of human nature. He wrote to Rufus King, a fellow member of the Constitutional Convention, "'Tis the lot of every thing human to mingle a portion of ill with the good."[64] Human motives and actions, in other words, are rarely pure. In many cases, the bad is the price one must pay for the good.[65] When Hamilton joined his friend John Laurens in an effort to create revolutionary battalions of black soldiers, he was connecting interest and justice. Writing to John Jay, then serving as the president of Congress, in support of Laurens's plan, he cited the interest of the nation and pointed out that troops were in short supply and the addition of these battalions would bolster American forces. He added that if the Americans failed to take advantage of the opportunity, the British would not hesitate to do so. Hamilton also appealed to higher motives, observing that the "contempt we have been taught to entertain for the blacks, makes us fancy many things that are founded neither in reason nor experience." The plan provided that the black soldiers would be emancipated after their military service ended. Hamilton remarked that "the dictates of humanity and true policy equally interest me in favor of this unfortunate class of men."[66]

His insistence that individuals of high character lead the nation was joined with his commitment to representative government. Perhaps it was with his personal experience and situation in mind that he expected the people to elect their representatives based on character and merit, not wealth or birth.[67] This sentiment for meritocracy is present throughout Hamilton's writings, and it belies the myth propagated by Jefferson and others that he was an advocate of hereditary government and monarchy. His confidence in the people's ability to choose meritorious leaders deteriorated with time, as the Federalists gave way to the Jeffersonians. He ardently defended the U.S. Senate, which was not directly elected, as a necessary check on popular will, and he warned that, without institutions that mitigated the democratic impulse in representatives, Congress would "become a mere mob, exposed to every irregular impulse, and subject to every breeze of faction."[68]

Hamilton accepted that character alone was insufficient to ensure good government: "Government being administered by Men is naturally like individuals, subject to particular impulses, passions, prejudices, vices; of course to inconstancy of views and mutability of conduct."[69] He asked, "What nation was ever blessed with a constant succession of upright and wise Administrators?"[70] Hamilton also knew that power could have a corrupting influence on human character. Anticipating Lord Acton's famous dictum on its potential for corruption, he stated, "A fondness for power is implanted in most men, and it is natural to abuse it when acquired."[71] The Constitution provides protections against these human failings, by dividing government into parts. Wrote Hamilton, "It can hardly happen, that all the branches or parts of it can be infected at one time with a common passion, a disposition, manifestly inimical to justice and the Public good; as to prostrate the public Credit by revoking a pledge given to the Creditors."[72] Hamilton's view is consistent with both moral realism and republican theories of government. Separated powers and a deliberative constitutional process are necessary because of the lower inclinations of human nature, but they also encourage the higher aspirations of human nature by compelling political leaders to hear the merits of rival interests as a prerequisite to promoting one's own interest. Hamilton recognized that republics are especially susceptible to the intrigues of demagogues and "the political-empyric" (the politically inflammatory)[73] who use the people's passions as the instrument with which to aggrandize power. As Hamilton noted: "It has been aptly observed that *Cato* was the Tory—*Caesar* the Whig of his day. The former frequently resisted—the latter always flattered the follies of the people. Yet the former perished with the Republic [and] the latter destroyed it. No popular Government was ever without its Catalines & its Caesars. These are its true enemies."[74]

If leaders do not possess the spirit of constitutionalism, politics is reduced to partisan bickering. In such circumstances, discord characterizes political conduct. Hamilton's objections to his political opponents, whom he often labeled "Jacobins," was that they were motivated not by patriotic disinterestedness but by factious partisanship. He called factions "the natural disease of popular Governments."[75] His concern regarding the Jeffersonians was that they would govern not in accord with the common good but in a way that promoted their ideological interests. Jefferson's sentiments toward the French Revolution revealed, so Hamilton thought, an ideological desire that was inimical to American interests. Likewise, Hamilton tended to view the states as reservoirs of parochial interests that inhibited the public good, which he saw as something national in character and scope. Hamilton considered events like Sears's Raid, Shays's Rebellion, the Whiskey Rebellion, the Virginia and Kentucky Resolutions, and Fries's Rebellion as indicative of the tendency in local communities for factious groups to disrupt the public order and undermine the public good. Not surprisingly, except for Sears's Raid and Fries's Rebellion, on which he was silent, Jefferson supported the rebellious factions.

Critics assert that Hamilton tended to emphasize the national interest and centralization of power to the extent that local interests and sectional groups end up subordinated to, if not obliterated by, a large and powerful national government. Stated in different terms, the issue pertains to diversity and uniformity.

Was Hamilton so intent on promoting a stronger union that he defined the national interest in a way that achieved unity by eroding the type of diversity on which it depends? Even in Hamilton's day, the American republic was a large and diverse nation. Climate, economy, and religious affiliation, to name a few factors, varied throughout the nation. Achieving unity among such diverse state and regional cultures required harmonizing these different and often competing interests. Harmony is something different from uniformity. It is accomplished not by destroying differences between local communities but by allowing them sufficient autonomy to flourish. Federalism aims to accomplish this objective by decentralizing power. As a consequence, state and local communities can tailor their laws and policies to fit the circumstances of their communities. To force local and state communities to conform to one uniform national way of life would mean the end of local autonomy and the cultural richness that stems from diversity. Harmony, then, is the mean between extremes of stifling uniformity that destroys local autonomy and a degree of decentralization that provides little or no common ground on which varied interests can unite.

Since the time of the Constitutional Convention, Hamilton has been accused of wishing to reduce the states to administrative appendages of the national government. That he is considered the father of loose constructionism adds to the suspicion that he was insufficiently attentive to individual rights, sectional interests, and constitutional checks on national power. Failing to win support at the Constitutional Convention for a unitary government, he used a loose interpretation of the Constitution to transform a limited federal republic into a highly centralized state. Critics who see Hamilton in this light find commonality between his political theory and those of Machiavelli, Hobbes, and Rousseau.

As long as states were small, Hamilton believed, their capacity to interfere with the common good was insignificant. In a 1799 letter that Chernow describes as "dark" and "vengeful,"[76] he suggested to Jonathan Dayton, the Speaker of the House of Representatives, that a constitutional amendment be created "enabling Congress on the application of any considerable portion of a state, containing not less than a hundred thousand persons, to erect it into a separate state." In order to discourage the use of such divisions to avoid fiscal obligations, Hamilton included in his proposal a provision for proportionally transferring existing state debt to the new state. He justified the amendment by arguing that the "subdivision of the great states is indispensable to the security of the General Government and with it of the Union."[77] His argument for why the security of the national government and the union depended on the fragmentation of large states reveals his view of federalism, which he called "the Gordian Knot of our political situation."[78] "Great States will always feel a rivalship with the common head, will often be disposed to machinate against it, and in certain situations will be able to do it with decisive effect. The subdivisions of such states ought to be a cardinal point in the Fœderal policy: and small states are doubtless best adapted to the purposes of local regulation and to the preservation of the republican spirit."[79] In other words, small states are better able to address local matters and are less likely to meddle in national affairs, because their capacity to encroach on the national government's sovereignty is prohibitively small. Interestingly, Hamilton declared small states better suited to embody the republican spirit than either large states or the national government. By "republican spirit" he meant the people's control of the government. Why does state population size matter in regard to the control that the people can exert on the government? The smaller the population of a state, the more attention its representatives must give to the popular will. By implication, Hamilton was suggesting that the national government is and should be less republican than the states.

Presumably, local concerns require more attention to the people's will than does the national interest. This assertion raises the question Why is the popular will any more worthy of consideration on a small scale than on a large scale? In *Federalist* 10, Madison claimed that enlarging the orbit of government is part of the solution to controlling the effects of faction. Hamilton, for different reasons, argued for the reduction of the orbit of state governments. The problem of majority faction exists at both the state and national level of government. How does Hamilton reconcile this contradiction?

What differentiates the local public good from the national

interest is that the latter must encompass and harmonize many disparate interests. The national interest cannot be encompassed by any regional interest group. Increasing popular input at the national level of government, thought Hamilton, would only exacerbate the difficulties of mitigating competing interests and controlling factions; and for Hamilton, factions were, by definition, always inimical to the common good. The local public good, by contrast, is more likely to be included in a uniform national interest that is expressed by the collective popular will. In other words, at the national level, popular pressure gives voice to the many competing local interests that aim to influence national policy. At the local level, assuming that the size of the state is sufficiently small, rather than a diversity of competing interests, there is more likely to be one overarching interest. Thus, because the popular will and the local interest are more likely to be in accord, it makes sense that state politics should be more democratic than national politics, the threat of faction being less intense at the state level.

If this is an accurate reading of Hamilton's view, then two important consequences follow. First, Hamilton would seem to discount the possibility of a local faction's taking control of state government and infringing the rights of numerical minorities. Did he not envision that something like a political machine run by the very demagogues he despised might dominate state politics and subject state communities to majority tyranny? Second, if large states were reduced in size precisely to weaken them and protect the national government from their meddling reach, then they would be too weak to play the role that Hamilton assigned them in *Federalist* 28. They would be incapable of providing the people with a protection against tyranny from the national government, unless several states were united in resistance to national tyranny, because their capacity to check it would be crippled by their diminished size and strength. This reading of Hamilton's view of federalism not only calls into question his commitment to a vibrant brand of federalism that uses the tension between state and national sovereignty to keep each level of government in its proper constitutional place, but it also suggests that Hamilton was insufficiently attentive to the danger that local popular factions can present to local autonomous groups and associations.

Hamilton's objective in proposing a constitutional amendment concerning state size was protecting the national government from large powerful states like Virginia. The proposal exposes Hamilton's theoretical and political blind side, the vulnerability of legitimate local and state interests to the power of a large and potentially overreaching national government.

Hamilton's constitutionalism is centered on the notion that there must be a permanent national will to counteract the whims of local and sectional democratic impulse.[80] By democratic impulse he had in mind such instances of disorder as the resistance in Virginia and Kentucky to the Alien and Sedition Acts. He noted to Speaker Dayton, "[The] late attempt of Virginia and Kentucke to unite the state legislatures in a direct resistance to certain laws of the Union can be considered in no other light than as an attempt to change the Government." Hamilton accused Virginia of preparing its militia to support its resolution by force.[81]

Living in the state of New York surely colored his perception of the place of states, especially large ones, in the federal system. George Clinton, six-term governor of New York, was representative of the pedigree of provincial leaders who routinely put local interests before national interests and who, after the American Revolution, treated Tories with disdain and injustice, using the sale of their property to avoid raising taxes and to win popular support. Hamilton, by contrast, defended dozens of Tories in his legal practice and successfully challenged the Trespass Act in *Rutgers v. Waddington* (1784). Hamilton, true to his belief that the central government should be primary in political affairs, argued that, because the Confederate Congress had ratified the peace treaty that ended the Revolutionary War in 1783, under the law of nations the terms of the treaty superseded state laws like New York's Trespass Act. Cicero, he reminded the court, had established that higher law, like the law of nations, supersedes what today is called statutory law when the two are in conflict.[82] Hamilton returned to this argument in *Federalist* 78. He also fought for the repeal of the New York acts that prohibited many Loyalists from practicing law in the state.[83] In 1782 he wrote to Robert Morris, then superintendent of finance for the United States, about New York, complaining that there was "no *order* that has a will of its own. The inquiry constantly is what will *please* not what will *benefit* the people. In such a government there can be nothing but temporary expedient, fickleness and folly."[84] He desired a more permanent standard for conducting political affairs, one that was derived from human nature and the natural law.

What Hamilton failed to recognize was the extent to which particular interests and groups are vital to the formation of the common good. If particular interests are brought together in a deliberative, constitutional process, rather than inhibiting the common good, they can potentially have a centripetal effect by synthesizing disparate interests in accordance with justice. In his statesmanship, Hamilton recognized the need to account for the realities and limits of politics; and, when necessary to win support for his policies, he was willing to compromise and incorporate the ideas of rival groups. Yet, his political theory fails to clearly embrace this central component of American constitutional government. In this instance, he seems not to have reflected upon something he discovered in his political activities and knew intuitively.

Hamilton, unlike Jefferson and the anti-Federalists, was far less concerned about the prospect of tyranny's emanating from centralized power. Consequently, he was somewhat insensitive to the possibility that decentralized communities, like states, embodied genuine interests that were a necessary counterweight to a dominant national will, which might insist on an artificial uniformity. As long as the national government was in the hands of men who possessed civic virtue, thought Hamilton, tyranny was unlikely. In regard to the national government, Hamilton's prejudice was to fear too little power more than too much power.[85] He stated, after successfully creating the national banking system and the assumption plan, "[M]y opinion has been and is that the true danger to our prosperity is not the overbearing strength of the Fœderal head but its weakness and imbecility for preserving the union of the States and controuling the eccentricities of State ambition and the explosions of factious passions."[86]

Hamilton was not unaware of the danger of concentrated national power. In his writings in *The Federalist*, he addressed the problem of a tyrannical central government. In *Federalist* 28, for example, he argued that "the people, without exaggeration, may be said to be entirely the masters of their own fate." Under the proposed constitution, power was "almost always the rival of power." The national government would "stand ready to check the usurpations of the state governments," which would "have the same disposition towards the general government." And the people were to take advantage of this balance of powers: "The people, by throwing themselves into either scale, will infallibly make it preponderate. If their rights are invaded by either, they can make use of the other, as the instrument of redress." Here Hamilton seems equally concerned with national tyranny as with local tyranny, and he assures his audience that the national government is incapable of imposing a tyranny on the states. He states with extreme confidence, "It may safely be received as an axiom in our political system, that the state governments will, in all possible contingencies, afford complete security against invasions of the public liberty by the national authority."[87]

To capture the spirit and significance of Hamilton's sentiment, it is necessary to recall that he was writing in circumstances much different from contemporary America. During the American Revolution and under the Articles of Confederation, a feeble national government struggled to provide the army with adequate supplies and to unite the states in managing political, military, and economic affairs. Hamilton witnessed the struggle firsthand. Shays's Rebellion, which he referenced in *Federalist* 28, illustrates the nature of the problem as Hamilton saw it. In his view, "seditions and insurrections are, unhappily, maladies as inseparable from the body politic, as tumours and eruptions from the natural body."[88] When a seditious insurrection breaks out, as it did in western Massachusetts in 1786, the people become the victims of anarchy unless a sufficient power exists to quell the rebellion. In the case of Shays's Rebellion, a state militia had to be formed to put down the rebellion because the national government was too weak to restore order. If Massachusetts had failed to stop the rebels, anarchy, like a tumor, might have spread to the surrounding states. In Hamilton's opinion, this made such situations of national concern.

CHAPTER 4

HAMILTON AND AMERICAN CONSTITUTIONAL FORMATION

A written constitution is but a scheme on paper. It sets the form
of government; but the form of a government is of less
consequence than its spirit, for it is the spirit that giveth life.
Among those who have given life to the language of the
Constitution Alexander Hamilton was the first in point of time,
and the existing government of the United States owes more to
him than most people realize.
—William Bennett Munro, *The Makers
of the Unwritten Constitution*

IT WAS DURING the Constitutional Convention, in the articles of
The Federalist, and in defending the ratification of the Constitution that Hamilton articulated the central aspects of his political
theory and demonstrated a willingness to compromise his ideal
constitution. Because he had to navigate the politics of constitution making, he was not always at liberty to speak his mind or to
advocate his most heartfelt ideas. After his June 18, 1787, proposal for a new constitution was largely ignored by the delegates
to the convention, he was compelled to move within the boundaries of the emerging consensus. Compromise and consensus
had much to do with Hamilton's subsequent arguments. That
he felt compelled to deviate from his pure theory does not depreciate the authenticity of his political ideas. An examination of
the existing circumstances reveals that Hamilton was not an un-
compromising idealist and that he took politics to be the art of
the possible. His political theory tends to avoid abstraction pre-

cisely because he was able to read the times and find ways to reconcile his first principles, which he was unwilling to sacrifice, with the exigencies and possibilities of particular circumstances.

To be experientially grounded, political theory must account for and accommodate the particular historical conditions in which it is derived and to which it is directed. It must also account for the historical and theoretical antecedents that provide its wider philosophical horizon. Hamilton's political theory is not ahistorically abstract but richly concrete and historical. It is embedded with historical evidence, appealing to what Hamilton called, in *Federalist* 6, "the accumulated experience of ages." Given its grounding in historical experience, Hamilton's political theory can be differentiated from rival theories that tend to be abstract due to their reliance on ahistorical principles or speculative theories. For example, unlike Jefferson, John Taylor of Caroline, and Thomas Paine, Hamilton did not affix himself to the proposition that popular government was appropriate in all places and circumstances. On the other hand, he did not believe, as some have said he did, that monarchy was the best form of government for every society; he found it especially wrong for the United States. Writing to Lafayette in 1799, Hamilton remarked, "I hold with *Montesquieu*, that a government must be fitted to a nation as much as a Coat to the Individual, and consequently that what may be good at Philadelphia may be bad at Paris and ridiculous at Petersburgh."[1] When Hamilton contemplated the best form of government for the thirteen states, he surveyed the particular circumstances as well as related historical experience and tailored the architecture of the proposed government accordingly.

THE BACKGROUND FOR *THE FEDERALIST*

Hamilton planned the project that became known as *The Federalist*; he wrote fifty-one of its eight-five essays, including all of those on executive and judicial powers, and he contributed to those on federalism, national security, political economy, the exclusion of a bill of rights, and the administration of government. He wrote his essays, totaling some 117,000 words, in seven months, while continuing to conduct his law practice. Biographer Ron Chernow aptly notes that he "wrote with the speed of a beautifully organized mind that digested ideas thoroughly, slotted them into appropriate pigeonholes, then regurgitated them at will."[2] Hamilton chose "Publius" as the pseudonym that he, James Madison, and John Jay would use for *The Federalist* essays, a name he had first used in 1778 when chastising Samuel Chase for his lack of republican virtue. The namesake of this "Publius" was Publius Valerius, also known as "Poplicola," which means "people-lover," a revolutionary founder of the Roman Republic. Plutarch remembered him as an enemy of tyranny and defender of republican government. He was known to be magnanimous, moderate, eloquent, and honorable.[3]

Hamilton began to contemplate the American political order, including the structure of its political institutions, while he was a soldier during the American Revolution. He was forced by circumstances to wonder why American troops were poorly equipped and why the Continental Congress was incapable of raising adequate revenue to fund the war. Such practical concerns led him to believe that the cause of American inefficiency was its highly decentralize political system combined with political leaders who lacked the gumption to use power effectively. The national government was beholden to state legislatures that were unwilling, in most cases, to recognize the national common good. Even as Americans were fighting for their lives and for independence for the colonies as a single political entity, the colonies seemed incapable of union. Parochial squabbles within and between states which seemed petty to Hamilton hampered efforts to win a war that was in nearly everyone's interest. The inertia of government under the Articles of Confederation pushed Hamilton in a direction to which he was already predisposed: promotion of stronger national government and weaker state governments. The circumstances in the period before the Constitutional Convention, as Hamilton saw them, are captured by historian John Fiske:

Congress was bankrupt, foreign nations were scoffing at us, Connecticut had barely escaped from war with Pennsylvania and New York from New Hampshire, there were riots and bloodshed in

Vermont, Rhode Island seemed on the verge of civil war, Massachusetts was actually engaged in suppressing armed rebellion, Connecticut and New Jersey were threatening commercial nonintercourse with New York. Spain was defying us at the mouth of the Mississippi, and a party in Virginia was entertaining the idea of a separate Southern confederacy.[4]

These interstate and international rivalries figure prominently in Hamilton's *Federalist* essays. They are the backdrop for his argument insisting that unless power was more centralized and the states unified, both civil and international conflict would plague the United States. Hamilton believed that republican government was faltering under the Articles of Confederation because of its ill-conceived organization of power and sovereignty. Reconfiguration of sovereignty was necessary, he believed, for republican government to succeed in the United States.

Not surprisingly Hamilton concluded that the solution to the inefficiency of fragmented government was to centralize power in a way that would provide energy and efficiency to political life without catering to democratic impulse or demagoguery. Energy would not be provided by the people pressuring government to act; it would emanate from expanding the scope of national government, combined with the effective administration of government. Government needed more energy and vitality than it had under the Articles of Confederation, Hamilton felt, but it also required a separation of powers—which did not exist under the Articles—to protect against the abuse of national power. Moreover, centralizing power did not mean obliterating the states but subordinating them to the national government in matters that he considered the proper province of central governments: military, international, and economic affairs. In other domains of governing, the states would remain exclusively sovereign. Although he changed points of emphasis in different circumstances, Hamilton advocated a federal system of government, a compound republic that divided sovereignty among the national, state, and local governments. In such a system, the states would be sovereign in the area of police powers and other local concerns but the national government would be sovereign where its power and scope mattered most, in national defense, economic development and trade, and foreign policy.

As Hamilton saw it, under the Constitution, national encroach-ment on state power would be highly unlikely, because the Con-stitution granted the federal government all it could possibly want.[5] Even assuming that the will to power controlled federal officials to the point that they would desire to usurp state pow-ers, no such encroachment would be possible. Because the states would always be more proximate to the people and because human nature creates greater affection for what is closest to one-self, the national government would be incapable of winning the affection of the people. It was, he believed, a fact of human na-ture that individuals' affections are greatest the more proximate the object. In *Federalist* 17, Hamilton gave one exception to this general rule regarding the people's feelings about the central gov-ernment: "much better administration" of the national govern-ment might create affection between the people and the national government. While he considered this contingency unlikely, be-cause the states would control the "great cement of society," the "ordinary administration of criminal and civil justice," he worked tirelessly as treasury secretary to make it a reality. What will be most immediate to the people, he predicted, is their state gov-ernment's role in the protection of their lives and property. By contrast, the work of the national government will be less im-mediate in the lives of the people.

Hamilton considered it a fact of human nature and historical experience that the people's affections rest with the most im-mediate level of government. In a speech to the New York Rati-fying Convention he explained:

> There are certain social principles in human nature, from which we may draw the most solid conclusions with respect to the con-duct of individuals, and of communities. We love our families, more than our neighbors: We love our neighbors, more than our countrymen in general. The human affections, like the solar heat, lose their intensity, as they depart from the centre; and become languid in proportion to the expansion of the circle, on which they act. On these principles, the attachment of the individual will be first and forever secured by the states governments.[6]

Hamilton was describing circumstances that were generally true, but it is less clear that his personal sentiments followed his theory of proximate affection. Because the United States was his adopted home and because so much of his attachment was forged in fighting the revolution and helping to form the national government, his greatest affection seemed to be toward the nation rather than subnational communities. It is a weakness of Hamilton's political theory that, while he recognized the affinity in human nature for the immediate, he failed to identify human nature's opposite affinity for distant things that provide a means of escape from immediate responsibilities. For instance, when criticizing Jacobins, he displayed a sense that they were inclined to meddle in the affairs of others, but he never raised that intuition to reflective awareness or applied it to the behavior of the United States.

John C. Miller writes that Hamilton's political theory underwent a "radical departure" from its earlier construction. Miller argues that prior to the Constitutional Convention, Hamilton's political theory was more balanced, in that it was concerned equally with increasing the power of government and ensuring that power was adequately checked and restrained. His fear of tyrannical government seemed to fade as the experience of British oppression was overshadowed by the impotence of government under the Articles of Confederation. "During the American Revolution, he had regarded the claim of the British Parliament to bind the colonies in all cases whatsoever as proof of its intention to reduce them to slavery." In devising a government to replace the Articles of Confederation, Miller asserts, Hamilton fundamentally changed his conception of political power. "There was no enumeration of the powers of government, no Bill of Rights, no safeguards for the 'natural rights' of man against the state. Instead, the national government was empowered to pass all laws whatsoever: sovereignty, absolute and uncontrollable, was vested in the government of the United States. The Constitution was not made superior to the government."[7]

Miller's argument has merit, but it overstates the case. Hamilton was indeed ambiguous at times in defining the powers of the national government and the specific limits on those powers. In *Federalist* 23, for example, he stated that "it is both unwise and dangerous to deny the federal government an unconfined authority, in respect to all those objects which are intrusted to its management." This statement implies that the Articles of Confederation confined the national government's sovereignty in a way that precluded energy in and effective administrative of government, but Hamilton was clear that power had to be "safely vested."[8] Safe vesting was achieved when power was divided and ensconced in an elaborate system of checks and balances buttressed by judicial review. In short, power must be confined by the rule of law. Government officials were subject to the Constitution, and the courts were designed to ensure that they remained within their designated constitutional boundaries. That Hamilton rejected the need for a bill of rights and was not enamored of natural rights theory does not mean that he disparaged civil liberties or individual rights. His defense of liberty did not emanate from the perspective of a civil libertarian. Parchment barriers were not, to his way of thinking, the best way to secure rights and liberties, nor did he believe that tyranny was prevented by making government weak and inefficient. In fact, he believed that weak government invites tyranny because it creates a vacuum of power that will be exploited by factions and men of intemperate mind, like demagogues and tyrants.

The new constitution's limits on government came from three basic sources: the law, the people (in the sense of the spirit of the times), and the character of leaders. Hamilton was not legalistic about rights or powers; he did not think of rights as absolute freedoms that could be defined in every manifestation by law and protected by legal sanctions. Politics for him was not an historical process by which human beings were progressing toward greater and greater freedom. Rights had to be repeatedly reconfigured to account for circumstances; they were, in a sense, malleable, which is why Hamilton opposed the addition of a national bill of rights, as he wrote in *Federalist* 84. Parchment rights were too inflexible to meet the demands of politics.

Forrest McDonald suggests that Hamilton's federalism was a system of divided sovereignty, in which each level of government was sovereign in its constitutionally designated domain.[9] Hamilton was convinced that even after the War for Independence was won, without an energetic central government, independence would be vulnerable to the machinations of the great powers that occupied the continent, the rivalries between the states, and those between the states and the national government. He used the experience of the ancients to remind Americans that loose confederations invite sectional violence. What possible motives would the states have to engage in frequent violence? Hamilton reminds his readers that "men are ambitious, vindictive, and rapacious." To expect the states to exist in peaceful harmony "would be to disregard the uniform course of human events, and to set at defiance the accumulated experience of ages." Regardless of their common republican regime type, (Hamilton reminded his readers that Sparta, Athens, Rome, and Carthage were all republics) the states were governed by men who possessed the common characteristics of human nature, "the love of power . . . the desire of pre-eminence and dominion . . . the jealousy of power." These lower motives of human nature would be fueled by rival commercial interests and interested political leaders, who, like Pericles, would lead their commonwealths to ruin. To be secure, the United States would have to become a great power as a nation. Hamilton could not conceive how American greatness would be possible unless the central government was in control of military and economic affairs. Even at its beginning, the country was too large to function well otherwise; "the extent of the country is the strongest argument in favour of an energetic government."[10] External security threats as well as the internal threat of rebellion and insurrection justified a strong and energetic central government.

Hamilton believed that the Constitution would remedy a fundamental problem with the Articles of Confederation by reformulating the relationship between the national government and the states. The Articles were doomed to fail because they rested on a fundamentally flawed conception of sovereignty that Hamilton classified as *imperium in imperio* (sovereignty within sovereignty), an arrangement he called, in *Federalist* 15, a "political monster."[11] In other contexts, he called it a "contradiction" and a "solecism," meaning that such an understanding of sovereignty can exist only in abstract theory, because in practice it defies the realities of political authority.[12] In "The Stand,"[13] he accused France of meddling in the affairs of other nations to produce an *imperium in imperio*. France's claims to assist other nations, he declared, were a way to disguise its intent to usurp their sovereignty. In the concrete world of practical politics, sovereignty divided within itself means that one governing entity must give way to the other. Under the Articles of Confederation, the national government gave way to the state governments, especially in the areas of taxation and raising armies.

Hamilton objected to the idea suggested by some anti-Federalists that the states were and should remain sovereign and completely independent from the national government in most matters and yet that the national government could be made stronger by giving it greater sovereignty in a few areas. As long as the states remained as sovereign as they were under the Articles of Confederation, he thought, the national government would be subordinate to them, because their sovereignty was exclusive. Under the Articles of Confederation, the national government had the power to tax the states, but in fact these taxes were "mere recommendations, which states observe or disregard at their option."[14] The national government's sovereignty was abated by the state governments' prerogative to comply with its requests or not at their pleasure. Likewise, the Congress had the power under the Articles to raise an army, but that power was contingent on the cooperation of the state governments; as Hamilton put it in *Federalist* 22, it was "merely a power of making requisitions upon the states for quotas of men."[15]

Drawing on his experience during the revolution, Hamilton explained, in *Federalist* 22, the difference between the parchment demarcation of sovereignty that gives the national government the power to raise armies by making "requisitions from each state" (Articles of Confederation) and the reality of practical conduct, in which national power is mitigated by the power of the states.

This practice [of raising armies], in the course of the late war, was found replete with obstructions to a vigorous and to an economical system of defence. It gave birth to a competition between the States which created a kind of auction for men. In order to furnish the quotas required of them, they outbid each other till bounties grew to an enormous and insupportable size. The hope of a still further increase afforded an inducement to those who were disposed to serve to procrastinate their enlistment, and disinclined them from engaging for any considerable periods. Hence, slow and scanty levies of men, in the most critical emergencies of our affairs; short enlistments at an unparalleled expense; continual fluctuations in the troops, ruinous to their discipline, and subjecting the public safety frequently to the perilous crisis of a disbanded army. Hence also, those oppressive expedients for raising men [quotas and bounties], which were upon several occasions practised, and which nothing but the enthusiasm of liberty would have induced the people to endure.[16]

As was evident during the war, the national government could not effectively raise taxes and troops to fight the war because its sovereignty was contingent on the voluntary compliance of state governments. Without practical sovereignty, (i.e., the ability to exercise power without the interference of the state governments) the national government lacked energy to exercise its responsibilities. The problem was rooted in *imperium in imperio*.

Hamilton saw a legitimate way to divide sovereignty within a nation while avoiding the problem of *imperium in imperio*. He had first considered the problem of divided sovereignty before the Declaration of Independence was written, while the colonies were still willing to reconcile their differences with England and remain in the empire. In "The Farmer Refuted," he argued that if the New York legislature possessed sovereign legislative power although New York remained within the British Empire, it would not create an *imperium in imperio*. In other words, it was possible for sovereignty to be divided without creating a contradiction of sovereignty.

> Let us, for a moment, imagine the legislature of New-York independent on that of Great-Britain, where would be the mighty inconvenience! How would government be frustrated, or obstructed, by this means? In what manner, would they interfere with each other? In none that I can perceive. The affairs of government might be conducted with the greatest harmony, and, by the mediation of the King, directed to the same end. He (as I before observed) will be the great connecting principle. The several parts of the empire, though, otherwise, independent on each other, will all be dependent on him. He must guide the vast and complicated machine of government, to the reciprocal advantage of all his dominions. There is not the least contradiction in this, no *imperium in imperio*, as is maintained; for the power of every distinct branch

will be limited to itself, and the authority of his Majesty over the whole, will, like a central force, attract them all to the same point.[17]

Hamilton suggested in this passage that as long as sovereignty is confined to separate and distinct entities, (e.g., parliament is sovereign over England and the New York legislature over New York), the line to *imperium in imperio* will not be crossed. It would be crossed if colonial assemblies and Parliament shared sovereignty to legislate for the same territory, as was the case with taxes and raising armies under the Articles of Confederation. The national government claimed the sovereign power to tax the states, and the states in turn claimed the sovereign right to refuse to pay them. Consequently, government was in conflict with itself, and in practice, only one sovereign part would end up with power when the conflict was resolved, regardless of what might be the case in theory or on parchment.

As colonists, the Americans argued, following Hamilton's line of reasoning, divided sovereignty between the colonies and the British Parliament was not only rational but reflected the reality of circumstances. Colonial assemblies governed their respective colonies in part, while Parliament governed them in part. The British, however, were wedded to the doctrine of indivisibility, which had been established, they argued, by the Glorious Revolution of 1688. Sovereignty resided exclusively in Parliament, which, having wrested it from the monarch, was not inclined to share it with the colonies. This way of thinking saw sovereignty as a zero sum proposition and excluded not just the idea of *imperium in imperio* but divided sovereignty in any form. Either Parliament was exclusively sovereign over the American colonies or they were independent states. The Declaratory Act of 1766 stated as much, but in ensuing years John Adams and John Dickinson, along with Hamilton, tried to articulate a doctrine of divided sovereignty, not as a way to break from England but in order to remain in the Empire. As Forrest McDonald explains the point, "what broke apart the empire was an inability to agree on the locus and nature of sovereignty."[18] The British refused to delegate a degree of sovereignty to their American colonies, which left the latter with no option but to declare their independence.

American independence meant that the debate over sovereignty did not end but became intramural. After declaring independence, the Continental Congress and the state governments had to grapple with the thorny problem of shared sovereignty. The Articles of Confederation were an initial attempt to provide constitutional definition to sovereignty. The rise of the Federalists was due in large part to their dissatisfaction with the Confederation in the conduct of the war and in its aftermath. The development of American political parties was determined, in part, by debates over the extent of division within American sovereignty. Hamilton was clearly on the side of those who wanted sovereignty to rest primarily but not exclusively in the national government. His opponents, especially Jefferson and Madison, wanted sovereignty to rest primarily in the states and the people. McDonald is correct to state that the Constitution "institutionalized a system of divided sovereignty,"[19] and he explains how, from that point on, Americans have fought political battles and a civil war to establish just what the Constitution means regarding sovereignty.

The Virginia and Kentucky Resolutions, written by Madison and Jefferson, respectively, in protest of the Alien and Sedition Acts, provide some sense of Hamilton's view of federalism and divided sovereignty, which had been publicly articulated more than a decade earlier in *The Federalist*. While Hamilton was not an enthusiastic proponent of the Alien and Sedition Acts, he did not question the federal government's authority to create them. He did question Virginia's and Kentucky's nullification power, and his reaction to the crisis is interesting, given his argument in *Federalist* 28, which suggests that states have the power to protect the people from a tyrannical national government.

Hamilton knew that some way of harmonizing the sovereign parts of government is necessary. In his constitutional theory, the executive serves this function. In his "The Farmer Refuted," he saw the king's role in much the same way as he later viewed the president's. The executive was the centripetal force in the American political system, pulling together the states and the branches of the national government so that they would move toward the public good, which was national in scope. Hamilton assumed that, in a system of divided sovereignty, the separated branches and levels of the government would typically not act in unison. Dividing power, which is necessary to safeguard liberty and prevent tyranny, results in a plurality of wills, corresponding to each part of the government. To bring these parts into harmony or to keep them from conflict requires the unifying force of executive leadership. What differentiates Hamilton's constitutionalism from Rousseau's is that in the former, the general will (regarded as a uniform standard that destroys diversity) should not govern society; it needs to be thwarted by separated powers, checks and balances, staggered elections, and the whole apparatus of constitutional government. In Hamilton's conception of national interest or public good, the various parts of society—parts that Rousseau viewed as obstacles to justice—are represented by different sovereign segments of government and given voice in the American constitutional system. With a variety of voices professing competing conceptions of the good, someone or something needs to direct them to the public good. For Hamilton, this role was played by the president.[20]

How did Hamilton reconcile rejection of *imperium in imperio* with support for federalism? Libertarian writer Frank Chodorov suggested that Hamilton, "would most certainly have preferred a national rather than a federal government, with undivided sovereignty, but the genius of the American people was decidedly against him."[21] How, then, does Hamilton believe that sovereignty can be divided between national and subnational governments without being in contradiction?

In *Federalist* 39, Madison described the Constitution as "neither wholly federal, nor wholly national,"[22] by which he meant that sovereignty was divided between the national government and the states. In *Federalist* 9, Hamilton explained that the Constitution, "so far from implying an abolition of the state governments, makes them constituent parts of the national sovereignty, by allowing them a direct representation in the senate, and leaves in their possession certain exclusive, and very important, portions of the sovereign power."[23] In *Federalist* 32, Hamilton again rejected the notion that the Constitution subsumed the states under national sovereignty, and he clearly agreed with Madison.

An entire consolidation of the states into one complete national sovereignty, would imply an entire subordination of the parts; and whatever powers might remain in them, would be altogether dependent on the general will. But as the plan of the convention aims only at a partial union or consolidation, the state governments would clearly retain all the rights of sovereignty which they before had, and which were not, by that act, *exclusively* delegated to the United States.[24]

These statements acknowledge that, under the new constitution, the states would have a degree of sovereignty nearly identical to what was theirs under the Articles of Confederation, a sovereignty separate and distinct from the national government. The states, however, lost some sovereignty when the new constitution was formed. In the final analysis of sovereignty, the states were net losers; some sovereignty was subtracted but none was added. It was this very subtraction that bothered many anti-Federalists and caused them to oppose ratification or to insist on the addition of a national bill of rights that clarified the distribution of sovereignty between the national government and the states. Most anti-Federalists acknowledged the need to add sovereignty to the national government but opposed the subtraction of state sovereignty. Hamilton's point, which was common among Federalists, was that the ineffectiveness of the Articles of Confederation could not be remedied unless state sovereignty was subtracted. Hamilton further insisted that particular sovereignty had to be subtracted from the states in order to prevent the *imperium in imperio* that existed under the Articles. In short, the national government needed to have exclusive sovereignty in some matters, and the only way to achieve that end was to deprive the states of some of their previously held sovereignty and ensure that the national government held "all the most important prerogatives of sovereignty."[25]

Hamilton refers to "concurrent jurisdiction"[26] in discussing some areas of taxation that are a consequence of divided sovereignty. In this concept, both levels of government share certain powers, like taxation of the same goods, but they do not, as was the case under the Articles of Confederation, share sovereignty in a way that makes one level of government dependent on the other for the efficacy of its power. In the case of concurrent taxation, each level of government can exercise its taxing power independently of the other level. What Hamilton objects to is not divided sovereignty or concurrent powers, as Chodorov suggests, but dependent sovereignty, that is, sovereignty that requires both levels of government to concur in order for power to be used with energy and vigor. Hamilton recognized that, in a federal system of divided sovereignty and power, the boundaries of state and national authority will not always be clear. If the national government and the states have exclusive powers as well as concurrent powers, how should their respective powers be demarcated? When disputes arise over constitutional power and sovereignty, the federal courts and the people will decipher which level of government has what powers. Both of these means of resolution are problematic. The people have no instrument other than elections with which to express their view, and elections are reserved to the selection of representatives, not used to decide policy or constitutional issues. The federal courts, as part of the national government, are apt to decide disputes between the national government and the states in favor of the former, as has been the case historically and as was feared by the anti-Federalists.

JUDICIAL POWER IN HAMILTONIAN CONSTITUTIONALISM

Hamilton's understanding of judicial power, including his theory of constitutional interpretation and the role of federal courts in the American political system, must be placed in the larger context of his constitutionalism, including its underlying philosophical anthropology, in order to clarify its meaning. His view of human nature provided the impetus for his theory of leadership and his understanding of judicial power: the imperfectability of human beings makes government and the constitutional restraints that guard against tyranny necessary. Hamilton's constitutionalism is ultimately held together by constitutional character and spirit, the personality type and corresponding spiritual substance that he saw as the animating force to political institutions.

A starting point for understanding Hamilton's constitutional theory is *Federalist* 78, which articulates a theory of constitutional interpretation and judicial power at odds with the common portrayal of Hamilton as an advocate of activist readings of the Constitution. *Federalist* 78 defends aspects of the Constitution, not only by explaining what the Philadelphia Convention created, but also by responding to arguments made by the anti-Federalists. Elbridge Gerry, a Massachusetts delegate to the Constitutional Convention, expressed a sentiment widespread among anti-Federalists when he stated his reasons for refusing to sign the Constitution: "[It] has few, if any *federal* features, but is rather a system of *national* government." In particular, he feared that "the judicial department" would be "oppressive."[27] "Brutus," likely New York delegate and judge Robert Yates, writing in the *Anti-Federalist Papers*, added that the national judiciary would be inclined to interpret the Constitution "according to its spirit and reason, and not to confine themselves to its letter."[28] The constitutionally stated ends of the national government were providing for the common defense and the general welfare as well as forming a more perfect union. The anti-Federalists feared that the federal courts would expansively read the national government's powers, using the spirit of the ends of government to justify most any specific power. "Brutus" claimed that the federal courts' power would "enable them to mould the government, into almost any shape they please."[29] He came to this conclusion because, when compared to British courts, American courts would be far more powerful. They would "give the sense of every article of the Constitution," have the final word on disputes regarding the meaning and application of the Constitution, and be "totally independent" and able to be removed only by impeachment for crimes. "Errors in judgement, or want of capacity to discharge the duties of the office,"[30] are not crimes and thus not subject to impeachment. In other words, federal judges might exercise their power outside the boundaries of checks and balances and beyond the reach of the people. The federal courts would, then, be administered by a body of aristocratic men who had no regard for the people's will or the Constitution. There was nothing in the new constitution to bind them to either one.

"Brutus"'s argument comes close to those later leveled against Hamilton's loose constructionism. Hamilton's reaction to these arguments, published in *Federalist* 78 and 81, formed as direct a response to the charge of "living constitutionalism" as exists. He aimed to reassure his readers that they had nothing to fear from the national judiciary. It would operate within the confines of constitutional checks and balances, and, because of the very nature of judicial power, it could become dangerous only if united with another branch of government. The ultimate check on the federal courts was the impeachment power given to Congress, which Hamilton considered "a complete security" against judicial encroachments on legislative power. He admitted, "Particular misconstructions and contraventions of the will of the legislature, may now and then happen," but he was confident that they could "never be so extensive as to amount to an inconvenience, or in any sensible degree to affect the order of the political system." The judiciary would be too weak to undermine the constitutional will of the people expressed by the Congress or in the document itself. The efficacy of its rulings depended on executive enforcement, because the judiciary had no power to support them. In some sense, Hamilton characterized the judiciary as the most cerebral but least energetic branch of government. As he stated in *Federalist* 78, the judiciary would "always be the least dangerous to the political rights of the constitution," having the "least in a capacity to annoy or injure them." The executive would have the power of the sword and the Congress the power of the purse and the power of law to compel citizens to bend to their will. By contrast, the judiciary would have "no influence over either the sword or the purse; no direction either of the strength or of the wealth of the society; and can take no active resolution whatever. It may truly be said to have neither FORCE nor WILL, but merely judgment."[31]

Hamilton's conception of judicial power is indicative of his political theory. He believed that energy in government was essential to controlling the tendencies in human beings toward disorder and anarchy. Courts lacked the very will to initiate and exercise power in a way that could do harm to liberty. The exception, it is worth repeating, is a judiciary that has united with either legislative or executive power, an example of centralized power that Hamilton opposed because it violated the principle of separated powers.

Federalist 78 makes clear that federal courts have the power of judicial review, but in evaluating Hamilton's theory of judicial power we must avoid reading back into the eighteenth century the contemporary practice and understanding of judicial review. History may not vindicate Hamilton's conception of judicial power—it would appear to favor "Brutus"'s arguments in many respects—yet in assessing Hamilton's political theory our objective is to discover why Hamilton conceived of judicial power the way he did.

Years before *The Federalist* papers were written, Hamilton had occasion to consider the relationship between the popular will and constitutional law. In the wake of the War for Independence, Hamilton took to defending the most unpopular clients imaginable, Loyalists who were being sued in New York courts for their actions during the British occupation of New York City. In such circumstances, Hamilton had every reason to subvert the notion that *vox populi* is *vox Dei*. In his "Letters from Phocion" (1784), he explained the role of a constitution in relation to the people and the legislature. He distinguished between the sovereign will of the people expressed in the constitution and the momentary will of the people. The two might be in conflict, just as the will of the legislature might contradict the constitution. In either case, the momentary popular will and the will of the legislature must be subordinated to the constitution, such a hierarchy being necessary for the rule of law. He admitted that "the constitution is the creature of the people" and added, "it does not follow that they are not bound by it, while they suffer it to continue in force; nor does it follow, that the legislature, which is, on the other hand, a creature of the Constitution, can depart from it, on any presumption of the contrary sense of the people."[32]

What made the American Constitution superior to statutory law in Hamilton's mind? Both forms of law derive from the popular will, which he believed was in some sense sovereign, but he did not find all expressions of the people's will equally valid or sovereign. Some, in fact, he though contrary to higher standards: the public good and natural law. These higher standards he considered not so much extra-constitutional, as they were what provided constitutional politics with direction and purpose. Public opinion could be delusional, especially when it was derived in the passion of the moment and incited by demagogues and factions. The purpose of constitutional government was to check the popular will so that "the deliberate sense of the community" could govern. What complicated the rule of law in constitutional systems of government that included federalism was that there was more than one process by which the deliberate will of the community was expressed. State and national legislatures would deliberate and create law. A separate and distinct process created the constitution. So why is constitutional law necessarily a superior standard compared to statutory law if both are the product of constitutional deliberation that is sanctioned by the people? Hamilton does not explicitly state why, but he does imply that constitutional law emanates from a more elaborate, substantial, and trustworthy deliberative process. The formation of constitutional law requires more time and a broader consensus than that for statutory law. Moreover, constitutional law pertains to fundamental matters, not everyday ones.

In short, what gives constitutional law more weight than statutory law is that the former is more apt to convey the permanent will of society and the latter is more apt to convey a transitory will. For the same reason, Hamilton placed great authority in the law of nations, because it embodied the deliberative experience of generations of human beings from different nations. It approximated the common human ground because it had been subject to extensive scrutiny. In the court of trial and error, it had been vindicated. In some rudimentary way, Hamilton seemed to recognize that deliberative constitutional process and transnational civilizational standards like the law of nations were part of human groping toward universality. At its best, then, law pulled individuals toward the enduring ends of politics: justice, happiness, order, and the like. For Hamilton, the American context required harmony among the states, or what he referred to as union. It served as a counter-tension to the spirit of anarchy, faction, and mere self-interest. As the dust settled from the American Revolution and the work of governing the new nation came to the fore, he wrote to Washington in 1783: "It now only remains to make solid establishments within to perpetuate our union to prevent our being a ball in the hands of European powers bandied against each other at their pleasure—in fine to make our independence truly a blessing. This it is to be lamented will be an arduous work, for to borrow a figure from mechanics, the centrifugal is much stronger than the centripetal force in these states—the seeds of disunion much more numerous than those of union."[33]

Hamilton's constitutionalism has led many to classify him as undemocratic because he refused to subordinate the actions of government to the popular will. Such an assessment is based on a false and misleading understanding of American constitutionalism that fails to differentiate between types of democracy and types of republics. As has been noted, Hamilton, like the other Framers, was opposed to pure or direct democracy. They tended to think of democracy within the narrow scope of direct democracy and to consider republican government as a separate, distinct, and irreconcilable regime type. The reasons why are telling. Hamilton did not believe that pure democracy could be justified by human nature and historical experience. He wrote to Washington in 1790 that "Man, after all, is but man."[34] Governments should not be constructed for angels, Madison asserted in *Federalist* 51, and Hamilton concurred. Hamilton's difference with Jefferson, Paine, and other populist thinkers is due to their more idealistic view of human nature and their progressive historicism. Unlike Hamilton, they believed that science and reason would create an age of improvement not only in the material well-being of individuals but also in their moral capacity. Paine's words provide a useful contrast to Hamilton on the meaning of the American quest for self-government. In the heat of the American Revolution, Paine wrote in *Common Sense:*

> We have it in our power to begin the world over again. A situation, similar to the present, hath not happened since the days of Noah until now. The birthday of a new world is at hand, and a race of men perhaps as numerous as all Europe contains, are to receive their portion of freedom from the event of a few months.[35]

Writing more than a decade later in support of the new constitution, Hamilton seemed, in *Federalist* 6, to suggest that times had indeed changed. Excessive idealism might have served some purpose in rallying support for the revolution, but it was time for sober reflection and action.

> Have we not already seen enough of the fallacy and extravagance of those idle theories which have amused us with promises of an

exemption from the imperfections, the weaknesses, and the evils incident to society in every shape? Is it not time to awake from the deceitful dream of a golden age, and to adopt as a practical maxim for the direction of our political conduct, that we, as well as the other inhabitants of the globe, are yet remote from the happy empire of perfect wisdom and perfect virtue?

Writing in 1793 to fellow New York lawyer and politician Richard Harrison, Hamilton commented that an age of perfection was impossible until the Second Coming: "The triumphs of Vice are no new things under the sun. And I fear, 'till the Millenium comes, in spight of all our boasted light and purification—hypocrisy and Treachery will continue to be the most successful commodities in the political Market."[36] Jefferson and Paine placed more trust in democratic political institutions because they placed more trust in human nature itself. While neither Jefferson nor Paine went so far as to claim that government was unnecessary (in fact, Paine calls government a necessary evil), they both tended to support the removal of institutional impediments to exercise of the momentary popular will. Jefferson thought the Constitution unsuitable for the very reasons that Hamilton considered it worthy of ratification, it placed significant checks and restraints on the popular will by vesting power and discretion in an independent executive and an independent judiciary; it balanced the popular sentiment of the House of Representatives with the more aristocratic sentiment of the Senate. Also, central to Hamilton's constitutionalism was the vital role played by the courts in checking the popular impulse of legislatures, while Jefferson had been far more influenced by Locke than had Hamilton and privileged the legislature over the judiciary. Hamilton's philosophical anthropology and constitutionalism are at odds with Lockean and Rousseaustic principles of legislative supremacy, on the one hand, and Hobbesian principles of absolute monarchy on the other.

These differences between Hamiltonian and Jeffersonian constitutionalism are often used to criticize Hamilton for placing too much trust in political elites. Hamilton has been identified as the progenitor of modern judicial activism. In their defense of Jeffersonian constitutionalism, William J. Quirk and R. Randall Bridwell suggest that Hamilton was too trusting of judges. He expected them to strike down statutory laws that were inconsistent with the Constitution, which is fundamental law. Quirk and Bridwell cite Justice Brennan's use of higher law and his comment to his law clerks, "With five votes around here you can do anything" as evidence that Hamilton was foolish to think that judges would uphold the Constitution rather than infuse their political or ideological desires into their reading of the Constitution. What ensures that judges, or presidents and representatives for that matter, will maintain fidelity to the Constitution? This is a key question to understanding Hamilton's constitutionalism.

Quirk and Bridwell argue that Hamilton, unlike Jefferson, was undemocratic, or at least significantly less democratic than Jefferson, in his conception of judicial power. In one sense, they are correct. Hamilton placed far greater trust in political elites to exercise power in accordance with the common good than did Jefferson. He figured that elected representatives were compelled to give more weight to the popular will than were unelected judges. Jefferson's assumption was that the people, in the form of voters at election time, want the Constitution to be upheld. On this assumption, there is a divide between Hamiltonian and Jeffersonian constitutionalism, because Jefferson was far more trusting of the people than Hamilton, and Hamilton was more concerned about the difference between the momentary popular will and the deliberative will of the people. This distinction helps to illuminate Hamilton's argument in *The Federalist* regarding judicial power. He was not in favor of giving judges license to change the meaning of the Constitution, and the primary check against such judicial indiscretion was impeachment.

THE DELIBERATE SENSE OF THE PEOPLE, MOMENTARY MAJORITY WILL, AND NATURAL ARISTOCRATS

Both Alexander Hamilton and James Madison distinguished between contrasting notions of the people's will. In *Federalist* 71, Hamilton explained,

> The republican principle demands, that the deliberate sense of the community should govern the conduct of those to whom they

intrust the management of their affairs; but it does not require an unqualified complaisance to every sudden breeze of passion, or every transient impulse which the people may receive from the arts of men, who flatter their prejudice to betray their interest.

Hamilton did not question the motives of the people so much as their ability to resist the passion of the moment or some over-whelming partisan interest. He conceded that "the people commonly *intend* the PUBLIC GOOD" but "their good sense would despise the adulator who should pretend, that they always *reason right* about the *means* of promoting it." Why do the people err in their judgment of the public good? Because they are continually "beset . . . by the wiles of parasites and sycophants; by the snares of the ambitious, the avaricious, the desperate; by the artifices of men who possess their confidence more than they deserve it; and of those who seek to possess, rather than deserve it."[37]

In this characterization of popular will, both the people and political elites are fallible and cannot be trusted with power. The problem stems from human nature and justifies the foundational elements of American constitutionalism: separated powers, checks and balances, representation, and judicial review. Constitutionalism does not eliminate the need for leadership and virtue, but it makes them more challenging than in nonpopular forms of government, because popular constitutionalism requires more not fewer leaders. American constitutional democracy relies on a much larger class of rulers than any form of government that existed at the time of its creation. Hamilton's view of human nature and constitutionalism is nearly identical to Madison's. In *Federalist* 55, the latter wrote: "As there is a degree of depravity in mankind, which requires a certain degree of circumspection and distrust: so there are other qualities in human nature, which justify a certain portion of esteem and confidence. Republican government presupposes the existence of these qualities in a higher degree than any other form." In Madison's classic statement in *Federalist* 51, because men are not angels, government is necessary; and because angels do not govern men, government needs to be limited by checks and balances, separated powers, and the like.

When Hamilton considered how to check and restrain the

people, he tended to place his faith in the presence of natural aristocrats, persons who would be good stewards of the commonweal. As *Federalist* 71 indicates, Hamilton was also sensitive to the existence of leaders who would betray the public good. He expected that external restraints (e.g., constitutional checks and separated powers) would confine political leaders, but he also placed a degree of confidence in the internal restraint of virtue. This point is evident in *Federalist* 71 when Hamilton writes:

> When occasions present themselves, in which the interests of the people are at variance with their inclinations, it is the duty of the persons whom they have appointed, to be the guardians of those interests; to withstand the temporary delusion, in order to give them time and opportunity for more cool and sedate reflection. Instances might be cited, in which a conduct of this kind has saved the people from very fatal consequences of their own mistakes, and has procured lasting monuments of their gratitude to the men who had courage and magnanimity enough to serve them at the peril of their displeasure.[38]

The momentary majority constitutes a concentration of power and a tyrannical inclination to subordinate all interests to one general will. Government therefore requires the restraining influence of individuals with sufficient perspective and virtue to constrain momentary public will, to the benefit of the common good.

Hamilton repeatedly expressed opposition to a "purely republican"[39] government, by which he meant one that subordinates government to the will of the people. In such a regime, the legislative branch exercises supreme authority, resisting opposition from the executive and judicial branches as contrary to the people's sovereign will. The legislature embodies the sovereign will of the people and the executive exercises no independent authority; it lacks the ability to check the legislature. Such a purely republican system is, in Hamilton's view, unbalanced, because the legislative branch dominates the government and is immune from the other branches' power to check and balance.[40] His opposition to the Articles of Confederation and both the Virginia and New Jersey Plans is consistent with his argument against purely republican government. Both plans were based on legislative supremacy and featured weak, dependent executives. The New Jersey Plan called for a plural executive, chosen by the national legislature, subject to a term limit, with no veto power. While the Virginia Plan created a single executive, it too confined the executive to one term and specified selection by the national legislature. The Virginia Plan's proposed "council of revision," which included the executive, would have added a degree of independence and veto power outside the legislature, but all in all, both plans were a far cry from the eventual makeup of the presidency. This was partly due to Hamilton's insistence that only a strong independent executive would serve the nation's interests. To Hamilton's thinking, the Virginia and New Jersey Plans were not much different from the Articles of Confederation. While they added executive and judicial branches, the legislative branch was still supreme. It is no wonder that Hamilton stated at the convention, "[W]hat even is the Virginia plan, but *pork still, with a little change of the sauce.*"[41] That the convention delegates moved so far away from these two plans to a constitution that was not based on legislative supremacy, created a strong independent executive, and was clearly at odds with purely republican government may indicate that Hamilton's influence was greater than has been typically assumed. For all the talk of Madison's being the father of the Constitution, his Virginia Plan was, in parts, strikingly at odds with the theoretical foundations of the Constitution with regard to executive power and the role of legislative power.

The American Constitution does not create a purely republican government and it is not based on legislative supremacy, as is Locke's or Rousseau's ideal regime. It creates a balanced and mixed government in which no one branch is supreme. The objective was to ensure that no one branch could concentrate power. Checks are placed on each branch in proportion to its power, to create a balance of power. In this framework, Hamilton's view of judicial power looks different if seen as the antecedent to twentieth-century judicial activism. An independent judiciary, like an independent executive, he regarded as necessary to prevent legislative tyranny. When Hamilton conceived of judicial power, he had in mind its role in the larger constitutional framework. To be a sufficient check on the legislative and executive branches, the judiciary must have enough independence to over-come the natural weakness of judicial power. Hamilton assumed that judges would rarely if ever encroach on Congress's law-making power because to do so would risk impeachment. "Brutus" argued that federal judges should be removable only for the commitment of crimes, but Hamilton proposed, in *Federalist* 81, that "deliberate usurpations on the authority of the legislature" also be subject to impeachment. In addition, Hamilton inferred that executives might choose not to enforce Supreme Court rulings. The history of the federal judiciary, it should be remembered, did not have to unfold the way it did. Had more presidents followed the lead of Andrew Jackson and ignored Supreme Court decisions; had more Congresses followed the lead of the Fourth Congress, which passed the Eleventh Amendment (passed March 4, 1794, ratified in 1795) and amended the Constitution to nullify a Supreme Court decision (*Chisholm v. Georgia*, 1793), things might have been different and more consonant with Hamilton's conception of American constitutionalism.

Hamilton on Executive Power and Monarchy

Hamilton had knowledge and experience in all branches of government. He wrote all of *The Federalist* papers dealing with executive power, and he spent most of Washington's presidency as secretary of the treasury. He had served in the New York state legislature, the Continental Congress, the Annapolis Convention, and the Constitutional Convention. His experience with judicial power was as an attorney arguing cases in New York courts, and he argued one case before the U.S. Supreme Court. Because he favored bold decisive action, executive power was more to his fancy than legislative power. In his June 18 speech at the Constitutional Convention, he argued for a single executive, elected indirectly by the people, who would serve for life, presuming good behavior.

Before moving to the details of Hamilton's conception of executive power, the frequent charge that Hamilton was an advocate of monarchy needs to be addressed. His monarchist leanings are traced primarily to four comments, none of which actually comes directly from Hamilton. He is reported by Madison to have stated at the Constitutional Convention, during his June 18 speech, that "the British Govt. was the best in the world: and that he doubted much whether any thing short of it would do in America."[42] Jefferson recounted a story from a 1791 dinner party in which John Adams professed his belief that the British system of government would be the best in the world if it was rid of corruption. Jefferson claimed in a letter to Dr. Walter Jones (January 2, 1814) that Hamilton's response was: "that the British constitution, with its unequal representation, corruption and other existing abuses, was the most perfect government which had ever been established on earth, and that a reformation of those abuses would make it an impracticable government."[43] At the same dinner party, Hamilton pronounced Julius Caesar to be "the greatest man that ever lived," according to Jefferson's account in a letter to Benjamin Rush (January 16, 1811):

> Another incident took place on the same occasion, which will further delineate Mr. Hamilton's political principles. The room being hung around with a collection of the portraits of remarkable men, among them were those of Bacon, Newton and Locke, Hamilton asked me who they were. I told him they were my trinity of the three greatest men the world had ever produced, naming them. He paused for some time: "the greatest man," said he, "that ever lived, was Julius Cæsar." Mr. Adams was honest as a politician, as well as a man; Hamilton honest as a man, but, as a politician, believing in the necessity of either force or corruption to govern men.[44]

The final stamp may have been applied by Hamilton's friend Gouverneur Morris, who eulogized Hamilton by stating, "He was on principle opposed to republican and attached to monarchical government."[45]

The creditability of Jefferson's story about the Julius Caesar remark is the topic of an essay by Thomas P. Govan and a comment by Ron Chernow, both of which shed light on the myth that Hamilton was a monarchist. "What makes the story suspect, if not downright absurd," writes Chernow, "is that Hamilton's collected papers are teeming with pejorative references to Julius Caesar. In fact, whenever Hamilton wanted to revile

Jefferson as a populist demagogue, he invariably likened him to Julius Caesar. One suspects that if Hamilton was accurately quoted, he was joking with Jefferson."[46] Govan cites and explains every written reference that Hamilton made to Caesar and concludes that Jefferson's story is highly questionable. Jefferson made just this one reference to the incident, as a sixty-eight-year-old man, after Hamilton had been dead for years. No corroborating evidence exists. And yet, based on Jefferson's story, Julian Boyd asserts that Hamilton "considered Caesar to be one of the greatest figures of history." Douglass Adair goes even further, declaring that Hamilton "admired Caesar above all men who had ever lived" and calling Hamilton "the one major leader among our Founding Fathers who had the desire, the will, and the capacity to attempt a policy of Caesarism in which he was the destined Caesar."[47] Adair goes so far as to accuse Hamilton of plotting a military coup and asks, "Is he not the one leading personality among the Revolutionary generation who had the potentialities, and who almost created for himself the opportunity, to try the role successfully played by his contemporary Napoleon?"[48]

Equally troubling is the analysis of Hamilton provided by J. G. A. Pocock in *The Machiavellian Moment,* a book that classified Hamilton as a Machiavellian. Pocock closely followed the view of Gerald Stourzh in *Alexander Hamilton and the Idea of Republican Government*[49] that "Hamilton's ambivalent use of Caesar's name is puzzling."[50] Pocock misinterprets Hamilton's observation, "*Cato* was the Tory—*Caesar* the Whig of his day. The former frequently resisted—the latter always flattered the follies of the people. Yet the former perished with the Republic [and] the latter destroyed it." In fact, Pocock turns Hamilton's meaning on its head. The context for the quote is revealing. In July 1792, President Washington asked Hamilton, then secretary of the treasury, to respond to accusations that Hamilton was conspiring to transform the republic into an empire. Washington did not reveal the identity of the accuser, who was secretary of state Thomas Jefferson. Jefferson specifically accused Hamilton of being at the head of a "corrupt squadron" that controlled Congress and aimed "to prepare the way for a change, from the present republican form of government, to that of a monarchy, of which the English constitution is to be the model."[51] Hamilton refuted the charges clearly. His letter to Washington included the quotation about Cato and Caesar, which was followed by, "No popular Government was ever without its Catalines & its Caesars. These are its true enemies."[52]

Hamilton's retort is a thinly veiled reference to Jefferson, implying that he flattered the people in order to gain power for himself and his faction, and to Burr, who he suspected would have willingly assumed the role of Caesar once disorder had set the stage.[53] Remarkably, Pocock, after making a distinction between "virtuous antiquity" and "commercial modernity," states that Hamilton's "tone is clearly one of preference for success [commercial modernity] over deservingness [virtuous antiquity], *virtù* over virtue; and it was language of this kind which persuaded Jefferson that Hamilton admired Caesar and wished to emulate him." Pocock adds that "Hamilton's feelings about Caesar . . . are rich in Machiavellian moral ambiguity." Yet, Hamilton is not being ambiguous by calling Caesar a Whig and he has Jefferson as much as Burr in mind when he does so. He is repeating a charge that appears throughout his writings:[54] those who claim to support the people often mask their will to power; their populism is a pretense.

Although Washington did not tell Hamilton who had made the charges against him, he surely knew their origin. He dated his written reply to Washington August 18, 1792, and on September 15 he penned his first "Catullus to Aristides" essay attacking Jefferson. In his third "Catullus" essay (published September 29), he aimed to reveal Jefferson's real character. Behind the façade of a "quiet modest, retiring philosopher," who appeared as "the plain simple unambitious republican" lay "the intriguing incendiary." Jefferson's real character, he wrote, was evident when "the vizor of stoicism is plucked from the brow of the Epicurean; when the plain garb of Quaker simplicity is stripped from the concealed voluptuary; when Caesar *coyly refusing* the proffered diadem, is seen to be Caesar *rejecting* the trappings, but tenaciously grasping the substance of imperial domination." Hamilton ends his essay with this flourish: "It has been pertinently remarked by a judicious writer, that *Cæsar*, who *overturned* the republic, was the WHIG, Cato, who *died* for it, the TORY of Rome;

such at least was the common cant of political harangues; the insidious tale of hypocritical demagogues."[55] If one reads the reply to Washington in the light of the "Catullus" essays, there is no ambiguity. Whigs like Jefferson are imperial wolves disguised in the sheep's clothing of populist republican modesty.

Even so, Pocock uses Hamilton to support his contention that the Classical sense of virtue was supplanted by a modern understanding of self-interest. He crystallizes the point by concluding that the "triumph of Caesar over Cato is the triumph of commerce over virtue, and of empire over republic. It is this historical role which transforms Caesar into an archetype of ambiguous *virtù*." Hamilton is cast by Pocock in the role created for him by Jefferson: a monocrat who secretly works to undermine the republic in order to create the opportunity for a military empire that he will lead to glory. Yet, Hamilton's very point in the disputed passage is that republics require leaders like Cato, who refuse to engage in demagoguery and who understand the primacy of order. In this as in other passages from Hamilton's work, Caesar is the enemy of order and particularly the enemy of the republic. Pocock, however, states that "Hamilton saw America as predestined to become a commercial and military empire, of a sort to which the figure of Caesar was indeed appropriate, but in which his role must be played by 'modern Whig' structures of government if it was not to be played by demagogues like Burr."[56] To suggest, as Pocock does, that there is some deeply hidden Machiavellian meaning to Hamilton's Caesar references belies not only common sense but the weight of Hamilton's writings and statesmanship.

If the four comments about Hamilton's inclination to monarchy are measured against the weight of his conduct as a statesman and his extensive public papers, the monarchist charge seems rather dubious. Simply put, while he expressed admiration for the British political system, he never advocated monarchy for the United States. He did favor a strong independent executive that would serve for life, presuming good behavior. This feature of his constitutional theory is a more substantive indication than the comments of Jefferson and Morris that Hamilton was enamored of strong executive power. A closer look at his theory of constitutional government helps to explain why Hamilton believed that strength and energy were essential characteristics of executive power and why he was not a monarchist.[57]

Hamilton's political theory and statesmanship had a way of irritating Jeffersonians. From their perspective, his politics were outside the mainstream of republican thought. They had similar suspicions about Washington but were reticent to express them directly because of his heroic stature. In behavior common to politics, many of Hamilton's foes exaggerated his penchant for national, military, and executive power to the point that their image of him resembled a monarchist. Add to these preferences his admiration for the British political system and his attention to aristocratic deportment, and the accusation does not seem so far-fetched. Contrary to this caricature of Hamilton, while the variety of republican government he favored was too undemocratic for those of Jeffersonian taste, monarchy was not his aim. He never wavered in his conviction that American sovereignty lay in the people and that government, including the executive, needed to be limited by the Constitution and the law.

It is interesting to note that Hamilton's support for the Constitution was second to none. No American did more to bring it into existence, ensure its ratification, and nurture it in its infancy than Hamilton. Jefferson, by contrast, was displeased with the Constitution and only made his peace with it because he expected the American people to correct its many flaws through the amendment process. He speculated that constitutions were legitimate for only one generation, because each generation should be free to create its own political system and laws without the prejudice of past generations.[58] Jefferson's often radical and utopian ideas are typically dismissed by his admirers as the intellectual trial balloons of a great creative mind. In practice, he was usually more sober and practical. Why, then, is Jefferson given great latitude where Hamilton is not? The answer is likely that Jefferson has greater appeal in a culture that has often been enchanted by the populist impulse. His seductive romantic sentiments about the people, natural rights, and equality flatter those who can then overlook his ideological excess. Hamilton, on the other hand, was sometimes disparaging toward the people and never a friend to democracy, in the pure sense. He was a sober realist whose political theory precluded the possibility of

Jefferson's world of man's natural goodness, abstract rights, and agrarian simplicity.

Only when one gets beyond the charge that Hamilton was a monarchist can his conception of federalism, the presidency, and republican government come to light. There are weaknesses in Hamilton's political theory, but they are obscured by the canard that he was a monarchist. The central weakness in his theory is that he failed to recognize what Tocqueville and others would later identify as the rich American tradition of state and local communities, including the place of sectional and private groups and associations in the affairs of the country. Hamilton overestimated the extent to which government can control and manage the lives of the people and communities it governs. Some critics charge that he masked his desire to create monarchy in America with a pretense of republicanism and that once the Constitution was implemented he began working to transform it into monarchy by way of loose constructionism. Construed broadly, government powers could be expanded to monarchical proportions. For such a conspiracy to be believable, though, Hamilton must somehow be cast as something he was surely not, a deceitful plotter who was a master of intellectual and political disguise. He was, by contrast, effusive to a fault regarding his motives and desires. In fact, the very charge of monarchism is based largely on his candid expressions at the Constitutional Convention. To some degree, Hamilton at times toned down his rhetoric to make his proposals more palatable to his audience, but by and large he was as forthright and honest as statesmen come, especially in the expression of political ideas.

Scholars who are intent on casting Hamilton as a thoroughly modern Enlightenment thinker tend to explain his affinity for monarchy as evidence that he was influenced by Hobbes. Gerald Stourzh, for example, links Hamilton's attitudes toward monarchy to Hobbes.[59] How such a claim can be made in light of Hamilton's insistence on separated powers and judicial review is difficult to fathom. John C. Miller explains why such critics are mistaken. "Hamilton was too levelheaded to fail to see that the British constitution was the product of a historical process that could not be duplicated in the United States and that the characteristics which so strongly attracted him to Great Britain were in many cases the peculiar contribution of the British people."[60] Hamilton spoke highly of the British system, but so also did John Adams, Benjamin Franklin, and many other Founders. As noted above, most of the evidence supporting Hamilton's alleged preference for monarchy in America stems from his comments about the British political system at the Constitutional Convention and a plethora of innuendo and slander propagated by his political rivals. What he admired about the British political system was not its hereditary characteristics but the fact that it had achieved what Hamilton desired for the United States: a free independent society that was economically prosperous, militarily strong, and efficiently administered. In that sense, the end was more important than the means, which is not to say that Hamilton dismissed the possibility of imitating some of England's political and economic characteristics. Thomas Paine, by contrast, could dismiss the British political system out of hand because he was rigidly ideological about the means of government; for him, regime type determined the legitimacy of governments. Paine was monistic about government whereas Hamilton was open to a wider variety of political systems, based on the circumstances of nations. It so happened that for America they both favored republican government, but in the cases of England and France they profoundly differed. What seems implausible to many of Hamilton's critics, but is precisely the case, is that he could admire monarchy as the best form of government for England and at the same time believe that republican government was the best form of government for the United States. This was the case even though Hamilton was not always confident that republican government would succeed in America.

In his speech to the Constitutional Convention on the Virginia and New Jersey Plans, he found them too purely republican. What he recommended was pushing American government closer to the British model, in order to give it greater permanence, by means of longer terms of office. He urged that greater permanence would be created not by imitating the hereditary component of the British system but by going "as far in order to attain stability and permanency, as republican principles will admit."[61] How far can republican principles allow terms of office to extend? He was suggesting life terms for one branch of the legislature (the Senate) and for the executive. What made Hamilton think that such a system was republican? Both the Senate and the executive would be elected, and all parts of the government would be subservient to the rule of law and the public good.

Federalist 71 follows the same pattern of thinking as Hamilton's June 18 convention speech. In both cases, three aspects of republican government are discussed: the separation of powers, the purity and balance of the republic and its branches, and the duration of terms of office. Hamilton insists that powers be separated into three branches of government and that they be balanced, so that one branch does not exert "imperious control over the other departments."[62] Unbalanced governments, for example pure republics, concentrate too much power into one branch of government. At the convention, he tried to push the delegates toward life terms, which he believed would check overly democratic impulses by creating a permanent will in the government. After he lost that argument, Hamilton continued to question the efficacy of shorter terms of office, even when writing as "Publius." In *Federalist* 71, he conceded, with regard to the president's term of office, "It cannot be affirmed, that a duration of four years, or any other limited duration, would completely answer the end proposed," (i.e., "the independence of the executive on the legislature"). How, then, did he reconcile himself to a shorter term of office for the president when he then campaigned for ratification of the Constitution? He argued that even the four-year term would contribute to the independence of the executive to "a degree which would have a material influence upon the spirit and character of the government."[63] In other words, the president would have sufficient independence, at least for a time, to promote measures that were prudent but unpopular. The president would have a window in which to act that would narrow as the next election approached. This understanding of executive duration may explain why, in his early tenure as treasury secretary, Hamilton acted so quickly to implement his financial policies. He did not want to see what he thought were essential policies be destroyed by the flux of election politics.

At various points in Hamilton's life, his republicanism was apparent. For example, when he argued against a bill of rights in *Federalist* 84, when he insisted at the Constitutional Convention that the House of Representatives be elected by the people, and when he argued in *Federalist* 78 that judicial and executive power should not mix. His much maligned plan for a new constitution, presented at that convention, created a republican system of government and included universal free male suffrage, an explicit prohibition against titles of nobility, and an impeachment process for removing the president.[64] To these examples should be added *Federalist* 9, which defended the Framers' choice of republican government even though historical evidence was scanty in its support. If the history of republics was a story of chaos, tumult, and faction, why would the Framers have the audacity to believe that republican government, that is free government, could succeed in America when it had failed in the ancient world? Hamilton asserted that the "science of politics" had advanced since the times of the ancients and that the principles of government were better known in the late eighteenth century than they had been in ancient Greece and Rome. This modern knowledge, combined with ancient insights and experience, made republican government possible in America. Improvements that Hamilton specifically cited were the separation of powers, checks and balances, an independent judiciary, representation and popular election, and the enlargement of the orbit of government made possible by construction of a "confederate republic" that combined republican institutions internally and monarchical institutions externally.

What is commonly misconstrued in Hamilton's political theory as advocacy of monarchy is his insistence that there be a permanent dimension to the government, an element capable of serving as a counterweight to society's democratic impulse. The problem with popular passion and impulse is that it pulls individuals and society into the flux. In political terms, the flux is the triumph of arbitrariness in the general affairs of life—at its extreme, anarchy. In these instances, power, not justice, determines right. Factions overwhelm legitimate interests and subvert the common good. Liberty is only possible if order reduces arbitrariness to a tolerable level. In this sense, then, political and social communities, like individuals, have centripetal and centrifugal forces working against one another at any given time. Hamilton was convinced that democratic impulse was part of the centrifugal aspect of politics; it was fleeting, ephemeral, and transitory. By contrast, the centripetal aspect of political life had a unifying effect. It harmonized disparate interests and pulled society toward an abiding and enduring standard that was, in Hamilton's words, "permanent."

The dichotomy between the ephemeral and the permanent is evident in various aspects of Hamilton's constitutionalism. When he discussed the role of the judiciary in the American political system he described the Constitution as "fundamental law,"[65] the implication being that statutory law is inferior to the Constitution. If the latter is in conflict with the former, the courts are obligated to declare the statute null. The Constitution serves as an expression of the society's permanent will. It is the standard by which the more fleeting will of the legislature is to be judged. What binds a political community is not the will of the moment but the enduring Constitution. However misconstrued it may have been, Hamilton's desire to have both the president and senators serve life terms was his attempt to establish an institutional mechanism that would promote the enduring standard of the nation while avoiding the pitfalls of faction. Hamilton defended his proposal at the Constitutional Convention by stating, "[W]e should have in the Senate a permanent will, a weighty interest, which would answer essential purposes."[66] He added that a president elected for life would be less apt to forget his "fidelity" to the Constitution. It is telling that, after making the argument for life terms in the Senate and presidency, he linked the people's "fondness for democracies" to the dissolution of the union.[67] He believed that the Articles of Confederation were incapable of unifying the states because the very structure they established encouraged the centrifugal passions of society and put states at odds with one another. Unity required permanence, and in the architecture of the Constitution that meant including specific provisions to give the more virtuous part of human nature a voice in government. The Constitution itself was to be the primary instrument of this voice, but it needed public officials who would promote *its* standards, as opposed to officials who would sacrifice it to what Madison called "temporary or partial considerations."

In his defense of the Constitution's description of executive power in *The Federalist*, Hamilton covered various aspects of the presidency, including the Electoral College, and compared the president to both the king of Great Britain and the governors of the states in order to demonstrate that the criticisms of the constitutional executive branch were greatly exaggerated. Much was made by the anti-Federalists of the fact that the president was not limited in the number of terms he could serve. Hamilton pointed out that, while the New York governor's term of office was three years rather than four, there was likewise no limit on the number of terms. Unlike the king of Great Britain, the president was subject to impeachment and removal from office. The checks on his office compared favorably with those of the governors of the states. The president would have a limited veto, while the king exercised an absolute veto; and the president would share war powers with the Congress, while the king held them exclusively. The president's war powers were greater than some governors' and less than others'. The president's treaty power would rely on the Senate for advice, consent, and ratification, but the king's treaty power was unilateral. Likewise the president's appointment power was dependent on the Senate's approval, while the king's appointment power was independent and of greater extent, including the power to grant titles of nobility, offices, and church preferments.[68]

Hamilton then took up the issue of energy in the executive branch. Jefferson, like many anti-Federalists, argued that energy is equivalent to capacity to tyrannize.[69] Hamilton, however, believed that "[e]nergy in the executive is a leading character in the definition of good government. It is essential to the protection of the community against foreign attacks; it is not less essential to the steady administration of the laws; to the protection of property against those irregular and high-handed combinations which sometimes interrupt the ordinary course of justice; to the security of liberty against the enterprises and assaults of ambition, of faction, and of anarchy."[70] Energy is something different from power. It has more to do with the vigor and efficacy with which power is exercised than with the quantity or capacity of power. Specifically, Hamilton explained, energy is constituted by "unity; duration; an adequate provision for its support; competent powers."[71] To be safely constituted, power must depend on the people's sovereign constitutional will and be exercised responsibly.

Given the nature of executive power, especially in the area of foreign affairs, the ability to act with "decision, activity, secrecy, and despatch" Hamilton considered essential.[72] The legislative branch benefits from plurality because deliberation and compromise are conducive to its functions and purposes. Executive power requires a different constitution because of the nature of its functions, none the least of which is the conduct of war, a function that should be exercised "by a single hand."[73] Executive power requires that responsibility rest squarely with a leader rather than with a council, in which responsibility can oscillate or hide. Executive committees make accountability difficult, because the people do not know to whom their scorn or praise, their approval or removal should be directed. Hamilton reasoned that, in a republican system of government, executive power is more safely contained in a single executive than a committee, and consequently the people know precisely who is responsible. In a monarchy, the people know who is responsible but they have no power to control the monarch. Attaching a constitutional council to a monarch would make sense, because without it, "there would be no responsibility whatever in the executive department."[74] Dividing executive power in a monarchy adds security to liberty, but doing so in a republic has the opposite effect. Hamilton concurred with Junius, an unknown writer and critic of George III, and Jean Louis de Lolme, a Swiss-born English political theorist, who advocated a mixed constitution and opposed pure democracy: "the executive power is more easily confined when it is one."[75] Hamilton concludes *Federalist* 70 by stating:

> When power, therefore, is placed in the hands of so small a number of men, as to admit of their interests and views being easily combined in a common enterprise, by an artful leader, it becomes more liable to abuse, and more dangerous when abused, than if it

be lodged in the hands of one man; who, from the very circumstance of his being alone, will be more narrowly watched and more readily suspected, and who cannot unite so great a mass of influence as when he is associated with others.[76]

The length of the president's term of office, four years and with no limit on number of terms, was especially bothersome to the anti-Federalists. They argued that the executive would be indistinguishable from a monarch. In a letter to John Adams shortly after publication of the Constitution, Jefferson compared the executive to "a bad edition of a Polish king."[77] Hamilton thought that a longer term of office was necessary for energy and that it comported better with human nature, that individuals are more attached to what they possess for a longer duration than a short one. He used the same argument to suggest that term limits on the president would run counter to those aspects of human nature that encourage diligence and industry. Hamilton responded to the argument that a shorter term of office would ensure that the president stayed attuned to "a prevailing current" in the legislature or the people by saying that those who make such arguments "entertain very crude notions . . . of the purposes for which government was instituted."[78]

Hamilton's response places his political theory in opposition to that of Rousseau, which includes three ideas that are contrary to Hamilton's political theory. First, is the notion that human beings are good or mostly good by nature. Consequently, government should reflect the popular will, as it embodies this natural goodness. Given man's natural goodness, Rousseau did not see much need for checks on democratic sentiment; his best regime provided the people with the ability to change the rulers and the political system every time the legislature met.[79] While Hamilton advocated a popular lower house of the legislature, he was at polar opposites from Rousseau when it came to duration of office. Second, from the foundation of man's natural goodness, Rousseau constructed his best regime on the principle of legislative supremacy. The legislative branch is the one that emanates most directly from the people and is therefore best suited to express their will. Third, the government's raison d'être is to actualize the people's momentary will as opposed to their deliberative will. Rousseau's philosophy is part of a liberal tradition that aims to free individuals from the authority of traditional institutions, including governments, that are not founded on democratic principles. An executive department exists in Rousseau's best regime, but it is subordinate to the legislature and merely carries out its will. Rousseau's executive is subordinate to both the popular will and the will of the legislature.

Hamilton, by contrast, believed that an independent executive was essential to good government. While the public good should be the aim of government and the people should exercise control of government through their representatives, he rejected pure republican government, which was what Rousseau espoused. In pure republican government, the legislature exerts "an imperious control over the other departments," because legislators claim to be the exclusive representatives of the people. For Hamilton, legislative supremacy united all power in the same hands and thus established legislative tyranny. He asked, "To what purpose separate the executive or the judiciary from the legislative, if both the executive and the judiciary are so constituted, as to be at the absolute devotion of the legislative?"[80] To maintain a balanced constitution, the executive and the judiciary must remain independent of the legislature and capable of checking it.

The executive veto, which Hamilton supported, is difficult to reconcile with Rousseau's or even Locke's political theory.[81] In *Federalist* 73 Hamilton states that without the executive veto "the separation of the executive from the legislative department, would be nominal and nugatory."[82] The veto power not only protects against legislative encroachments on executive power, but it also allows the president to block legislation that is motivated by factious interest or is inconsistent with the public good. Hamilton assumes that the legislature "will not be infallible" and that "a spirit of faction may sometimes pervert its deliberations." Moreover, like the popular will, Congress may be influenced by the passion of the moment and "hurry it into measures which itself, on mature reflection, would condemn."[83] Hamilton acknowledged that the veto power opened the prospect for the opposite problem. The veto could be used to nullify a good law. No doubt, such instances would occur, he observed, but they would be far fewer in number than their opposite. Presidential judgment is vital to a properly functioning constitutional system. Legislation that violates the public good must first withstand the president's scrutiny and then the courts'.

Unlike the president, however, the judiciary cannot nullify legislation prior to an injury brought before them and can nullify legislation only on legal and constitutional grounds, not for reasons of policy. Laws may be inimical to the public good yet be constitutional. The courts are powerless to check Congress in such instances. Consequently, the responsibility to uphold the public good falls on the president. Hamilton's defense of the executive veto illustrates his larger view of constitutional government. Because of the veto, it "is far less probable that culpable views of any kind should infect all parts of the government at the same moment, and in relation to the same object, than that they should by turns govern and mislead every one of them."[84] This benefit of separated powers is also why it makes sense to rest the veto power in the president alone as opposed to vesting it in a council, the structure Hamilton knew in New York. If judges were to share the veto power with the president, they would then, in some instances, be exercising policy judgments, not legal ones. If a bill were vetoed by a council of judges and the executive and the legislature voted to override the veto, the courts could conceivably later hear a case, on legal and constitutional grounds, on which some or all of its members had previously passed judgment on policy grounds. Hamilton, again, remained true to a strict (yet not absolute) separation of powers, something he deemed necessary to the sufficient restraint of energetic government. He recognized that the way the Constitution assigned treaty-making power was considered by some to be a violation of the separation of powers, but in *Federalist* 75 he suggested that it was appropriate for the president and Senate to share the power, as treaties involved both legislative and executive power.

HAMILTON AND THE BILL OF RIGHTS

Hamilton is commonly characterized as neglecting individual rights for the sake of political and social order. In *Federalist* 84, he defended the Framers' decision to exclude a bill of rights from the Constitution. His argument is multifaceted and reveals both his view of rights and his understanding of the "unwritten constitution." Hamilton argued that a national bill of rights was unnecessary not because rights were unimportant but because, like the New York constitution, the national Constitution included protections for rights, He also cautioned that a bill of rights could prove inimical to the rights of the people.

Hamilton went to great lengths in *Federalist* 84 to enumerate the particular rights included in the body of the Constitution. Among the rights he identified were the writ of habeas corpus (which Hamilton supported by quoting Blackstone), no bills of attainder or ex post facto laws, no titles of nobility (Hamilton called this provision "the corner stone of republican government"), trial by jury, that a treason conviction requires the testimony of two witnesses, and that the punishment for treason cannot extend to family members or family property after the death of the person convicted of treason.[85]

Hamilton pointed out that bills of rights developed as a way to clarify what rights were not surrendered to the king by his subjects. He cited the Magna Charta (aimed at King John), the Petition of Right (Charles I), and the declaration of right of 1688 as examples. He concluded that bills of rights had "no application to constitutions professedly founded upon the power of the people, and executed by their immediate representatives and servants." The difference in the two cases is that in bills of rights the people surrender rights to monarchs but under the American Constitution "the people surrender nothing; and they retain every thing." A bill of rights would turn the relationship between the people and the government on its head. After citing the preamble to the Constitution, he stated that "this is a better recognition of popular rights, than volumes of those aphorisms, which make the principal figure in several of our state bills of rights, and which would sound much better in a treatise of ethics, than in a constitution of government." This characterization of the Constitution illustrates the great distance between Hamilton's day and the present. The Constitution he described was "merely intended to regulate the general political interests of the nation" not to regulate "every species of personal and private concerns."[86]

Hamilton's words also reveal how significantly different his view of bills of rights was from the anti-Federalists' when he asserts that a bill of rights was "not only unnecessary in the proposed constitution, but would even be dangerous." It seems counterintuitive to suggest that denying specific powers to government can depreciate rights and liberty. Yet Hamilton does exactly that, because he believes that specifying exceptions to government's power leaves the impression that government can do anything except what the document specifically prohibits it from doing. "[W]hy declare that things shall not be done, which there is no power to do? Why, for instance, should it be said, that the liberty of the press shall not be restrained, when no power is given by which restrictions may be imposed?" What would be added to protection for the liberty of the press by including in the Constitution a provision denying government the power to regulate it? Hamilton candidly stated that the liberty of the press could not easily be defined, and he added, "Who can give it any definition which would not leave the utmost latitude for evasion?" If this be the case, then what assurances are there that liberties like freedom of the press will be upheld? In answering that question, Hamilton invoked what some have called the unwritten constitution, the elaborate web of customs, traditions, and attitudes that are the substance of a nation's culture. Regardless of what protection may be inserted into a parchment constitution, rights like freedom of the press "must altogether depend on public opinion, and on the general spirit of the people and of the government. And here, after all . . . must we seek for the only solid basis of all of our rights."[87] He cited England as the nation with the freest press in the world, and yet the British government taxed publications. Was this a violation of the right of free press? Hamilton did not think so and added that even a provision that prohibited excessive government taxes on publications would be subject to interpretation (i.e., what constitutes an excessive tax), which is itself determined by the unwritten constitution.[88]

How, then, did Hamilton expect civil liberties to be protected and their boundaries to be identified if not by means of a bill of rights?[89] His famous defense of journalist Harry Croswell on a charge of libel in 1804 sheds some light on the question. In the course of defending Croswell, Hamilton defined the liberty of the press directly from Blackstone as "publishing the truth, from good motives and for justifiable ends." He emphasized that "free and elective government" depends on the ability of the people to know what is true and to express their views accordingly. Tyranny is advanced as the freedom of the press contracts. Hamilton acknowledged, however, that the freedom of the press does not extend to slander, and thus he argued: "I contend for the liberty of publishing truth . . . even though it reflects on government, magistrates, or private persons. I contend for it under the restraint of our tribunals.—When this is exceeded, let them interpose and punish."[90] The courts, he said, held the discretion to determine when the limits of the liberty of the press had been violated. These boundaries could not be defined a priori, other than to set general standards for what constitutes legitimate expression; and the availability of judicial discretion was necessary, because the particular circumstances of a given dispute were essential to determining if the standard of truth had been met.

Was Hamilton a Loose Constructionist?

There is a lingering question regarding the strictness of Hamilton's reading of the Constitution that gets to the heart of the frequent characterization that he was a loose constructionist, that he saw the Constitution as open to wide-ranging interpretation. People finding fault with his loose constructionism have often connected it to his desire for a strong central government led by an energetic executive. These aspects of Hamilton's political theory have been used by some of his more recent critics to link him to modern judicial activism and liberal progressivism. Richard B. Morris, for example, expressed the common view that "Hamilton anticipated the later assumption by the Supreme Court of powers for the federal government on the basis of three clauses in the Constitution—the necessary and proper clause, the general welfare clause, and the commerce clause." Morris not only connects Hamilton's reading of the Constitution to the expansion of Congress's power to regulate the economy and create the welfare state, but he also claims that, "to Hamilton the enormous expansion of the power of the Presidency by the mid-twentieth century would have been less a surprise than a vindication of his notions of the need for administrative power, energy, and efficiency."[91]

Herbert Croly, one of the intellectual fathers of progressive constitutionalism was more ambivalent in connecting Hamilton to progressive ideas. He recognized that, while Hamilton's political theory promoted strong central government that placed the national interest above local interests, it was undemocratic and insufficiently egalitarian. The objective of progressive constitutionalism, Croly believed, should be to join Hamilton's preference for strong central government with Jefferson's egalitarian democratism.[92] Croly's reservations about Hamilton's political theory suggest its incompatibility with liberal progressivism and suggest that Morris was wrong to identify these Hamiltonian traits as sharing a pedigree with modern progressivism. Important aspects of Hamilton's thought call into question key features of modern liberalism, such as the administrative state, the welfare state, and judicial activism.

Hamilton, in arguing that there is no need to prohibit powers that government is not given and that a bill of rights would be dangerous because it would imply that the people have only those rights therein enumerated, leaves the impression that government is strictly limited to enumerated powers and that the Constitution should be interpreted narrowly. However, in promoting the constitutionality of a national bank, he argued to President Washington from a seemingly different perspective.

[I]t appears to the Secretary of the Treasury, that this *general principle* is *inherent* in the very *definition* of Government and *essential* to every step of the progress to be made by that of the United States; namely—that every power vested in a Government is in its nature *sovereign,* and includes by *force* the *term,* a right to employ all the *means* requisite, and fairly *applicable* to the attainment of the *ends* of such power; and which are not precluded by restrictions & exceptions specified in the constitution; or not immoral, or not contrary to the essential ends of political society.[93]

Compared to Hamilton's statements in *Federalist* 84, this comment on the national bank appears to advocate a much looser reading of the Constitution. Are Hamilton's two statements contradictory or can they be reconciled?

In the case of rights, Hamilton viewed the problem of scope (the extent of a power or right) and the problem of meaning (what power is granted or restrained) from different perspectives. It should be kept in mind that Hamilton did not think that the Alien and Sedition Laws were unconstitutional even with the Bill of Rights added to the Constitution. Why not add to the Constitution specific prohibitions on government that protect the people's rights? The answer is that Hamilton, like Burke, was sensitive to the need for discretion in governing because he understood that circumstances dictate what prudence requires. In other words, both government power and rights are limited by law and circumstance. Constitutions cannot account for all circumstances, and therefore, discretion is necessary in determining the boundaries of power and rights. Rightly or wrongly, Hamilton thought that the national bank was necessary to carrying out Congress's enumerated powers. When it came to declaring rights in the Constitution, Hamilton did not object to *all* parchment protections for rights. Part of his argument in *Federalist* 84 is that the Constitution *is* a bill of rights, because it protects specific rights like habeas corpus. The freedom of the press, for example, is different, because it is far more difficult to define than a procedural right like habeas corpus. How, then, does one know if a right has been violated by government? Hamilton's answer is that the "propriety of a law, in a constitutional light, must always be determined by the nature of the powers upon which it is founded."[94] Presumably, if Congress passed a law restricting the freedom of the press, it could only be justified if it was done as a means to carry out a legitimate constitutional power; otherwise, it has no legal authority to restrict civil liberties.

Federalist 33 provides some insight into the problem. There Hamilton took up the anti-Federalist charge that the necessary and proper clause and the supremacy clause would render the national government's powers unlimited. He responded that "the constitutional operation of the intended government would be precisely the same, if these clauses were entirely obliterated." As a way of deciphering the extent of constitutional power, Hamilton then asks, "What is a power, but the ability of doing a thing? What is the ability to do a thing, but the power of employing the *means* necessary to its execution?" Hamilton suggested in *Federalist* 33, as in his letter to Washington on the national bank, that as long as the Constitution gives specific power to government, it has (within reason) the means that prudence deems necessary to execute that power unless specifically prohibited by the Constitution. This is clearly his argument regarding the bank. Congress has the enumerated power to borrow money, coin money, and regulate commerce, and consequently, it is necessary and proper for it to exercise the implied power to incorporate a bank.

Hamilton was fully aware that legal documents could be interpreted in a way that subverted their original meaning in order to promote a partisan objective. In the aftermath of the War for Independence, he noted the tendency of some New Yorkers to "mould the Treaty with Great-Britain, into such form as pleases them, and to make it mean any thing or nothing, as suits their views." Against such loose interpretations of the treaty he offered a candid reading of the document and consideration of the context in which it was created. With these standards in mind, Hamilton was certain that "the plain and authentic language" of the document was a superior measure of its meaning than "loose recitals of debates in newspapers."[95] Writing as "Pacificus," he argued for not a merely literal interpretation of the Constitution but "a reasonable construction."[96]

When arguing for a national bank, that the power of incorporation had been considered and rejected by the Constitutional Convention seems not to have troubled Hamilton. He acknowledged that the "moment the literal meaning is departed from, there is a chance of error and abuse," but he recognized that "an adherence to the letter of its powers would at once arrest the motions of the government." He searched for the mean between unlimited license and paralyzing legalism. He considered this mean to be "a reasonable latitude of judgment." In short, original intent matters but it must be found in the law itself and applied with a reasonable degree of discretion. No "government has a right to do *merely what it pleases*," yet government officials should not be strictly bound by original intent when interpreting the meaning of the Constitution to discover the extent of their powers. "Nothing is more common than for laws to *express* and *effect*, more or less than was intended." Applying these principles of constitutional interpretation to the case of the national bank, Hamilton concluded, "If then a power to erect a corporation, in any case, be deducible by fair inference from the whole or any part of the numerous provisions of the constitution of the United States, arguments drawn from extrinsic circumstances, regarding the intention of the convention, must be rejected."[97] To his way of thinking, the creation of the bank added no additional power to what the Constitution provided. The government's powers are fixed but the means to execute those powers are flexible.

It is this flexibility that has been construed as Hamilton's desire to read the Constitution loosely so that government power could expand beyond the limits of the Constitution. His notion of flexibility, however, was not the same as that of twentieth-century progressives' loose constructionism.[98] To Hamilton's thinking, implied powers are tethered to the limits of their antecedent enumerated powers, so an action like incorporating a bank is consistent with the original meaning of the Constitution. By contrast, progressive "living constitutionalism" aimed to break with the original meaning of the Constitution by changing the nature of constitutional powers and rights. Progressives argued that both the fundamental powers and the means to use them were flexible and not limited to any sense of originalism, or to the text of the Constitution for that matter. In short, they aimed to break the tether that connects government power and individual rights to the historical constitution. Like Hamilton, they argued for discretion, but of a different variety. Hamilton's discretion exists within the boundaries of constitutional checks and balances and the rule of law, as originally conceived by the Constitution's Framers. Progressive discretion frees the democratically elected president, senator, representative, or the appointed federal judge from the burden of following historically established norms like the Constitution and the rule of law. For the progressive loose constructionist or noninterpretativist, the discretion of the judge, member of Congress, or the president acting as the voice of the people is the standard of legitimacy. The Constitution, then, becomes what the judges who interpret it say it is. The judges may be bound by some sense of broad principles that emanate from the Constitution, but they have license to apply and interpret those principles as they deem necessary in given circumstances. Hamilton may have encouraged loose constructionism when he wrote in *Federalist* 22, "Laws are a dead letter, without courts to expound and define their true meaning and operation."[99]

When Croly synthesized Hamilton and Jefferson, he was attempting to tear Hamilton's constitutionalism from its foundations. Like Woodrow Wilson and other progressives, he wanted to preserve Hamilton's penchant for powerful, centralized, energetic government but at the same time remove it from the moorings of its philosophical anthropology. What was especially unacceptable to Croly was Hamilton's moral realism. As long as human beings were perceived as fallen creatures that could not be trusted with power, the progressive project of tearing down the Framers' system of separated and checked powers faced a philosophical obstacle. If the human condition could be cast in a different light, one that promised freedom from the tension between good and evil, then, Croly believed, government could be trusted with far more power than could be justified by the Framers' philosophical assumptions. To transform Hamilton into a progressive, requires the emasculation of his political theory; his sober historically based moral realism must be replaced by the abstract dream of human perfectibility. As Croly stated the new vision of American government: "Democracy must stand or fall on a platform of possible human perfectibility . . . it must have some leavening effect on human nature."[100] In Hamilton's view, it was not within the capacity of political institutions to change human nature; rather, it was the task of statesmen to craft and use political institutions in a way that recognized the limits of human nature and politics.

CHAPTER 5

HAMILTON'S FOREIGN POLICY

> It is not meant here to advocate a policy absolutely selfish or
> interested in nations; but to shew that a policy regulated by their
> own interest, as far as justice and good faith permit, is, and ought
> to be their prevailing policy.
>
> —Alexander Hamilton, *Pacificus Number IV*

ALEXANDER HAMILTON'S international relations theory stems
from the realistic and historical view of human nature that serves
as the foundation of his political economy and political philosophy. Some commentators push Hamilton's realism to the point
that it shares significant theoretical ground with Machiavelli. This
argument is present most notably in John Lamberton Harper's
American Machiavelli and it is suggested by Eric Voegelin in his
History of Political Ideas.[1] While Hamilton sometimes favored
bold and audacious use of power, in most instances he was more
reluctant about its use internationally than domestically. His economic policies pushed the national government's powers to the
brink of, or beyond, their constitutional boundaries in domestic
matters. In foreign affairs, however, Hamilton was far more cautious and reserved. When he advocated building up arms and
preparing for war, it was usually as a deterrent or as a last resort
when diplomacy seemed futile. He rarely advocated the use of
force in international relations except as a defensive measure,
and while he welcomed and even courted the glory of war as an
instrument of his personal social and professional progress, like
Washington he deplored the ravages of war, especially the loss of
social, political, and economic order.

Hamilton's overarching principle in foreign affairs was prudence. He was not infatuated with ideological conceptions of a transformed world. Ron Chernow calls Hamilton "the first great skeptic of American exceptionalism," because "he refused to believe that the country was exempt from the sober lessons of history."[2] In *The Continentalist*, Hamilton stated, "[W]e have no reason to think ourselves wiser, or better, than other men."[3] Writing during the quasi-war with France in 1796, he argued that it was "not the interest of the United States to be engaged in any war whatsoever."[4] If ever Hamilton had reason to promote war against a nation for ideological reasons it was with France in the aftermath of the French Revolution; his writings are filled with polemics against Jacobins. In the conduct of foreign policy, however, he remained wedded to the primacy of national interest; and in the decade of the 1790s, he saw the national interest to be preserving American independence by staying out of European political turmoil.[5] With Washington he promoted what came to be known as "the great rule": the United States would aim to maintain friendly and active commercial relations with other nations while avoiding entanglement in their political affairs.

One notable exception to Hamilton's general tendency to consider war as contrary to American welfare and interest was what John C. Miller calls Hamilton's "empire building" efforts in the last two years of John Adams's presidency.[6] Hamilton was not only intent, at times, on war with France—such a position could be construed as defensive, given the actions of the Directory—but he conspired with the Venezuelan revolutionary Francisco de Miranda to invade and acquire Louisiana and the Floridas. Hamilton's plan aimed to capture from the French and Spanish territories that he considered vital to American security. The two men's objectives overlapped, as most of the territory each desired was controlled by Spain. Miranda had come to the United States in 1783 looking for sympathetic military men who would join his plan to liberate Latin America from Spain. He traveled to England and for years tried to gain the support of the British, to no avail. As time passed, Miranda's plan seemed more and more far-fetched, and Hamilton's interest in it faded.[7] Gilbert L. Lycan disagrees with Miller's characterization of Hamilton's relationship with Miranda. He argues that, while Hamilton took some interest in Miranda's scheme, his focus was not liberating Spanish subjects but securing western territory that would advance commerce and provide security.

The plan to acquire western territory was connected to the increasing likelihood of war with France and possibly Spain. If war materialized, the French would likely invade through Louisiana. Hamilton wanted to take advantage of the opportunity to eliminate from the continent as much of the security threat from European powers as possible. His plan, which had the support of Washington, was to fortify the western army, relying on "the gifted intriguer" General James Wilkinson (who, unknown to Hamilton, was an agent of the Spanish government) for his knowledge of the western territory and of Spanish defenses. Hamilton learned that Spanish defenses were weak. In the mix of ideas circulating among Federalists about western expansion was a plan supported by Rufus King, minister to Great Britain, and John Jay to consort with England to remove Spanish forces from the continent.[8]

As long as the French and Spanish were on the continent, the Americans would have to be on guard against them. Hamilton was especially concerned about gaining free navigation of the Mississippi River, an objective repeatedly denied by Spain. The "Spanish Conspiracy" also created some concern by Hamilton. By not ceding navigation rights to Americans, the Spanish could entice western settlers to become Spanish subjects, thus creating a drain on the American population and economy. With these economic and security concerns in mind, Hamilton wrote to Secretary of War James McHenry, "[W]e ought certainly to look to the possession of the Floridas and Louisiana—and we ought to squint at South America."[9] This statement has been construed by some as a desire for American empire. Hamilton went so far as to consult with British officials about assisting the Americans against the French, who were at war with England and had a depleted military presence on the continent. Hamilton was willing to run up substantial debt in this enterprise, and he volunteered to come to Philadelphia to work with McHenry and Secretary of State Pickering to craft the plan, yet it is unclear that Hamilton's objective was empire.

American defense would provide the pretext for territorial expansion. Political scientist Richard K. Matthews insists that Hamilton planned "to create an American empire, based on capitalism" and that he spared "no ink in spelling out his unique dream of power, wealth, and empire."[10] Hamilton did refer to American empire, but he did not mean that the United States should become either a British-style territorial empire spanning the globe or an ideological empire, as revolutionary France aspired to be. Some commentators, like James F. Pontuso, attribute to Hamilton imperial designs that are inconsistent with his political theory and statesmanship. Pontuso claims that Hamilton's conception of national greatness combined "a prosperous economy and a vigorous military" that "would make it possible for the United States to control the destiny of other nations and even of all mankind."[11] There is no documentary support for the proposition that Hamilton desired this type of empire, whatever may have been the consequences of his economic or military reforms. When he used the word "empire," he referred to a range of political entities: large American states,[12] the United States, great European powers like Britain, and ancient regimes like Rome. He used the term to indicate a political unit made up of smaller entities; both the United States under the Articles of Confederation and imperial Rome could be considered empires. Once, when comparing the United States under the Articles of Confederation to great historical empires, Hamilton remarked on the "wide difference between our situation and that of an empire under one simple form of government, distributed into counties, provinces or districts, which have no legisla<tures>, but merely magistratical bodies to execute the laws of a common sovereign." He feared that if the American states did not form into a more centralized political unit, the larger states would form separate empires and frequently be at war with one another.[13]

Hamilton called the United States "the embryo of a great empire,"[14] which has led some to believe, with Pontuso, that he envisioned an American empire that was characterized by both territorial and ideological expansionism. Yet, he criticized France for attempting to create a "universal empire."[15] Even in the case of Hamilton's desire to expand American territory in North America, his justification was not to spread ideology or to become a colossus but to provide for the security and economic health of the nation. His focus was inward; for him, expansion was justified only if it created unity and security at home. He explained: "I have always held that the Unity of our empire and the best interests of our Nation require that we should annex to the UStates all the territory East of the Mississippia, New Orleans included."[16]

Two points are worth making regarding Hamilton's political theory and his character, especially in the domain of military and foreign affairs. First, when it came to military matters Hamilton was much more like Plato's timarchic man than a philosopher king. His ruling passion in such instances was a mix of ambition for glory and honor, on the one hand, and concern for vital American interests, on the other. His thoughts and rhetoric on American expansion were, at times, immoderate. Second, Hamilton often repeated his belief that too little power was as dangerous as too much power. In the context of life under the Articles of Confederation and efforts to create and ratify the new Constitution, the point is apt. But, as time passed and the federal government amassed power by creating the assumption plan, the national bank, a standing army, the Alien and Sedition Laws, and significant taxing power, Hamilton ought to have recalibrated his assessment of power and liberty. Instead, he continued to push for greater and greater national power, to the point that he became somewhat isolated, not only in the larger context of American politics but even within the political party he had created and nurtured into dominance.

It was in public policy debates that three important aspects of Hamilton's life converge: his political thinking, his character, and his statesmanship. In his political thinking, he consistently believed in the imperfectability of human nature and the permanent presence of evil in political life, yet his statesmanship was at times animated by a self-confidence that was at odds with his view of human nature. Granted, he believed that there were individuals of exceptional talents and virtue who seemed to rise above their nature, but he never indicated that such leaders were immune from the depravity that defined the human condition. Hamilton tempered such thoughts with concern that the "ungoverned spirit"[17] that ascended during revolution would refuse to subordinate itself to law or virtue. He was quick to find fault in his fellow members of the American leadership class, but he seemed at times blind to his own weaknesses and tendency to crave power. Prone to overestimate the possibilities of politics when power rested in his hands, he underestimated them when power lay with his rivals. He was as sure that he could win the Louisiana territory by virtue of his military leadership as he was that Jefferson could not buy it from Napoleon. This criticism expects a great deal from Hamilton. It should be noted, however, that he expected as much from his nation and his peers. If he had been more attuned to his own shortcomings, he might have been more sober and modest in his expectations and conduct. Like any other statesman or political thinker, Hamilton navigated the world of politics as one whose spiritual life and character influenced both how he conceived of politics and how he conducted its affairs.

Hamilton's attitude toward domestic disorder, like the Whiskey Rebellion and Fries's Rebellion, was remarkably different from his view of international disorder. While he believed that American security depended on the nation's rise to the level of a great power, he knew that it would take time to reach such a point. Military and international power, he believed, would result from economic development and the consolidation of political power at home. Until these objectives were accomplished, it was best to steer clear of other nations' squabbles. Yet, unifying and building the nation might require breaking domestic factions by force. The seeming inconsistency in Hamilton's views disappears when his consistent objective is kept in mind. His reluctance to involve the nation in international disputes was because such involvements would stifle its growth by dividing it politically and amassing debt. Quelling domestic unrest was another matter. Hamilton viewed resistance to domestic law and policy as cancers on national unity and prosperity. Rather than stifling national growth and prosperity, crushing domestic insurrections was necessary to advance the national agenda. Moreover, while the nation was relatively weak internationally, the federal government under the Constitution was relatively strong, compared to the states, especially to a state like Pennsylvania, home of both the Whiskey

Rebellion and Fries's Rebellion. In domestic affairs the government could be bold, while it had to be cautious or even timid in international affairs.

Whether in domestic or foreign affairs, Hamilton gave paramount attention to order and security. The formation of the Constitution in 1787 was justified in part, he thought, by both domestic and international security concerns. In *Federalist* 6 Hamilton responded to the argument that greater consolidation of the states was unnecessary because their common regime type would lead them to concord and peace. The "visionary, or designing men" who advocate such ideas, he said, claimed that the "genius of republics . . . is pacific" because "the spirit of commerce has a tendency to soften the manners of men, and to extinguish those inflammable humours which have so often kindled into wars." Commercial republics, the claim went, are governed by "mutual interest" that breeds harmony. This is an argument made by Montesquieu and Thomas Paine, among others. Hamilton, however, identified the causes of violence and conflict between nations not as differences in regime type but as the human condition itself. Passion has as much to do with the behavior of nations as does interest. Although the "true interest" of every nation is "to cultivate the same benevolent and philosophic spirit," he argued, "momentary passions, and immediate interests, have a more active and imperious control over human conduct, than general or remote considerations of policy, utility, or justice." Hamilton asks poignantly:

> Have republics in practice been less addicted to war than monarchies? Are not the former administered by men as well as the latter? Are there not aversions, predilections, rivalships, and desires of unjust acquisition, that affect nations, as well as kings? Are not popular assemblies frequently subject to the impulses of rage, resentment, jealousy, avarice, and other irregular and violent propensities? Is it not well known, that their determinations are often governed by a few individuals in whom they place confidence, and that they are of course liable to be tinctured by the passions and views of those individuals? Has commerce hitherto done any thing more than change the objects of war? Is not the love of wealth as domineering and enterprising a passion as that of power or glory?[18]

He then appealed to the standard he considered the least fallible, historical experience, to answer the questions. Ancient republics like Sparta, Athens, Rome, and Carthage were at times as belligerent as any nation. Commercial intercourse does not pacify nations. Geographic proximity and the passions of human nature, including economic rivalry, overshadow what little if any benefit results from common regime type. There is no escape from the discord and danger of international politics. The best nations can do is build their economic and military strength and mind their own business.

Hamilton also argued, in *Federalist* 11, that European powers recognized that, as a rising power, the United States presented a threat to their North American territories and their trade. Without a unified nation, these European powers would do what they could to play the American states off one another, to gain advantages against their military and economic rivals. Security lay in a strong union that could defend the nation and enforce the rights of neutrality, in part with a navy, which Hamilton regarded as requisite to the nation's interests. "A nation, despicable by its weakness, forfeits even the privilege of being neutral."[19] How prescient Hamilton's analysis seemed when Europe raged with the French revolutionary wars.

During Hamilton's brief tenure as a member of the Continental Congress, he tried to address both the substance and the apparatus of the government's foreign policy, including trade. The circumstances at the time allowed Hamilton to speak about the needs of American security and the machinations of European diplomacy. With other members of a committee, he recommended the establishment of a department of foreign affairs that would devote its exclusive attention to the formation and conduct of foreign policy. The department would be headed by a secretary who would lead a diplomatic corps.[20] As might be expected, near the end of the Revolutionary War and in its immediate aftermath, Hamilton considered France to be a more reliable ally than Britain, but England was more important as a trading partner. His assessment was based not on any sense of ideological compatibility with the two nations but on the extent to which their national interests coincided with those of the United States. American and French interests had overlapped more when France was a monarchy than as a republic. Hamilton understood that the French had not helped the Americans during the war out of kindness or common cause in American ideals. On balance-of-power considerations, making England weaker would make France stronger. The objective for America should be to make itself stronger before it was devoured by any of the great European empires, three of which remained on the North American continent after the War for Independence. They, along with the Indian nations, were the most immediate threat to American security, and in each case Hamilton counseled reconciliation of differences and peacemaking.

In wars between other nations, he argued for neutrality. War should be a last resort for the country, because it would exert economic pressure on the new nation and require a national unity that it did not yet possess. The prelude to American greatness was solidification of the union. Until that point was reached, the nation should avoid unnecessary involvement in European affairs. In Hamilton's first draft of Washington's Farewell Address, he sketched several points regarding foreign relations that related to the great rule: "That foreign influence is one of the most baneful foes of republican Governt . . . The great rule of conduct for us in regard to foreign Nations ought to be to have as little *political* connection with them as possible . . . Permanent alliance, intimate connection with any part of the foreign world is to be avoided so far as we are now at liberty to do it."[21]

Hamilton favored a standing army as necessary to defend the nation's borders and to deter European powers from preying on the fragile republic, and he faced opposition from the Jeffersonians in promoting it. They feared that a standing army would encourage war and tempt government leaders to use it against their own people. The Whiskey Rebellion was often cited by Jeffersonians as evidence that Hamilton and even Washington were prone to this political vice. Hamilton believed that the nation's increasing trade would require a navy to protect its economic interests.[22]

Hamilton learned from his experience in Congress that the national government was too weak to conduct effective foreign policy. It had proved unable to keep New York State from violating the peace treaty, for instance. In *Rutgers v. Waddington*, Hamilton argued that New York's Trespass Act, which gave New Yorkers the right to sue British citizens or Loyalists who had confiscated their property during the war, was in conflict with the peace treaty. As "Phocion," he wrote to convince New Yorkers that it was time to put the animosity of wartime behind them and to live as a united people. As was often the case, in his choice of pseudonym Hamilton revealed something about his political theory. Phocion was an ancient Athenian statesman whom Hamilton likely knew from reading Plutarch. Honesty, frugality, and stubborn independence were considered his main attributes. Hamilton's efforts to defend Tories and Loyalists in the wake of the revolution were not only unpopular but also contributed to the charge that he was overly sympathetic to Britain, if not an agent of its government. Like Phocion, Hamilton fought against the current of elite and public opinion because he was convinced that they were mistaken about the public good.

Vermonters' quest to be free of New York's claims on their land[23] combined domestic insurrection and the potential for British acquisition of American territory, but Hamilton's assessment of the situation did not follow a rigid ideological template. He cautioned that policy should account for both "the existing state of things, and the usual course of human affairs."[24] In other words, prudence requires that both circumstances and historical experience be taken into account. Circumstances represent the particularities of contemporary life, while patterns of human experience over time suggest an enduring order that humans can to some degree know but not change. As part of the unchanging aspect of reality, human nature provides limits to the possibilities of politics. If statesmen ask more from men and women than their nature allows, then failure is certain.

In the case of the Vermont crisis, New York insisted that the national government use force if necessary to help it bring the protesting Vermonters, including Ethan Allen and his supporters, into submission. The state government of New York had few options. Hamilton characterized the situation: "our governments are feeble and distracted; . . . the union wants energy [and] the nation concert . . . our public debts are unprovided for; our federal treasury empty; our trade languishing."[25] Britain knew of these circumstances and wished to pull Vermont into her empire. When considering these factors, Hamilton rejected following the example of Rome and forcing Vermont into an American empire, as suggested by a law colleague, Richard Harison. Hamilton concluded: "Neither the manners nor the genius of Rome are suited to the republic or age we live in. All her maxims and habits were military, her government was constituted for war. Ours is unfit for it, and our situation still less than our constitution, invites us to emulate the conduct of Rome, or to attempt a display of unprofitable heroism."[26] The American character, its political culture, and its habits were not imperial but republican. The point was not that republican America would never expand its borders or use military force but that when it did engage in such behavior, its animating spirit would not be that of an empire governed by hubris. The American character in the early republic was more modest than Rome's, not merely because its means were likewise modest, but because the nation was born in opposition to empire, not in quest of it. What Hamilton found objectionable about European imperialism was that Europe seemed to consider "the rest of mankind as created for her benefit."[27] America's encounter with the world would presumably be different, because the United States would base its foreign relations on mutual interest, not the *libido dominandi*. Hamilton's solution to the Vermont crisis was not to force Ethan Allen and his supporters into a union with New York; rather, he introduced a bill in the state legislature supporting statehood for Vermont. He then negotiated a compromise that would compensate New York landholders who stood to lose property as a consequence of Vermont independence, giving them cash from Vermont and land from the western part of New York State.

That Hamilton favored republicanism over imperialism did not mean that he agreed with anti-Federalists[28] and Republicans who argued for a governmental modesty that would exclude standing armies and navies, territorial expansion, a national debt, a national bank, and long terms of office without term limits. The debate in the early republic was intramural, in the sense that it was about what kind of republican government was appropriate for the nation. Included in that debate was the extent to which Americans should concern themselves with external affairs. Hamilton did not want the United States to meddle in the affairs of

Europe or any other part of the world, but unlike many anti-Federalists he believed that protection from the outside world would result if there was military and economic strength at home. Foreign nations would have to respect and even fear the United States if the country was to avoid being drawn into international conflict. Likewise, modesty and peace required sufficient economic and military strength to deter European powers from meddling in America's business and to reduce American dependence on foreign nations. Even before Hamilton helped Washington create the neutrality policy in 1794, he advocated neutrality as essential for American prosperity. In *Federalist* 11 he insisted that neutrality was not simply a matter of unilaterally announcing one's intent to stay out of foreign disputes. "The rights of neutrality will only be respected when they are defended by an adequate power."[29]

THE NEUTRALITY PROCLAMATION

Shortly after Washington took office as the first president, events in France created great concern, if not a crisis. Not only did the French Revolution destabilize European affairs, but France was intent on reacquiring the Louisiana territory, at that time held by Spain, and everything west of the existing American border.

In the aftermath of the Revolutionary War, Americans also had to contend with acts of Parliament that placed restrictions on trade with England. The British were intent on keeping the Americans from trading with the British West Indies. In some cases the British were willing to allow American goods into their country, but only if transported by British ships. Trade with the French was not much better. Protection of domestic markets was the general practice in Europe.[30]

As hostilities between France and England reached the point of war, the Americans were sure to be a pawn in the power politics of Europe. Washington and Hamilton were steadfast in their efforts to remain aloof from European squabbles. They were convinced that the nascent republic could not withstand the economic, political, and military expense of war. The United States was a long way from the degree of power necessary to flex its

muscle in international affairs.[31] At this early stage in the development of the American republic, the president and his treasury
secretary seemed to understand that war would be destructive to
constitutional government and the domestic tranquility it provided.
They decided that the president should issue a proclamation declaring American neutrality in the French revolutionary wars.

At this early stage in the life of the Constitution, some, like
Jefferson and Madison, believed that only Congress could decide the nation's policy with regard to war. This interpretation
of the Constitution coincided with the view that the Americans
should support the French for three basic reasons: France had
been instrumental in aiding American independence, the Americans were obligated by treaty to assist the French, and the French
were fighting for the same ideological objectives that had inspired the American Revolution. Unlike Jefferson and Madison,
Hamilton's imagination was not prejudiced by an affinity for
France and its emerging ideological state. Although he was an
admirer of many things British, he was more likely to view foreign affairs through the prism of national interest, and this instance was no exception. Forrest McDonald explains, with some
irony, the underlying differences between Hamilton and Jefferson in this matter.

> Jefferson liked to talk about the force of reason in human affairs,
> but his political attitudes were visceral, not rational, at their base. He
> had what Hamilton described as "a womanish attachment to France
> and a womanish resentment against Great Britain," and his for-
> eign policy initiatives were always colored by those emotions . . .
> Hamilton was the opposite: he talked of men being driven by their
> passions and their interests but based his [policies] on reason and
> careful calculation. In the face of war in Europe, he saw neutrality
> as the great desideratum, but not because, having known war, he
> cherished peace. Rather, he understood that war, in the emotional
> and ideological climate of the United States during the 1790s,
> would divide the nation against itself and sap the strength of its
> infant national government.[32]

When Hamilton used his pen to defend the neutrality proclamation, he engaged the constitutional, political, and ideological
aspects of the debate. The result was a series of articles in which
Hamilton, writing as "Pacificus," and Madison, writing as "Hel-

vidius," debated the meaning of the Constitution and the prudence of the president's policy. Five years earlier they had joined as "Publius" to defend and support ratification of the Constitution. Now, as party and ideological fissures developed—orchestrated in part by Hamilton and Jefferson—the former allies were in opposing roles. At stake was the setting of precedent that would shape the conduct of American foreign policy and executive-legislative relations for decades to come.

As was typically the case when Hamilton argued about foreign affairs, he invoked both constitutional law and the law of nations. Apart from its legal justification, the purpose of the proclamation was to notify the warring nations of America's policy and intentions, and to warn Americans that they were obligated to the duties that accompanied neutrality. He reminded his readers that the law of nations provided guidelines in matters relating to war goods and the impressment of seamen. He asserted that the neutrality proclamation did not preclude compliance with existing treaties as long as fulfilling specific treaty obligations did not compromise American neutrality. This comment responded to the argument that neutrality would require violating the American treaty with France. He invoked Vattel and argued that, because the treaty had been made long before the current war, American compliance with the treaty, even if it meant supplying France with troops or ships, would not violate neutrality. Because the treaty required no such obligation, the Americans need not worry about such a predicament; they had made no such promises to France. To supply troops or ships would, under the circumstances, then, be a violation of neutrality. Compliance with the clause of guarantee in the eleventh article of the treaty would violate neutrality, because it would make the U.S. a military "*associate* or *auxiliary* in the War."[33]

Who is constitutionally authorized to determine if neutrality is an appropriate policy for the government? Hamilton argued that the president, not the Congress, is constitutionally justified in creating foreign policy, apart from specific powers given to Congress, like declaring war. Congress "is not the *organ* of intercourse between the UStates and foreign Nations," he wrote. The president makes treaties and enforces them. The executive is, therefore, the "*organ*" of foreign affairs and, Hamilton implied, the sole organ. While the Senate exercises some executive power in foreign affairs, like ratifying treaties, such powers are intended to be checks on the use of executive power not the power itself. As a matter of constitutional interpretation, Hamilton asserted that Congress's executive powers ought to be construed "strictly," whereas the president's executive powers ought to be construed broadly. Executive power rests in the president who is the sole organ of the nation. Where the Constitution limits and checks executive power, there is a specific clause to serve the purpose. In the case of proclaiming neutrality, no constitutional limitation exists, because it falls under the broad powers of the president. Why, if Congress can declare war, is it prohibited from declaring its opposite, neutrality? Hamilton answered:

> If the Legislature have a right to make war on the one hand—it is on the other the duty of the Executive to preserve Peace till war is declared; and in fulfilling that duty, it must necessarily possess a right of judging what is the nature of the obligation which the treaties of the Country impose on the Government; and when in pursuance of this right it has concluded that there is nothing in them inconsistent with a *state* of neutrality, it becomes both its province and its duty to enforce the laws incident to that state of the Nation.

Because the president, and not the Congress, is obligated to interpret treaties (a position accepted by the Supreme Court in *Missouri v. Holland*, 1920), and because he alone decides to continue or suspend a treaty, he must determine if neutrality is consistent with the nation's treaty obligations. The treaty with France creates a defensive alliance; according to the great writers of international law (especially Burlamaqui), it only obligates the U.S. to assist France if she was attacked. Because France initiated war with England and other nations, it was not incumbent on the United States to provide military assistance, for the war was of an offensive nature. Hamilton concluded the constitutional part of his argument by declaring that, in the system of separated powers, "[i]t is the province and duty of the Executive to preserve to the Nation the blessings of peace. The Legislature alone can interrupt those blessings, by placing the Nation in a state of War."[34]

Hamilton's defense of the neutrality proclamation moves from legal and constitutional issues to the policy realm. The United

States could not easily engage in a distant war, given that it had no navy and France was in no position to transport American troops. Apart from any legal consideration, entry into the war was contrary to American interests, especially in regard to trade with Britain, America's leading trading partner. As Hamilton stated the point, "self-preservation is the first duty of a Nation." Given the circumstances of the war, Hamilton believed that it was "impossible to imagine a more unequal contest, than that in which we should be involved in the case supposed; a contest from which, we are dissuaded by the most cogent motives of self preservation, as well as of Interest." Assisting France would put at risk the very existence of the United States, and to what end would such a risk be taken? Hamilton thought the answer was clear: to secure for France "her West Indian Islands and other less important possessions in America."[35] He invoked Vattel to argue that treaty obligations may be broken if honoring them would result in the disintegration of the nation. According to Hamilton, France was intent on spreading its revolutionary doctrines to other parts of the world, and her enemies were intent on protecting their regimes. He would later write that France "betrayed a spirit of universal domination" that aimed to impose her "moral political and religious creeds" on other nations.[36] He correctly sensed during the Pacificus-Helvidius debates that American prosperity required as much distance from France as was possible.

Some opponents of the neutrality proclamation argued that the gratitude the United States owed to France warranted assisting her war efforts. Hamilton replied that national interest, not gratitude, should dictate foreign policy, for the latter might require sacrificing the former. It may be consistent with the virtue of individuals to forego self-interest for the sake of gratitude, but nations operate by different standards of morality. Hamilton felt compelled to qualify his argument by stating, "It is not meant here to advocate a policy absolutely selfish or interested in nations; but to shew that a policy regulated by their own interest, as far as justice and good faith permit, is, and ought to be their prevailing policy." Nations were not free to do as they pleased; following the dictates of national interest and self-preservation was not license to commit injustices against other nations. Here the differences between Hamilton and Hobbes are apparent.

For Hobbes, the anarchy of the state of nature leaves individuals free to behave any way they choose. Because morality is a mere convention (i.e., an artificial instrument created and used by the leviathan to impose order), prior to the social contract it does not exist. For Hamilton, morality was both natural and conventional. Human beings and nations were obligated to follow the dictates of justice. As is evident from Hamilton's writings and behavior during the American Revolution, he believed that individuals never exist in a pure state of nature; they are always bound by the moral laws of nature, conscience, and their creator. Nations should follow their interests, but with the boundaries of justice and good faith as mitigating factors. France helped the Americans win their independence because it was in her interest to do so, not because she was filled with the spirit of benevolence, he commented.[37] Moreover, what gratitude was owed to France had been earned by Louis XVI, not the revolutionary government that beheaded him.

In the debates, Hamilton also responded to the argument that America should support the spread of the revolutionary spirit and the liberty it aimed to engender. He cautioned his countrymen to mind their own business and suggested that they were too wise to be seduced by "foreign or domestic machinations." Rather, they would "support the government they have established, and . . . take care of their own peace, in spite of the insidious efforts . . . to detach them from the one, and to disturb the other." He then previewed a point that would be central to Washington's Farewell Address. The information from the French Convention (the governing body before the Directory) "ought to teach us not to over-rate *foreign friendships*—to be upon our guard against *foreign attachments*. The former will generally be found hollow and delusive; the latter will have a natural tendency to lead us aside from our own true interest, and to make us the dupes of foreign influence."[38]

"No Jacobin"

When Hamilton wrote as "Pacificus," he was trying to steer the nation away from partisan attachment to European powers that he feared would drag the nation into war. In the wake of the controversy over the neutrality proclamation, partisan tension heightened, as the United States was caught between warring European empires. Many Republicans were clamoring for war with England, as Federalists stood firm in their opposition to France. The Republicans were encouraged by Edmond Genêt, a French diplomat who exuded revolutionary pathos. Serving as the French minister to the United States, he was intent on recruiting Americans and securing ships and weapons for the French efforts against the British. Genêt was also plotting to capture British territory north of the American border and Spanish territory south of it. He was bold, defiant, and, the Federalists thought, obnoxious. The neutrality proclamation had no effect on his efforts to recruit American support for the French cause. He traveled throughout the country and was treated with enthusiasm and celebrity. He armed French cruisers in American ports that were used to capture British ships. England demanded that the Americans put a stop to Genêt and that the captured ships be returned. Miller explains, "More and more he began to behave like an apostle preaching a crusade against kings, priests and aristocrats—and among the last he included Federalists."[39]

Genêt was plotting an attack against Spain's North American territories, the Floridas, and Louisiana. He lobbied Hamilton to accelerate American payments on outstanding French loans worth more than five million dollars. When the secretary of the treasury refused, he castigated him as a monarchist who was intent on saving British monarchy from French efforts to liberate England from that vile form of government. Genêt was the kind of Jacobin that brought out the Burkean side of Hamilton. In July 1793, Hamilton wrote as "No Jacobin" to expose Genêt's criminal and subversive behavior. He argued in painstaking detail that the outfitting of vessels violated the Treaty of Commerce with France and that the seizure of British ships within the jurisdiction of the United States violated the custom of international law. Hamilton aimed to prove that Genêt's penchant for skirting the law was indicative of the Jacobin ideology he espoused. He charged that, rather than comply with American and international law, Genêt openly conducted a demagogic appeal to the American people that aimed to undermine President Washington's authority and policies by directing public opinion against him. The following month, Washington decided to demand Genêt's recall. By this point, even Jefferson agreed. However, because of tumult in France, the revolutionary government, more than willing to recall Genêt, was probably going to send him to the guillotine. Once again, Hamilton demonstrated extraordinary civility and magnanimity to a political opponent by helping Genêt receive sanctuary in America, after which he became a citizen and married one of New York governor George Clinton's daughters.[40]

"AMERICANUS"

The Genêt affair served to heighten partisan tensions between Federalists and Republicans. In early 1794, Madison, who opposed Washington's neutrality policy, proposed a bill in the House of Representatives that would initiate a trade war with England. The British did not recognize the principle of "free ships make free goods." As a naval power, they were reluctant to hamstring their chief military advantage and went so far as to include food as war contraband. Hamilton feared that if the bill was adopted the trade war would push Britain into a real war. The neutrality policy devised by Hamilton and Washington was designed not only to avoid potentially disastrous military conflicts with great powers, but also to take advantage of the opportunity to trade with the warring powers under circumstances that highly favored the Americans. Madison's efforts in Congress would likely defeat both objectives. Hamilton, again, took to his pen, this time as "Americanus,"[41] and tried to avert another war with Britain. He cast a dismal future for the United States if they joined the French, and he reminded Americans of the advantages of their commercial intercourse with the British Empire.

Hamilton argued that the tide of the French Revolution had turned; its immoderate features were deplorable and would breed a government of like manner. He wrote, "[A]fter wading through seas of blood, in a furious and sanguinary civil war, France may find herself at length the slave of some victorious Sylla, or Marius, or Caesar."[42] The United States was ill equipped to assist France in war, and doing so would mean setting the United

States against England and Spain, a situation contrary to American national interest. In particular, America was experiencing a period of great economic progress that, if continued, would "place our national rights and interests upon immovable foundations."[43] American prosperity would occur because, while Europe warred, the United States would gain the economic and military might required to protect its own interests. The expansion of American commerce was fueling tax revenues, thus reducing the need for additional taxes. War would depress commerce and would require a greater tax burden on the people. War with England and Spain would also incite Indian wars and destabilize the border territories. A final threat to America was the "violent resentment" that would result from "a wanton and presumptuous intermeddling" in the affairs of Europe that did not impinge on American interests. To those who argued that France's enemies would turn on the United States once they finished subduing France, Hamilton responded that the differences in the two cases were clear.

> If left to themselves they [European powers] will all, except one [France], naturally see in us a people who originally resorted to a revolution in government, as a refuge from encroachments on rights and privileges *antecedently* enjoyed, not as a people who from choice sought a radical and entire change in the established government, in pursuit of new privileges and rights carried to an extreme, irreconcilable perhaps with any form of regular government. They will see in us a people who have a due respect for property and personal security; who, in the midst of our revolution, abstained with exemplary moderation from every thing violent or sanguinary, instituting governments adequate to the protection of persons and property; who, since the completion of our revolution, have in a very short period, from mere reasoning and reflection, without tumult or bloodshed, adopted a form of general government calculated, as well as the nature of things would permit, to remedy antecedent defects, to give strength and security to the nation, to rest the foundations of liberty on the basis of justice, order, and law; who have at all times been content to govern themselves without intermeddling with the affairs or governments of other nations.[44]

This distinction between contrasting national characters would be lost if the United States joined the French cause, not only in the view of foreign powers but in the conduct and character of the American nation. Nothing less than the identity of the nation was at stake.

What is impressive about Hamilton's argument is that it reveals understanding of the American Revolution and the meaning of American identity. Unlike the contemporary philosopher Richard Price[45] and others who looked on the revolution as an ongoing project dedicated to the progress of universal liberty, Hamilton was clear that the American Revolution ended when the guns and cannons fell silent. Moreover, he identified the cause of the war as the recovery of ancient rights and privileges, not the acquisition of new ones. Finally, he connected the modest objectives of the American Revolution with a national character that was modest in its foreign relations, minding its own business rather than meddling in the affairs of other nations.

THE JAY TREATY

In 1794, John Jay was sent by Washington on a diplomatic mission to England to negotiate a treaty that would, it was hoped, improve Anglo-American relations by resolving outstanding violations of the Treaty of Paris and by encouraging greater commercial concord. Jay's assignment was complicated by the French revolutionary wars, initiated by France in 1793, and heightened tensions at home between pro-French Republicans and pro-British Federalists. While the Federalist Jay was negotiating in England, the Republican Monroe was in France serving a similar role and also sent by Washington. The festering treaty violation issues included British occupation of Great Lakes forts that were south of the post-treaty border and American failure to compensate Loyalists for property losses incurred during the war. The border problem was exacerbated by American settlers pushing beyond the western border and British encouragement of Indian attacks on American settlers. The British also accused the Americans of failing to honor their prewar British debts, which some southerners refused to pay in retribution for deliberate efforts by the British to free their slaves. The British prevented American ships from trading in the West Indies, and they refused to compensate American slave owners for losses that resulted from British efforts to emancipate slaves. American neutrality was challenged by both French and British treatment of American ships, crews, and cargoes. Seizure of American ships and impressment of American sailors became common, to the point that war at times seemed certain. Jay's mission was an effort to avert war with England without instigating war with France.

Although Hamilton had left his position at the Treasury Department by this time, Washington and other members of the cabinet confided in him as if he had never resigned his post. Consequently, Hamilton was still intimately involved in shaping American foreign policy, including the Jay Treaty. Like Washington, he believed that the new republic could ill afford war with any European imperial power. American foreign policy should, he thought, be guided by national security and national interest. With these objectives in mind, Hamilton counseled Washington to resolve the border problems and to do what could be done to free American shippers from British restrictions. Hamilton especially desired an unguarded, disarmed border to the north, which would require British compliance with the boundaries established by the peace treaty. He understood that some enticements would encourage compliance. It seemed reasonable to Hamilton for the United States to assure that American prewar debt owed to England would be honored. He knew that any agreement would hinge on the mutual benefit that England and the United States received from trade. Each side was vital to the other's economic health.

The Jay Treaty was met with widespread opposition; the Senate approved it by the slimmest of margins only after deciding to keep the terms of the treaty from the public. The House of Representatives tried to kill the treaty by denying it funding and demanded that Washington show them Jay's instructions. In the treaty as Jay negotiated it, the British agreed to leave the Great Lakes forts south of the U.S. border and to enter arbitration by mixed commissions to settle prewar debt and Loyalist compensation cases. A provision, Article 12, to marginally open the British West Indies to American trade was rejected by the Senate, in large part because it prohibited American export of sugar and other goods produced in the West Indies. The list of war contraband was expanded to include timber, hemp, and some food-stuffs. Such items could be seized during shipment to enemies of England or to the United States. No agreement was reached on compensation for slaves lost during the Revolutionary War, shipping rights for American vessels, or British impressments of American seamen. Republicans were incensed by the treaty, and partisan passion reached a new level of acrimony and vitupera-tion. Washington's popularity hit its nadir at this time. Hamil-ton, never one to back down from a good political fight, wrote as "Camillus" and defended the Jay Treaty, but not before he struggled to find the virtues of its agreements. He worried that rejection of the treaty would move the nation closer to war with England. The Republicans thought that approval of the treaty would have the same effect with France.

"CAMILLUS"

The "Camillus" essays are vintage Hamilton. In the face of wide-spread opposition to the Jay Treaty so vehement that Hamilton was pelted with stones while speaking in its defense and chal-lenged to a duel,[46] he wrote twenty-eight essays aimed at win-ning public and political support for it. Republicans thought that Jay's treaty conceded too much at a time when the British were weak. They attributed what they perceived as lopsided terms to the Federalists' desire for a closer political and commercial relationship with England. Specifically, they criticized the com-mercial terms of the treaty as an unconstitutional encroachment by the executive on Congress's power to regulate commerce; they found it appalling that the treaty failed to win acceptance of the principle that "free ships make free goods" (including an end to British seizure of food destined for France as war contra-band) and an end to the impressment of American seamen; they considered American agreement to honor prewar debts while the British ignored the losses incurred by slave owners whose slaves were freed by the British as preposterous. Some Republicans thought the treaty so dishonorable that they considered war with England a better alternative than acceptance of the treaty.

Hamilton began his defense of the Jay Treaty in July 1795, writing as "Horatius" in a New York City newspaper then titled *The Argus or Greeleaf's new daily advertiser*. He argued that the "permanent welfare" of the nation would be protected by the treaty. The concessions to be made pertained to transitory things. The commercial part of the treaty would expire two years after the conclusion of the war between England and France. What harm might be done to American commerce in the West Indies would be temporary. The opening of trade with Canada would be permanent.[47]

He began his "Camillus" letters to *The Argus* by noting that public opinion was skewed in favor of France and against Britain, a problem both caused and exacerbated by men who, "actuated by an irregular ambition," placed their self-interest above the national interest.[48] The sequestration of prewar debts was a case in point. Consequently, passion not reason was determining the public's view of the treaty and "time, examination and reflection would be requisite to fix the public opinion on a true basis."[49] The treaty must be understood in context: "Few nations can have stronger inducements than the U States to cultivate peace. Their infant state in general—their want of a marine in particular to protect their commerce[—]would render war in an extreme degree a calamity."[50] Without the treaty, Spain, as an ally of Britain, would consort to inspire Indian wars on the frontier and continue to prohibit navigation of the Mississippi. Hamilton estimated that in ten to twelve years the United States would be in a position to conduct a more assertive foreign policy. Until then Americans needed to recognize that Britain, not France, was vital to the nation's economic development. American hearts were sympathetic to France but their heads should recognize that without England most of American trade would evaporate, as would American prosperity.

Hamilton appealed to national interest and a realistic assessment of the circumstances. This attitude was especially evident in his view of the shipping rights that were due to America as a neutral power. Britain's strategy in its war with France included starving the enemy into submission. American food shipments to France were an obstacle to the strategy. The British were not going to agree in a treaty to forgo an essential war strategy, especially given that the Americans lacked the naval power to defend their commercial ships. Hamilton reminded his Francophilic opponents that French treatment of American ships violated another treaty, one that the two nations had signed in very different circumstances. He observed that nations could be expected to act in accordance with their perceived interest; parchment agreements were no guarantee that law or principle will overcome the dictates of self-interest. Such reasoning harked back to Hamilton's *Federalist* 23. There he argued that the powers of national security "ought to exist without limitation" because circumstances are too unpredictable to account in advance for the needs of the nation. "The circumstances that endanger the safety of nations are infinite; and for this reason, no constitutional shackles can wisely be imposed on the power to which the care of it is committed."[51] What is true of constitutions and national security is surely true of treaties and national security; nations will not negotiate away their ability to defend their vital interests, the first of which is survival. British impressment of American seamen was a case in point. Though the laws of nations prohibited British impressment of Americans, to the British it was "a question of *national safety*" and to the United States it was a matter of "commercial convenience & individual security."[52]

Hamilton did not suggest that treaties were held together only by overlapping interests and that compliance was wholly dependent on the continuation of common interest. National interest may be paramount but specific aspects of interest may vary in importance. Nations will sacrifice lesser interests to protect more vital interests. It is also requisite on nations to consider their character and reputation when they conduct foreign relations. Honor and interest usually coincide; both require that nations demonstrate fidelity to both law and commitment. Nations that are in the habit of breaking their word will find it difficult to win the confidence of other nations, a necessary condition for the promotion of national interest. With regard to such issues, Hamilton often invoked the importance of national character. To possess a magnanimous character, nations must honor their agreements except in extraordinary circumstances. Hamilton explained the point and then applied it to the circumstances of the Jay Treaty: "The truth is, that though nations will too often evade their promises on colorable pretexts, yet few are so profligate as to do it without such pretexts. In clear cases, self-interest dictates a regard to the obligations of good faith. Nor is there any thing in the history of Great Britain which warrants the opinion that she is more unmindful than other nations of her character for good faith."[53] Hamilton would later argue that it would be best for the United States to dissolve the treaty with France by mutual consent, saying, "It is bad to be under obligations which it will be a violation of good faith not to perform."[54]

Again writing as "Camillus" and defending the Jay Treaty, Hamilton explained that foreign relations require virtues that transcend mere self-interest. He echoed Cicero's belief that honorableness is both rational and consistent with moderation.

> True honor is a rational thing. It is as distinguishable from Quixotism as true courage from the spirit of the bravo. It is possible for one nation to commit so undisguised and unqualified an outrage upon another, as to render a negotiation of the question dishonorable. But this seldom, if ever, happens. In most cases it is consistent with honor to precede rupture by negotiation, and whenever it is, reason and humanity demand it. Honor cannot be wounded by consulting moderation. As a general rule, it is not till after it has become manifest that reasonable reparation for a clear premeditated wrong cannot be obtained by an amicable adjustmen[t], that honor demands a resort to arms. In all the questions between us and Great Britain, honor permitted the moderate course; in those which regard the inexecution of the treaty of peace, there had undoubtedly been mutual faults. It was therefore a case for negotiation and mutual reparation. True honor, which can never be separated from justice, even requires reparation from us to Great Britain, as well as from her to us. The injuries we complain of in the present war were also of a negociable kind. . . To have taken, therefore, the imperious ground which is recommended, in place of that which was taken; would have been not to follow the administration of honor, but to have submitted to the impulse of passion and phrenzy.[55]

The United States negotiated the Jay Treaty with two primary objectives in mind: move toward compliance of the Paris Peace Treaty of 1783 and settle disputes regarding British seizure of American goods shipped to France. Both objectives were achieved by the treaty, as well as British agreement to leave northwest posts, a commercial treaty, improved trade with England and India, and the creation of a mixed commission to settle territorial disputes. To get these British concessions, Jay had to agree to

> renounce the "freedom of the seas" at least for the duration of the war; enemy property not contraband was admitted to be subject to capture from American vessels; the contraband list was extended to include foodstuffs under certain conditions; the United States agreed not to export cotton, sugar and other West India products; it was stipulated that there should be no confiscation of bank deposits; the question of prewar debts was handed over for arbitration to a mixed commission; and to guard against a repetition of Citizen Genêt's activities, it was provided that no privateers were to be fitted out in United States ports and that no prizes were to be brought in and sold.[56]

Jay might have been able to accomplish more, but Hamilton was convinced that the Americans were negotiating from a position of weakness and should take what they could get, unless the terms were grossly one-sided. In the end, he decided that the benefit of averting war with Britain justified the treaty.

THE ADAMS YEARS

Once Washington left office, Hamilton exerted his influence by continuing to advise the cabinet, which came easily because the new president decided it was his duty to retain the members of Washington's cabinet. As tensions with Britain subsided as a result of the Jay Treaty, they mounted with France, which was furious that America was negotiating with its enemy and which had its own grievances about unpaid debts from the American Revolution. France broke off diplomatic relations with the United States and started capturing American ships. An undeclared war developed, often called the Quasi-War.

ALIEN AND SEDITION ACTS

The Alien and Sedition Acts were created in response to the circumstances surrounding the Quasi-War with France and a resulting suspicion of aliens, especially the French. They limited some basic rights, including freedom of speech (especially in criticism of the president or Congress), and aroused much controversy. The president was empowered to deport dangerous aliens, and the residency requirement for naturalization was increased from five to fourteen years. Hamilton was not involved in their creation, although John Adams, shortly after he became president in 1797, falsely accused him of sending a memo advocating such measures. Hamilton commented in writing on aspects of each of the four bills as they were being considered by Congress. His reaction to them illuminates aspects of his political theory that relate to civil liberties and foreign policy. As we have seen, Hamilton could be remarkably merciful toward his opponents but rarely showed that virtue toward individuals of Jacobin persuasion. Because the Alien and Sedition Laws were directed at Jacobins, one would expect Hamilton to have been a strong advocate of them. As was often the case with Hamilton, careful scrutiny of his attitudes reveals unexpected complexity.

When the Senate was considering the Sedition Act, Hamilton wrote to Oliver Wolcott, the secretary of the treasury, and to Timothy Pickering, the secretary of state. To Wolcott he expressed his reservations about the Sedition Act.

> There are provisions in this Bill which according to a cursory view appear to me highly exceptionable & such as more than any thing else may endanger civil War . . . I hope sincerely the thing may not be hurried through. Let us not establish a tyranny. Energy is a very different thing from violence. If we make no false step we shall be essentially united; but if we push things to an extreme we shall then give to faction *body* and solidarity.[57]

To Pickering he expressed his reservations about the Alien Act in a postscript.

> If an alien Bill passes I should like to know what policy in execution is likely to govern the *Executive*. My opinion is that while the mass ought to be obliged to leave the Country—the provisions in our Treaties in favor of Merchants ought to be observed & there ought to be *guarded* exceptions of characters whose situations would expose them too much if sent away & whose demeanour

among us has been unexceptionable. There are a few such. Let us not be cruel or violent.[58]

Several months later, when the Congress was considering a revision to one of the Alien Acts, Hamilton wrote to Theodore Sedgwick, a member of the Senate: "On a recent though hasty revision of the Alien law it seems to me deficient in precautions against abuse and for the security of Citizens. This should not be."[59]

Hamilton did think that a provision in the Sedition Act that allowed those accused of libel to use truth as a defense was a welcome reform. It was with this provision in mind that he defended Harry Croswell, editor of a New York newspaper called *The Wasp*. Croswell had been arrested and convicted in New York of libel against President Jefferson and others. Hamilton defended him in his appeal, arguing that truth was a defense in libel cases and that on that ground his client was not guilty. Because the case was prosecuted under New York law, the federal law did not apply; but Hamilton argued, unsuccessfully, that common law was unclear on the matter and that, in a republic, truth was a defense in libel cases. In the course of Croswell's defense, Hamilton predicted that the Sedition Law, with its allowance of truth as a defense, would "one day be pronounced a valuable feature in our national character. In this we find not only the intent, but the truth may be submitted to the jury, and that even in a justificatory manner."[60] Hamilton lost the case, but Croswell's conviction, while upheld, did not result in sentencing; and in the following year, the New York legislature passed a law incorporating Hamilton's argument for truth as a defense against libel into a statute. In the ensuing years, similar provisions were incorporated into the laws of the other states.[61]

Hamilton's comments on the Alien and Sedition Laws were not all as seemingly prescient as those quoted above.[62] In a 1799 letter to Senator Jonathan Dayton, an old classmate from Elizabethtown Academy, Hamilton surveyed the political landscape and drew a bleak assessment of the situation. He lamented the influence of the French Revolution in America and added, "[P]ublic opinion has not been ameliorated; sentiments dangerous to social happiness have not been diminished; on the contrary, there are symptoms which warrant the apprehension that among the most numerous class of citizens, errors of a very pernicious tendency have not only preserved but have extended their empire." As Hamilton reflected on and enumerated the various responses that might be taken by Federalists, he criticized President Adams for not using the Sedition Act and made the following statements to Dayton:

> It will be useful to declare that all such writings &c which at common law are libels if levelled against any Officer whatsoever of the UStates shall be cognizable in the Courts of UStates.
>
> To preserve confidence in the Officers of the General Government, by preserving their reputations from malicious and unfounded slanders, is essential to enable them to fulfil the ends of their appointment. It is therefore both constitutional and politic to place their reputations under the guardianship of the Courts of the United States. They ought not to be left to the cold and reluctant protection of state courts always temporizing and sometimes disaffected.
>
> But what avail laws which are not executed? Renegade Aliens conduct more than one of the most incendiary presses in the UStates—and yet in open contempt and defiance of the laws they are permitted to continue their destructive labors. Why are they not sent away? Are laws of this kind passed merely to excite odium and remain a dead letter? Vigor in the Executive is at least as necessary as in the legislative branch. If the President requires to be stimulated those who can approach him ought to do it.[63]

Hamilton's reservations about the Sedition Act faded as time passed. He was increasingly incensed at the treatment he received in the Republican press, and he feared that public opinion would be swayed by it, like a mob by a demagogue. He encouraged a lawsuit against David Frothingham, who reprinted in the *Argus*, a New York newspaper, an article previously published by another paper falsely accusing Hamilton of trying to buy the *Aurora*, a Philadelphia paper, in order to deprive Republicans of a means by which to criticize Federalists. The article dredged up Hamilton's extramarital affair with Maria Reynolds and accused him of being a British agent and being able to afford to buy the *Aurora* because he was on the payroll of the British secret service. Hamilton testified in the case; Frothingham was fined one hundred dollars and imprisoned for four months.[64]

LOUISIANA PURCHASE

As events continued to unfold in Europe and France acquired the Louisiana territory from Spain, Hamilton played the role of the loyal opposition. As a consequence of the transfer of sovereignty over Louisiana, Spanish authorities closed the port of New Orleans to American shippers, in violation of existing treaty agreements. Hamilton reacted by arguing for a combination of military force and diplomacy. His preferred plan was to acquire the Floridas and New Orleans by force and then negotiate from a position of strength. The alternative was to negotiate first in an effort to purchase the territories from France and only if the talks failed would military force be used. In either case, Hamilton considered the strategic and economic importance of the Floridas and Louisiana to be so vital to the national interest that decisive action was warranted. Gaining control of the territory would mean unencumbered access to navigation of the Mississippi River and the northern part of the Gulf of Mexico.

When Jefferson effectively negotiated the purchase of the Louisiana territory from France, Hamilton put aside his partisan feelings, to an extent, and supported the president's decision.[65] Both of them correctly believed that removing France from the immediate geopolitical neighborhood would transform Franco-American relations, because the greatest cause of the tension between the two nations, France's efforts at North American expansion, was thereby removed. Hamilton was unwilling, however, to give Jefferson credit for skilled diplomatic maneuvering. The Louisiana deal, he claimed, was the consequence of good fortune, not wise leadership. Without the slave uprising in San Domingo and the turn of the tide in France's war with Britain, the deal would never have been done. The sale was an act of desperation by Napoleon more than a shrewd diplomatic victory for Jefferson. Hamilton preferred to credit Providence than his chief political rival. He also raised questions about the effect that the Louisiana Purchase would have on the efficacy of the national government. In particular, he suggested that expanding the nation by too great an extent too quickly would strain the administrative and economic capacity of the government. The greatest number of economically and militarily strategic benefits would have come from acquiring a smaller portion of new territory than Jefferson had obtained. Hamilton wondered if Jefferson, who was somewhat averse to both professional armies and the development of economic institutions, understood the implications of governing such a vast territory. It surely would have implications not only for the economy but for migration, slavery, and the balance of power in Congress as new states were added to the union and new regional interests emerged in their wake. Hamilton could have gloated that without the national financial system he had designed, the Louisiana Purchase would likely have been impossible; and he could have chided Jefferson, as some of his Federalist allies did, for raising the national debt to record levels in order to consummate the deal with Napoleon.[66]

COSMOPOLITAN PATRIOT OR A NATIONALIST?

Hamilton favored unilateralism and advocated what Walter McDougall classifies as the "Old Testament tradition" of American foreign policy.[67] This approach to America's role in the world tended to conceive of foreign policy as a derivative of domestic concerns. In the aftermath of the American Revolution, the United States was in no position to exert its influence in the world. It had no navy and no standing army. The Jeffersonian Republicans opposed the development of both for nearly two decades. Even the Federalists, led by Washington and Hamilton, understood that it would take time to build the military capabilities of the nation. Doing so would depend on economic development and political stability. No one understood this point better than Hamilton. The new republic was no match for the empires of Europe in traditional realms of national strength.

Remaining distant from European affairs was justified not simply by this imbalance of power. Ideological dangers also made it a wise move, in Hamilton's view. Republics, he thought, were not immune from the allures of power and glory. To conduct sensible foreign policy, the United States would have to remain focused on national interest and avoid ideological attachment to particular European movements. The greatest temptation came from French Jacobinism, and Hamilton was intent on steering

Americans away from its path. In some sense, Hamilton was like Burke, a sober-minded conservative who recognized, much earlier than others did, that Jacobinism was incongruent with American republicanism. He opposed Jacobinism not with a counter-ideology but with the virtue of prudence. He understood, at least implicitly, that ideology obscures one's view of national interest. It stimulates the passions and either muffles the voice of reason or makes it a slave to its wiles. Generally speaking Hamilton did not regard America as an ideological experiment that required continual revolution. The nation was not moved by the current of some great historical force that would lead to a transformed world. The closest Hamilton got to the crusader state is a statement made in his "Letters from Phocion."

> The world has its eye upon America. The noble struggle we have made in the cause of liberty, has occasioned a kind of revolution in human sentiment. The influence of our example has penetrated the gloomy regions of despotism, and has pointed the way to inquiries, which may shake it to its deepest foundations. Men begin to ask every where, who is this tyrant, that dares to build his greatness on our misery and degradation? What commission has he to sacrifice millions to the wanton appetites of himself and the few minions that surround his throne?
>
> To ripen inquiry into action, it remains for us to justify the revolution by its fruits.
>
> If the consequences prove, that we really have asserted the cause of human happiness, what may not be expected from so illustrious an example? In a greater or less degree, the world will bless and imitate! . . .
>
> But if experience, in this instance, verifies the lesson long taught by the enemies of liberty; that the bulk of mankind are not fit to govern themselves, that they must have a master, and were only made for the rein and the spur: We shall then see the final triumph of despotism over liberty. The advocates of the latter must acknowledge it to be an *ignis fatuus*, and abandon the pursuit. With the greatest advantages for promoting it, that ever a people had, we shall have betrayed the cause of human nature.[68]

As he did in *Federalist* 1, Hamilton acknowledged that the American experience might have global implications. Yet, two points should be kept in mind. First, in both cases, "Phocion" and "Publius" indicated that Americans must prove the virtue of their revolution by their conduct; the fruits of the revolution had not yet ripened. In addition, the change from the American exceptionalism of "Phocion" to the sober realism of "Publius" was illustrated by the American example of not meddling in the affairs of other nations. A few years after the "Phocion" essays were written Hamilton, would learn, before most Americans did, that not all revolutions in sentiments or regimes that profess to be in the cause of liberty are what they claim to be. The French Revolution, more than anything else, differentiated Hamilton's political theory from that of Jefferson. While the former's revolutionary passion subsided and was replaced by sober realism, the latter's revolutionary pathos gave birth to the American ideology called global democracy.

World politics would always be rife with violence and the machinations of great powers, said Hamilton. The objective of statesmanship was to navigate carefully in such an environment, protecting the ship of state from ideological and imperial powers. In Hamilton's day, the former was represented by France and the latter by England. Steering a path that avoided both was the objective of his foreign policy. He imagined the day when the United States would become a great nation, but greatness required sufficient power to tend to the prosperity and happiness of the nation with little threat of foreign interference. America was not yet a great nation precisely because it was forced by its relative weakness to endure the intrigues of the great European powers that occupied parts of North America and provided markets for goods produced in the United States. In his economic policies, Hamilton intended to create a degree of self-sufficiency that would help to insulate the nation from the outside world, not draw it into a web of entangling connections to foreign nations.

This foundation for American foreign policy was especially present in Washington's Farewell Address, which was primarily the work of Hamilton. In his first draft of the address, Hamilton invited Washington to annunciate that "[t]he great rule of conduct for us in regard to foreign Nations ought to be to have as little *political* connection with them as possible."[69] The great rule figured prominently in the final draft, as did several other admonitions against foreign entanglements, both "inveterate antipathies against" other nations and "passionate attachments" to them.[70] Such passionate antipathies and attachments, in Hamilton's assessment, inspire policies contrary to justice and interest. Avoiding foreign entanglements did not mean abandoning existing treaties and agreements nor did it mean that alliances should never be developed. Washington and Hamilton were not advocating isolation. Far from it; the United States should honor its current obligations to other nations and join alliances, as long as they were temporary and served the national interest. Prudence, it was implied, would dictate the course of action, but with a strong prejudice toward the great rule. Remarkably absent from the address is advocacy of a prejudice toward republican or any other specific type of government. Rather, "religion and morality" as well as "good policy" commanded that good faith and justice animate relations with all nations. Abiding by this principle would provide an example to mankind and the blessings of Providence. "Who can doubt that in the course of time and things the fruits of such a plan would richly repay any temporary advantages wch. might be lost by a steady adherence to it? Can it be, that Providence has not connected the permanent felicity of a Nation with its virtue? The experiment, at least, is recommended by every sentiment which ennobles human Nature. Alas! Is it rendered impossible by its vices?"[71] One hears the echo of Cicero in the marriage of virtue, benefit, and happiness.

Most every scholar who has written about Hamilton has classified him as a nationalist, but few, if any, devote much attention to explaining how they are defining "nationalism" and in what sense Hamilton's political theory and statesmanship fit the category. Nor is much attention devoted to distinguishing between types of nationalism or competing conceptions of nationhood. The meaning of "nationalism" has changed significantly since Hamilton's day. The rise of totalitarianism, fascism, certain types of authoritarianism, and imperial democracy, has altered the political and ideological landscape in such a way that Hamilton, if he was a nationalist, was of a variety that needs to be differentiated from its modern derivatives. By one measure, modern nationalism is given birth in Jacobin France. Hamilton recognized

Jacobinism as an ideological movement engendered by a national hubris that prone to meddling in the affairs of nations it considers less enlightened. In this sense he was one of the first antinationalists, because he recognized that nations are not the ultimate measure of goodness or justice. He often found fault in his own nation while recognizing virtue in other nations. He was aware that nations, like individuals, must be judged by transnational standards that embody the wisdom of historical experience. Hamilton's variety of nationalism may have something to do with his origins. Unlike most of the other Founding Fathers, Hamilton, not born in one of the original colonies, lacked the familial and community ties that bound them to one state and caused the members of the founding generation to think of their state as their nation. He did, however, marry into one of the most prominent New York families, the Schuylers. Soon after he arrived in the Colonies, he was engaged as a soldier in the War for Independence, and he traveled wherever the war took him. He spent a great deal of time in Philadelphia in the early days of the republic. Hamilton's nation was the United States,[72] a political entity that he had a hand in creating and that gave him the opportunity to rise to the level of his talents, something that would not have been possible had he lived in Europe. Yet Hamilton was acutely aware, as he mentioned repeatedly in *The Federalist*, of the importance of geographical proximity (e.g., *Federalist* 17). Although he may have been more attached to the nation because he lacked a childhood home in America, he saw how Americans were wedded to what was most immediate and meaningful in their lives. Family and birthplace were sources of discord for him. Hamilton never returned to his childhood home in the West Indies, and he remained distant from his father and brother.

Historian of the twentieth century John Lukacs considers nationalism to be "the most powerful and enduring" influence of that century. His use of the term "nationalism" indicates the desire to differentiate between patriotism and something similar to it in some respects but different in others. Patriotism, viewed in this way, is more modest and more cosmopolitan; it is less inclined to jingoism, racism, and nativism and is restrained by transnational standards like natural law and conceptions of transcendence. Lukacs explains:

> Patriotism is defensive; nationalism is aggressive. Patriotism is the love of a particular land, with its particular traditions; nationalism is the love of something less tangible, of the myth of a "people," justifying many things, a political and ideological substitute for religion. Patriotism is old-fashioned (and, at times and in some places, aristocratic); nationalism is modern and populist. In one sense patriotic and national consciousness may be similar; but in another sense, more and more apparent after 1870, national consciousness began to affect more and more people who, generally, had been immune to that before—as, for example, many people within the multinational empire of Austria-Hungary. It went deeper than class consciousness. Here and there it superseded religious affiliation, too.[73]

Twentieth-century nationalism was often opposed to liberalism and sometimes included an anti-Semitic component. In Germany and Italy, nationalism and socialism were bound together, as they were in Russia. Communism was never able to break the hold of nationalist identities. In democratic nations, the rise of the welfare state constituted the union of nationalism and socialism within the confines of democratic political institutions. Contemporary nationalists can hold great disdain for the state but unwavering loyalty to the nation. Nationalists tend to embrace abstraction, (e.g., the idea of America) rather than the historical particulars of a nation's customs and traditions.

Aristotle's political theory embodies the roots of patriotism when it connects love of family and village to the love of the polis. Each more immediate and proximate part is a subset of the most distant community, the city-state. Social and political attachment to the human beings in these immediate political entities is what gives life purpose and meaning. Attachment to the polis is unthinkable if it is emptied of its community-forming constituents, that is, households and villages. Modern nationalism, by contrast, tends to empty the loved community of its particular characteristics and to substitute principles, creeds, and propositions. Whether in Orwell's fictional portrayal of totalitarianism in *1984* or in the historical regimes in mid-twentieth-century Germany, Russia, and China, totalitarian nationalism is characterized by an obliteration of intermediate groups and associations. Individuals are not permitted loyalty or affection to any group that serves as a rival to the nation, which is considered indistinguishable from the state. At its extreme, nationalism is a pseudo-religion that replaces love of God, mother and father, and one's neighbor with love of the nation. David Gelernter's *Americanism: The Fourth Great Western Religion* describes and promotes this pseudo-religious nationalism.

Hamilton's nationalism does not contain the characteristics of modern nationalism. While it certainly included a preference for the nation over the states and tended to conceive of the public good as a national rather than local phenomenon, neither the state nor the nation was the ultimate measure for Hamilton. And although he was intent on adding to the powers of the national government and giving it more energy and influence, these enhancements were not to be done to the exclusion of intermediate groups and associations, at least not to the extent of obliterating or co-opting them, as was done by totalitarians in the twentieth century.

Hamilton's nationalism was not a plea for centralized power in any form. In fact, one of his objections to the government under the Articles of Confederation was that it concentrated power in one branch. While the national government must be equipped with requisite powers, it must be formed in such a way that power is fragmented. He recognized the dangers of concentrated power, especially in the hands of demagogues. For centralized power to be conducive to liberty, it must be adequately separated, balanced, and checked; it must be part of the rule of law and subject to judicial review. Consequently, Hamilton's contributions to *The Federalist* argued for energy in the national government while assuring that in exercising its power, that national government would be constrained, by itself, the states, and the Constitution. The case is illustrated by Hamilton's defense of the judiciary. Tepidly and grudgingly, Hamilton embraced the need for a compound republic, one in which the states played a vital role. His pleas for more centralized power were made in circumstances far different from those that engendered modern nationalism. By the mid-twentieth century, the centralization of government had evolved well beyond anything Hamilton could have imagined. To push national power forward in such circumstances would be to invite the tyrannical concentration of power, but to do so in the context of the Articles of Confederation, when the thirteen states were arguably not yet a nation, is another matter. Nationalism, in Hamilton's sense of the word, meant joining the states into a tighter political form and equipping the national government with sufficient power to defend and develop the nation. Specifically, Hamilton wanted the nation to be strong enough to make its debt payments, create a currency and banking system, and build a standing army large enough to deter European powers from encroaching on American interests. These policy objectives are hardly the stuff of modern nationalism. Among other things, they lack the messianic pretentions in twentieth-century varieties of nationalism like Wilsonianism and the New Deal or totalitarian ideologies like those of Nazi Germany, the Soviet Union, and Maoist China.

CHAPTER 6

HAMILTON'S POLITICAL ECONOMY

The Constitution marked the limits of governmental power;
those limits must not be crossed. We need to bear in mind that
the Constitution was actualized as a living fact by translation into
tangible institutions. To comprehend now the importance of this
early transmutation is not easy; but the fact is plain; every step
taken, every principle announced or acted upon, was important
in giving life to words; conduct was creative; practice and
procedure soon became constitutional reality.

—Andrew C. McLaughlin, *A Constitutional*
History of the United States

THE AMERICAN ECONOMIC system was not created by the Constitution; it was part of the unwritten constitution that existed at
the time of constitutional formation and in the years following
its implementation. The Constitution does not mandate a particular economic system, although it provides protections for
private property and contracts that presume both property rights
and the liberty to engage in economic intercourse. Congress is
given the explicit power to regulate interstate and international
commerce, borrow money, and coin money. The national government was obligated to honor the debts incurred by the government under the Articles of Confederation. The Bill of Rights
added additional protections for private property, most notably
in the Fifth Amendment's due process and takings clauses. Consequently, as with other aspects of the Constitution, a balance or
tension was created between order and liberty; economic freedom
as constitutionally envisioned is not absolute, but neither is government's power to regulate it. Within the boundaries of this ten-

sion there exists a range of possible relationships between government and the economy. Some of Hamilton's political opponents accused him of expanding the national government's power to regulate the economy outside of its constitutional purview.

Of course, Hamilton was not free to mold the American economy and government's relationship to it any way he pleased. To some extent he was able to shape both elite and public opinion on those subjects, but the circumstances of the day and the spirit of the times limited both Hamilton's thinking and the acceptance of his policies. The Constitution would have a bearing on the conduct of economic affairs, but parchment descriptions of the limits and powers of government were subject to interpretation. Because the Constitution says very little about economics, debates over the federal government's powers to regulate economic activity were vital to setting the practical precedents that would shape economic policy for decades. What role government was to play in the development of the American economy would be determined by the exigencies of the day and the leadership of individuals in both private and public life who were willing to push for economic constructs they believed were compatible with the Constitution. Once the Constitution was in place, few, if any, Americans played a more vital role in the development of the American economy and the ideas on which it is based than Alexander Hamilton. As the first treasury secretary, he developed policies and institutions that involved debt management, including assumption by the national government of state debts incurred during the War for Independence, a national bank and currency, a tax system, trade policy, and the expansion of manufacturing.

Hamilton did not limit his work as treasury secretary to finance and economy, and he did not create economic policies in isolation from other areas of government. His economic policies were connected to national defense, solidifying the union, and shaping the national character. Each policy was part of a larger effort to build a prosperous nation that could withstand challenges from European powers that were bent on controlling the economy of North America and using the American republic as a pawn in the competition between empires. The scope of Hamilton's vision is one reason he is considered a central figure in the early republic. It is also why his opponents considered him so dangerous. He was compared to Sir Robert Walpole, the first de facto prime minister of England, because of his reported control of the cabinet and his supposed control of President Washington. He did exercise an extraordinary amount of influence in the government, even though unelected. Serving in such a role, Hamilton could orchestrate not only the policies of the Washington administration but of the Congress as well. His involvement was not limited to issues of public finance and economic regulation; it encompassed the whole of national policy. His correspondence during his tenure as treasury secretary reveals regular communication with members of Congress. Moreover, while influencing the president, his cabinet, and members of Congress, he was also actively shaping public opinion by writing numerous essays for newspapers. The extent of his sway, combined with his open advocacy of an energetic government, led many to believe that Hamilton was attempting to transform the constitutional system into something more akin to what he argued for at the Constitutional Convention. His "loose reading" of the Constitution heightened fears that he was intent on turning the American government into a replica of the British Empire.

Hamilton's experience in the War for Independence, as tax collector of New York for the national government in 1782, and as a representative in the Confederate Congress in 1782–83 left him with the impression that the government lacked sufficient power and energy to adequately serve the public good. He was especially concerned that the voluntary nature of the national tax system made it incapable of generating the revenues needed to finance an effective central government. He often juxtaposed the provincially oriented, who opposed a more energetic government, with those who thought "continentally" and consequently supported a government with sufficient power to meet the challenges of the new nation.[1] Thinking continentally meant transcending local interest and embracing the national interest. Putting the national interest before parochial interests was an inversion of what came naturally to most individuals, Hamilton believed. The success of his economic vision was contingent, to some extent, on subordinating local interests to the national interests, or harmonizing them.

It is common to think anachronistically about Hamilton's political economy, identifying him as the father of the big, intrusive federal government that became prevalent in the twentieth century. While Hamilton's policies share common ground with modern monetary and industrial policies, something like the welfare state or the modern administrative state would have been unthinkable to him. More important to understanding Hamilton's political economy is the spirit and purpose in which it was cast. What ultimately differentiates Hamilton's political economy from twentieth century conceptions of big government is that the latter were based on a view of human nature that called into question the Framers' principles of separated powers and checks and balances. Progressives, for example, wanted energetic government but they also wanted to remove many of the restraints on government power in order to make government more centralized. Hamilton was a strong advocate of separated and checked power. Energy stemmed from bold leadership within the system of separated powers and checks and balances, not from removing constitutional protections against tyranny. But if there is one area of overlap between Hamilton and twentieth-century Progressives it is their mutual distrust of local communities and interests and their willingness to subordinate them to the national interest.

At the forefront of his economic plan, Hamilton placed the development of the economy, especially its diversification and consequent expansion of productive capacity. While his economic theory and policies are not identical to Adam Smith's, he shared with Smith a paramount concern for the wealth of his nation.[2] Increasing the nation's wealth was a prerequisite to providing for its military defense and domestic tranquility. Economic growth required a more diverse economy that was less dependent on agriculture and more open to manufacturing, a view Hamilton articulated in his 1791 *Report on Manufactures*. As the economy grew in size and scope, it would have the capacity to fund the national debt and provide for a government that was capable of protecting the nation's interests in an international environment dominated by European empires intent on territorial expansion. While Hamilton worked to provide a tax system that would ensure ample revenue for the government, he was generally in favor of moderate taxes. Ron Chernow considers Hamilton's view of taxes to be a precursor to supply-side economics, because Hamilton believed that if tax rates went too high, taxes revenues would begin to decline.[3] The relationship between tax rates and tax revenues becomes inverse because the tax burden stifles economic activity and encourages shady bookkeeping. Writing as "The Continentalist," Hamilton made the case that Congress's taxing power was limited by market forces. The members of Congress could have "no temptation to abuse this power" of taxation; the "motive of revenue" would "check its own extremes," he explained. "Experience has shown that moderate duties are more productive than high ones. When they are low, a nation can trade abroad on better terms—its imports and exports will be larger—the duties will be regularly paid, and arising on a greater quantity of commodities, will yield more in the aggregate, than when they are so high as to operate either as a prohibition, or as an inducement to evade them by illicit practices."[4] Hamilton was not a libertarian, but he was not an advocate of the managerial state either. His view of human nature would not have allowed either the faith in economic anarchy suggested by libertarians or the heavily regulated state advocated by Keynesians. Hamilton's policies lack enough of the gnostic flavor of Jacobinism or Progressivism to consider his political economy an antecedent to modern American liberalism. They were not designed or intended to eradicate poverty, fear, and want, as FDR's New Deal was designed to do, and they did not aim to dramatically change the scope of government's role in individual lives. Hamilton's objectives were far more modest. To some of his contemporaries they seemed immodest because they were his, and he had built American economic institutions virtually from the ground up. Yet, taken in the context of its supporting theoretical foundations, Hamilton's political economy becomes sober to the point of being incompatible with later ideologies and developments in American history, like the New Deal, the welfare state, and the managerial state.

Hamilton, never one to rely solely on the self-interest of citizens, understood that individual conduct is the result of a mix of higher and lower motives. To expect human beings to follow only their higher inclinations was utopian, and it was unrealistic to assume that self-interest alone could foster the public good.

Whatever mixture of private and public initiative became part of economics, Hamilton wanted to maximize economic growth. He favored a diverse economy engaged in trade, agriculture, and manufacturing that was self-sufficient in producing goods essential for national defense. Hamilton's economic theory synthesizes mercantilism and capitalism, because it uses the instruments of free markets to promote the development and interests of the nation. When urgent or vital national interests are at stake, government involvement in the economy is acceptable; otherwise, the state should not interfere much in the economy.

In the aftermath of the revolution, several interrelated problems presented Hamilton with his greatest challenges as treasury secretary. Both the national government and the states were in debt—combined, roughly eighty million dollars—and both were struggling to make payments on the interest owed, apart from paying down the principal. An effective tax system was needed to both fund these debts and provide for government operations, like the military, postal service, and transportation projects. The nation had little available capital, in large part because its credit markets were insufficient. Money was in short supply. There was no national banking system and no currency system. Making matters more difficult, the revolution had inspired a suspicion of distant government that possessed taxing power and a standing army, two things that Hamilton thought were essential to the public welfare. It was apparent from the beginning of his tenure as secretary of the treasury that in trying to tend to these problems he would face a range of obstacles that would require stubborn perseverance to overcome.

As the electorate's division into rival political parties and factions unfolded, it became clear that many of Hamilton's policies were opposed because they violated particular interests and/or ideological assumptions regarding the republic, including the meaning of the American Revolution and delineation of government's role in managing economic affairs. For example, southern agricultural interests clashed with Hamilton's efforts to develop manufacturing and his plan for a national bank. Both prejudices were exhibited by Jefferson, who nearly blocked the creation of the first national bank. The bank was established, in 1791 with a charter for twenty years; but when time for renewal came, during Madison's presidency, Congress initially failed to approve a new charter.

Jefferson is classified as an advocate of "country ideology," which opposed Hamilton's economic plan. As explained by historian Drew R. McCoy, "Hamilton's economic system, tied to a funded debt, a national bank, and the mobilization of mercantile capital, was based on assumptions and beliefs that not only offended 'country' ideologies but also explicitly denied the efficacy and wisdom of commercial discrimination."[5] "Commercial discrimination" in this instance refers to a trade policy advocated by Madison and Jefferson to bolster trade with France and reduce it with England, to reflect political not economic objectives. Hamilton considered such policies misguided, in part because Britain was America's leading trading partner; it produced goods that Americans needed and in his view the United States was in no position to engage in a trade war with the world's premier economic and naval power. He believed that trade policy should be determined not by the politics of factions but by what served the public good, which was national in scope.

Because of his reputation for organization and detail, one might expect to find in Hamilton's political economy a penchant for economic systems. Enlightenment thought encouraged the development of rational, abstract systems that were the products of scientific investigation. As political scientist Peter McNamara points out, however, Hamilton was not inclined to the kind of abstract speculation that produced comprehensive systems. Hamilton was skeptical of political and economic theories that lacked experiential texture. Something that is "geometrically true," he pointed out, may prove to be false when measured against the standard of historical experience and actual circumstance. In making a point *for* a theory at the Constitutional Convention, he stated, "Theory is in this case fully confirmed by experience."[6] As Hamilton surely knew from Hume, passion clouds human judgment and wreaks havoc on the purity of mathematical exactness, and he noted, "illusion mixes itself in all the affairs of society."[7] As McNamara explains the point, "geometric, or deductive, reasoning is of limited utility, because it cannot take into account the complexity of economic reality." Generally speaking, human beings act in accordance with their self-interest, but in fact they are also prone to act against it, because they some-times are confused about what is in their self-interest or are beset with a stronger passion for another course of action. Men and women are not predictable in the way that machines and math-ematical equations are. Consequently, economic policies can es-timate human behavior based on historical experience, but pol-icy makers must be prepared as circumstances change to read the times and adjust their plans accordingly. In economic policy, Hamilton was influenced by Jacques Necker (1732–1804), finance minister to Louis XVI, and British economist James Steuart (1712–1790) more than by Adam Smith.[8] Recent scholarship also identifies a connection between Hamilton and Aristotle in re-gard to commerce and statesmanship.

David Hume, Jacques Necker, Malachi Postlethwayt, James Steuart, and Aristotle

As in other aspects of his thought, Hamilton tended to dispar-age theoretical speculation and abstract systems in his economic philosophy. David Hume was in some ways his model in believ-ing that a certain degree of technical support and study was nec-essary for economic planning but that economic policies and ideas were best worked out in practical theories that were based on historical experience and common sense. Like Hume, Necker[9] and Steuart were skeptical of theorists' ability to systematize eco-nomic principles. Steuart argued in his *An Inquiry into the Prin-ciples of Political Economy* that theories that fail to account for changing circumstances "are mere conceits; they mislead the understanding, and efface the path to truth." The book, which was in Hamilton's library, is a collection of Steuart's thoughts and experiences, in various countries, on topics that were of paramount concern to Hamilton as treasury secretary: "popula-tion, agriculture, trade, industry, money, coin, interest, circula-tion, banks, exchange, public credit, and taxes." Steuart deduced principles from his consideration of experiential evidence, but he did not devise a system of economics. *Principles of Political Economy* reads more like an open exploration of practical ideas than a closed system of highly refined theories. Steuart modestly claims no greater objective than to "present this enquiry to the public as nothing more than an essay which may serve as a canvass for better hands than mine to work upon."[10]

Scholars by no means agree on how Hamilton's political economy should be classified. McNamara identifies the similarities among Necker, Steuart, and Hamilton. Stanley Elkins and Eric McKitrick emphasize the continuity between Hamilton and Hume. Louis M. Hacker insists that Hamilton's political economy is nearly identical to Smith's, and John C. Miller considers Hamilton to be more of a mercantilist than an advocate of laissez-faire capitalism and, like Elkins and McKitrick, believes that Hume had the greatest influence on Hamilton's political economy. According to Miller, Hume's political economy was a mix of mercantilism and what might be called common sense economics. Hamilton saw the need for government intervention in the economy, including protection of domestic producers, and he was an economic nationalist. "[Hume] placed the greatness of the state above the happiness of its citizens," Miller observes.[11] Whether or not Hamilton embraced this aspect of Hume's political theory is unclear. Hamilton certainly thought that national greatness was important, but there is little evidence that he was willing to sacrifice the happiness of citizens to achieve it, especially in regard to their economic well-being. It is more likely the case that he saw these two objectives as intertwined to the point that one was necessary for the other.

Michael D. Chan finds significant commonality between Hamilton's view of commerce and that of Aristotle. Both thinkers emphasized the importance of ancient prudence, which is characterized by a regard for particularity, the formation of public opinion, and concern for morality and virtue. Chan, thus, challenges the conventional view that Hamilton's political economy represents a break from the classical theory of virtue. Hamilton's conception of virtue was not identical to Aristotle's, but he synthesized Classical and modern virtue in a way that led him to believe that commercial virtue could have an uplifting effect on character. Commerce cultivated liberality, which replaced the ancient virtues of courage and military glory. Like Aristotle, Hamilton believed that liberality requires acquisition of wealth. Commerce and industry can encourage virtue in two ways, by encouraging the character necessary for wealth accumulation and by creating the means for liberality. Chan also agrees with McNamara in Hamilton's aversion to abstraction. "Hamilton and Aristotle were . . . in agreement on the dangers of theoretic politicians who treat political things as if they were abstractions that can be as easily manipulated as a set of numbers." Chan concludes that Hamilton "was arguably the best of the founders in endeavoring to combine American acquisitiveness with virtue, justice, and the love of fame to achieve immortal glory and happiness."[12]

Hamilton's political economy shares some theoretical ground with Edmund Burke, who was also skeptical of economic and political systems derived purely from a rationalistic impetus. The similarity is not so much a commonality of particular policy prescriptions but a sharing of philosophical assumptions about human nature and the possibilities of politics. Compare, for example, Burke's comment in *Reflections* regarding primitive natural rights derived from a state of nature with Hamilton's preference for prudent policies as opposed to rational systems. The passage not only shares common theoretical ground with Hamilton's view of rights as expressed in *Federalist* 84, but it also shares an understanding of the complexity of human nature and society that is difficult to reconcile with a preference for economic systems.

> These metaphysic rights [natural rights] entering into common life, like rays of light which pierce into a dense medium, are by the laws of nature refracted from their straight line. Indeed, in the gross and complicated mass of human passions and concerns the primitive rights of men undergo such a variety of refractions and reflections that it becomes absurd to talk of them as if they continued in the simplicity of their original direction. The nature of man is intricate; the objects of society are of the greatest possible complexity; and, therefore, no simple disposition or direction of power can be suitable either to man's nature or to the quality of his affairs.[13]

Hamilton stated, in reference to the controversy over the national bank, that "[i]n all questions of this nature the practice of mankind ought to have great weight against the theories of Individuals."[14] Burke struck a similar note: "What is the use of discussing a man's abstract right to food or to medicine? The question is upon the method of procuring and administering them. In that deliberation I shall always advise to call in the aid of the farmer and the physician rather than the professor of metaphysics."[15]

In reference to trade, Hamilton insisted that the objective was not to follow some abstract ideological theory but to use human experience to craft a prudent policy. Principles were useful in developing policy but not in controlling it. Principles were prejudices that moved policy in a general direction, but they were, in themselves, incapable of steering through the waters of circumstance, because they could not anticipate every specific detail of life. The winds of fortune required adjustments that varied with circumstance. Generally, then, free trade ought to be the aim of economic policy, but circumstances require government regulation of trade. Such regulation is not a violation of principle per se, because principles do not exist outside the demands of historical circumstances. On this subject, Hamilton shares theoretical ground with Machiavelli as well. The latter did not dismiss principles, but he insisted that they be subordinated to the exigencies of circumstances. In other words, principles should be followed up to the point at which continuing to do so would undermine their raison d'être, to realize the ends of politics (e.g., justice, order, happiness). Machiavelli may have pushed discretion to an extreme, but like Hamilton, he had an aversion to ahistorical abstraction manifested in reified principles. Burke commented:

> I cannot stand forward and give praise or blame to anything which relates to human actions, and human concerns, on a simple view of the object, as it stands stripped of every relation, in all the nakedness and solitude of metaphysical abstraction. Circumstances (which with some gentlemen pass for nothing) give in reality to every political principle its distinguishing color, and discriminating effect. The circumstances are what render every civil and political scheme beneficial or noxious to mankind. Abstractedly speaking, government, as well as liberty, is good; yet could I, in common sense, ten years ago, have felicitated France on her enjoyment of a government (for she then had a government) without inquiry what the nature of that government was, or how it was administered?

Can I now congratulate the same nation upon its freedom? Is it because liberty in the abstract may be classed amongst the blessings of mankind, that I am seriously to felicitate a madman, who has escaped from the protecting restraint and wholesome darkness of his cell, on his restoration to the enjoyment of light and liberty? Am I to congratulate a highwayman and murderer who has broke prison upon the recovery of his natural rights?[16]

Hamilton's and Burke's shared aversion to abstraction was inspired by the assumption that historical experience is the standard for judging the prudence of political action and ideas.

Because Hamilton was the first secretary of the treasury, he spent much of his time in Washington's cabinet developing economic policies and institutions. His official writings of the time, including *Report on Manufactures*, the assumption plan, reports on a national bank, and *Report on Public Credit*, contain the various elements of his political economic philosophy. These parts of his fiscal program were intended, according to Forrest McDonald, to engender a "social revolution" that would stem from an economy in which markets determined values and money was the instrument of value. Consequently, "power would derive from merit and industry rather than, as in the existing scheme of things, from inherited wealth or social position."[17] In this attitude Hamilton was less like Burke and more like Adam Smith. Such an economy would privilege industry and entrepreneurial skill. The aim was to build the nation by creating a meritocracy. He believed that the national government should play a significant role in the development of the national economy, but he was generally in favor of free markets.

The mercantilist and economic nationalist Malachy Postlethwayt (1707–67) was an early influence on the development of Hamilton's political economy. Hamilton's pay book, which he used to take notes on his wartime readings, includes comments on Postlethwayt's two-volume *Universal Dictionary of Trade and Commerce*. The book was a reference source that contained a wealth of information about various economic and political subjects, including banking, currency, taxes, and debt. It recorded statistics about population and mortality rates in various parts of the world and quoted widely from a wealth of sources. Hamilton learned from Postlethwayt the virtues of the mixed economy and especially the value of manufacturing.[18]

Hamilton's economic philosophy does not fit neatly into any ideological category. He embraced elements of mercantilism and protectionism as ways to shield the new republic from international competition that might stunt the growth of its emerging industries. In some instances, his economic ideas were intimately bound up with two overarching objectives: solidifying the nation and providing for its defense. Navigation of the Mississippi and trade with Britain were examples. They were both vital to the security and economic prosperity of the nation. Too much dependence on trade with one nation was problematic. Hamilton's goal was for the United States to be as economically independent as possible, in large part because economic independence would help to protect political independence.

HAMILTON'S ECONOMIC REPORTS AND POLICIES

Hamilton's financial policies were articulated in three major reports that addressed the debt crisis, the health of the economy, and the prospects of the American economy. Management of the debt was rather haphazard during the revolution and in its immediate aftermath. Delinquency was eroding American credit and jeopardizing the growth of the economy. Hamilton wanted to centralize the debt while creating a system of public securities to pay the foreign debt at par as soon as possible and to finance the domestic debt over a longer period of time. Integral to his plan for the American economy was the creation of a national bank, the development of currency and a mint, and the diversification of the economy through the encouragement of manufacturing.

Discrimination among Creditors

As debate raged about how to organize and finance the debt, it was clear from the Constitution that the debts incurred under the Articles of Confederation would have to be honored by the new government.[19] One important issue was whether or not to discriminate among the holders of debt, and if so, how. In many cases government securities had changed hands over the years. Many original owners of debt had watched its value decline and decided to sell it, at a fraction of the cost. Many of the original holders of the securities were Revolutionary War veterans or their widows, and many of the subsequent holders were speculators. To some people, paying the current holders at full value (par) seemed to reward a far less deserving class of people. Hamilton believed in honoring the contracts as they were; Madison and others wanted to avoid paying securities that had been bought far below par by speculators, who would reap great profits once Hamilton's plan was operational. Hamilton believed that tracing the original holders of the securities would be administratively unfeasible. War veterans and others who had sold their securities had shown little faith in the nation's future, he pointed out. Whatever else might be said about the speculators, they had demonstrated a willingness to invest in the nation at a time when it was most needed. Their reward was proportionate to their risk. However worthy the original holders, they had sold their securities and thus forfeited legal right to them. In Hamilton's view, regardless of the motives of the current holders, they were legally entitled to reap the benefits of their actions, regardless of their virtue.

The intent of Hamilton's opposition to discrimination was not to benefit speculators, as some recklessly charged; he agreed that they were, for the most part, wholly self-interested. Hamilton had the public good at heart, and in particular he was promoting an economy that, unlike speculators, produced goods and thus expanded both the wealth of the nation and its capacity to produce wealth. McDonald explains: "Hamilton could not leave the speculators out of his reckoning, but on the whole he found them a sorely troublesome nuisance, for their interests and his were diametrically opposed. His interest—establishing public credit on the best possible footing—was bullish: it lay in getting the market prices of securities up to par as rapidly as possible and holding them there: Their interest was bearish: it lay in getting the Dutch market as high as possible while keeping the American market low and unstable."[20] Hamilton's opposition to discrimination contributed to the charge that he favored the moneyed class over the class of common laborers or farmers. Madison, among others, was concerned that Hamilton's debt plan would disproportionately benefit northern speculators and merchants at the expense of people in the southern states, particularly those most dependent on agriculture. He feared that Hamilton's policies would give rise to the kind of financial corruption and financial class that plagued the British Empire by diverting its resources away from the public good and toward the moneyed classes. Whatever merit there was to the argument made by Madison and others, it was tinged with hypocrisy in many cases. Madison, for one, was engaged in land speculation that could have influenced his decisions about debt policy and about the location of the nation's capital, but he seems to have been able to separate his private economic interests from the vices of securities speculation. Hamilton, for his vision to succeed, would have to overcome the argument that his plan would usher in a regime of speculators, hustlers, and scofflaws. The debate was about much more than the technical details of public finance; it incited passion, because it went to the heart of American identity and character. Politically, it helped divide the nation into parties that conducted their politics based on where their self-interest lay and on the parochial interests of regions, states, and economic class. This outcome was not what Hamilton had desired; it was the unintended consequence of the messy process of creating the first national economic policy under the Constitution.

The discrimination debate was part of a struggle in the wake of the Constitutional Convention to clarify contract law. Hamilton's view of contracts would find its way into constitutional law when the Supreme Court decided *Fletcher v. Peck* (1810), a ruling that upheld the integrity of contracts, in that case, ones that were mired in the political corruption of the Georgia legislature's Yazoo land deal. Like the Revolutionary War debt, the Georgia land deals created a web of transactions occurring over a period of years that made ex post facto invalidation administratively cumbersome and unfair. Such cases of economic shadiness did not surprise Hamilton. Given human nature, some degree of greed and corruption was inevitable. Hamilton had no interest in encouraging such vices, and he recognized the hypocrisy in arguments made by southern plantation owners like Jefferson and Madison, who had built their wealth off the sweat and toil of slaves. He was not about to cede the moral high ground to such moral hypocrites, who in turn were convinced that he was enriching himself by using Treasury Department information to speculate. The criminal speculation of Assistant Treasury Secretary William Duer, who made personal use of public monies and information only to end up heavily in debt and in prison, along with the legal speculation of Secretary of War Knox and Hamilton's father-in-law, General Schuyler, appeared to provide evidence that Hamilton was part of a conspiracy to use his office to enrich his friends, his political party, and the speculating class. However, in 1794, Hamilton and the Treasury Department were investigated by a House of Representatives select committee, composed mainly of Republicans, which found no wrongdoing by Hamilton.

To help reestablish American credit, Hamilton insisted on making past due debt payments first. He considered payment of the debt to be something more than an economic concern; it was a matter of national honor and constitutional integrity that would build national character and consequently benefit the United States in its future economic and political endeavors. Hamilton also insisted that new debt be incurred only if accompanied by the means for paying it off. Taxes, in the form of duties and imposts, would be necessary to generate revenue to finance the debt. A national bank was part of Hamilton's plan, as it would serve, with the Treasury Department, as an institutional mechanism for implementing fiscal and monetary policies. Congress would have to approve such policies, but they should be initiated and directed by the Treasury Department and the national bank.

Hamilton faced significant opposition to his financial plan. Because the debt system mirrored, and to some extent was modeled on, the one in England, Jeffersonian Anglophobes were quick to argue that national debts made war and empire more likely. Because Hamilton was also in favor of a standing army, the argument seemed to fit their image of the treasury secretary as an Anglophile monarchist. In truth, Hamilton went to great pains to avoid war; he saw the funding system as a way to support war only if war became necessary and saw a standing army as a means to deter European powers from meddling in American affairs. A national debt was worth incurring to create these defenses soon. Without them, the United States would be at the mercy of foreign powers for protection. Jeffersonians were lax when it came to military readiness because they tended to subscribe to the theory, rejected by Hamilton, that republics were peaceful and, if they minded their own business, would be left alone. They also believed that diplomacy and economic sanctions (e.g., embargos) could be used to influence the behavior of rival nations and thus avert not only conflict but the need for a standing army.[21]

"Report Relative to a Provision for the Support of Public Credit"

Hamilton's first "Report on the Public Credit," submitted in January 1790, was intended to address the debt that was largely a consequence of the Revolutionary War and the failure of the government under the Articles of Confederation to raise enough revenue to make regular interest payments on the national debt. In 1789 Congress requested that the secretary of the treasury create a plan that could be used as the basis for legislation to create a public credit system. In a few months, Hamilton produced a document that was typical of his work as treasury secretary. It provided what Congress wanted, a blueprint for the institutional creation of an American credit system. But it did much more. Hamilton's report addressed the theoretical and ethical foundations of public credit. Nothing less than the honor and national character of the American republic was at stake. Good credit must be earned by punctual payment inspired by good faith. Andrew C. McLaughlin explains that for Hamilton the "proper and honest handling of the debts meant more than financial stability or economic well-being in any narrow sense; there was a moral obligation."[22] Hamilton insisted that the interest on the domestic debt be paid on a regular basis, but he was less concerned about paying off the principal and retiring the debt. Making regular interest payments would restore American credit and monetize the debt, providing a desperately needed substitute for money.

He separated the debt into foreign and domestic debt. In his plan, the interest on the former would be paid and its principal refinanced. The latter would also be refinanced, by issuing new government securities. Reconfiguring the debt would reduce the effective interest rate on it and provide the government with a means to influence market prices for securities by using a sinking fund to stabilize security prices.[23] The sinking fund would be provided with permanent revenues (e.g., post office revenues) and inviolable funds. Hamilton figured that having the sinking fund would boost public belief in the government's ability to pay off the debt. The government could wait for the price of securities to drop and then use the sinking fund to buy debt at a reduced price, thus accelerating its payment. Hamilton, however, was also interested in using the fund to ensure that the price of securities remained high enough to attract investors and to reward their faith in the government.[24] The objective was not to pay off the debt as much as it was to keep the nation's credit rating high and to keep interest rates stable. A high credit rating would keep money circulating in the economy, which Hamilton believed was essential for economic growth; stable interest rates would help entrepreneurs gauge future risks. Having revenues that were committed to the debt could not be siphoned off to fund other projects, as occurred in the twentieth century with the Social Security budget. In a somewhat crude way, Hamilton had created a system for government control of the money supply. The sinking fund could be used to increase or decrease the money supply. The system also allowed for an infusion of foreign capital. As American securities became an increasingly good investment, foreign money would flow to the United States, providing much needed capital for economic development. The funding system alone was not sufficient to control credit and currency; it needed to be buttressed by a national banking system like the one in England.

In 1795, Hamilton produced a report that disparaged reckless and unnecessary spending by government, endless debt, and high taxation.[25] Hamilton's financial plan had reorganized the debt, but it also created a new taxing system that relied mostly on indirect taxes, like import duties and excise taxes. The latter were especially controversial and led to the Whiskey Rebellion. In 1798, after Hamilton had left office, a direct tax on property and slaves was created and proved to be even more unpopular than the indirect taxes. The direct taxes led to Fries's Rebellion. Hamilton was not naïve about taxes. He knew that there would be resistance to new taxes, of whatever type, but he hoped that it would become clear that without new taxes the nation could not finance the debt, provide for national defense, and place the economy on sounder footing. He also knew that the new tax system would require an efficient administrative system that would minimize the expense of collecting the tax and ensure its enforcement. Many Republicans thought that state militias were sufficient for the national defense and much cheaper than Hamilton's desired professional army and navy. They also opposed excise taxes because they were politically volatile and in some cases, such as the whiskey tax, burdened a class of Americans who did not have a great ability to pay taxes.

Hamilton's Assumption Plan

Hamilton not only insisted on federal assumption of state debts incurred during the Revolutionary War but that the debt be funded in full. He realized that, while the various states benefited equally from independence, neither their particular debts, nor their practices for paying them off, nor their contributions during the war were equal. Some states had greater debt than others and some had paid their debt down much more than others had. Virginia had paid off most of its debt, while Massachusetts still held most of its debt. Some states had made greater sacrifices during the war and consequently were deeper in debt. Hamilton argued that what minor injustices might occur from national assumption of the debt would be outweighed by its benefits. Independence was a national endeavor, and the debt created to make it a reality should be addressed nationally. Always mindful of the problem of union, Hamilton believed that without the assumption plan the national government and the states would compete for tax revenues, driving the states apart rather than into the union. As tax burdens would vary from state to state, migration would flow to lower-tax states. Moreover, although implemented retroactively, the new funding system would provide a systematic approach to the disposal of the nation's debts when the next war came. The experience of desperation about funding the Revolutionary War should never be repeated. Hamilton defended the funding system by stating that war "offers but two options—Credit or the devastation of private property."[26] As Karl-Friedrich Walling and E. J. Ferguson have estimated, "half the cost of the Revolutionary War was 'paid' for through military impressments of private property."[27] To avoid such violence to private property and domestic life, it was necessary to create a system of public credit. The new securities issued as part of the assumption plan would have the added benefit of serving as a form of money, which was in short supply in the early republic. Because some of the debt would be financed by foreigners, the effect would be an influx of money into the American economy that could be used as investment capital.

Hamilton's philosophy about national debt is one of the most misunderstood aspects of his political economy. His Republican opponents tended to eschew all public debt. Consequently, they were prone to misstate and distort Hamilton's view. Hamilton believed that the national debt could be constructive to both the government and the economy if it was managed properly. First and foremost, Hamilton insisted that the debt not grow beyond the fiscal means of the nation. While taxes were a necessary part of financing government, they could become destructive to the nation's economic health if they were too high. In other words, Hamilton believed that the amount of debt a nation could responsibly handle depended on the size and strength of its economy and the efficiency of its revenue system. He did not believe, as some of his critics charged, that the national debt should be pushed to an extreme. War, being an inevitable part of political life, would sooner or later occur. When it did, the public debt would be pushed to an extreme, as had been the case during the War for Independence. If the nation was already deeply in debt when war came, the financial capacity of the nation to fight would be greatly reduced. Keeping the debt at a responsible level was not only important for the economy but a matter of national security. This is one of the reasons Hamilton was willing to go to great lengths to avoid war in the 1790s. The size of the debt in the wake of the revolution was enormous. His top priority, then, was to organize the debt in such a way as to create confidence in the national government and in the United States as a place to prosper. As long as Americans continued to default on public debt, these objectives would remain out of reach.

Hamilton's policies were successful because the value of government securities rose with the rising prosperity of Americans. Hamilton understood that prosperity was contingent on the psychology of the merchant and investing classes not only in the United States but also abroad. Because the debt was being managed responsibly, confidence was high and financial risk seemed worthwhile. Money began to flow from Europe to America. In some circumstances, the United States was preferred to Europe for investment. When Europe was shortly mired in the volatility and uncertainty of war and revolution, the United States became a refuge for investors who craved stability. Hamilton expected that as the nation grew economically, the debt would shrink as a percentage of national production even if the principal remained the same. The extent to which Hamilton's funding system was the catalyst for economic growth is explained by John C. Miller, who writes that it

> provided the means of creating wealth. Every three months, almost a million dollars was pumped into the national economy; and this money, drawn from the taxpayers of the United States, made possible capitalistic enterprise on a scale hitherto unknown in the republic. And the fact that the money thus extracted from the taxpayers was concentrated in a comparatively few hands accelerated the growth of capitalism: it made available for purposes of investment and exchange a sum estimated at ten times the amount of all the specie circulating in the country. Thus Hamilton activated the springs of national credit and a torrent began to roar down the dry creek bed.[28]

"Report on the Subject of Manufactures"

Hamilton helped to establish the Society for the Encouragement of Useful Manufactures to inspire manufacturing in the United States. Its founders chose Paterson, New Jersey, as the location for the endeavor because it was close to New York City's capital resources and it contained a large river and waterfall to supply power for production. Although in this and other endeavors Hamilton supported the development of manufacturing, he was not, as some have charged, opposed to agriculture. He wanted to diversify the economy and considered the development of manufacturing one way to become less reliant on foreign producers. Manufacturing was also critical to military preparedness, as Hamilton had learned from American dependence on French supplies during the War for Independence. To make a go of manufacturing, it was necessary to have a supply of what today is called venture capital and the technical knowledge that was carefully guarded by European manufacturers. Hamilton's economic vision included not only attracting investment capital into the American economy but also finding a way to bring trade secrets across the Atlantic. The United States would have to engage in industrial espionage, not as an instrument of war, but in order to create greater economic independence.

Hamilton's argument for a diversified economy that was less dependent on agriculture was based primarily on the belief that manufacturing would yield as much productivity and profit as agriculture. Industrial productivity was enhanced by a production process that could run day and night and that could also employ women and children. In his December 1791 report on manufacturing, Hamilton explained the benefit to farmers: "The husbandman himself experiences a new source of profit and support from the encreased industry of his wife and daughters; invited and stimulated by the demands of the neighboring manufactories." In addition, idle persons who are "a burthen on the community" might be employable in manufacturing although unemployable in agriculture. Hamilton adds that children become more "useful" at an earlier age, as they were doing in English cotton factories. He observed that nearly half of those employed in such factories were women and children. Manufacturing would also encourage immigration, as the demand for skilled labor would attract workers to employment opportunities in the United States. On the whole, the development of manufacturing would create a "new energy" that would promote the "spirit of enterprise" beyond what was possible in an economy dominated by agriculture. This energy and spirit would be "less in a nation of mere cultivators, than in a nation of cultivators and merchants; less in a nation of cultivators and merchants, than in a nation of cultivators, artificers and merchants." In short, a diversified economy would make labor and resources more productive and the nation wealthier. "The bowels as well as the surface of the earth are ransacked for articles which were before neglected. Animals, Plants and Minerals acquire an utility and value, which were before unexplored."[29]

As was often the case, Hamilton had his sights set on national objectives, in this case building a diverse and productive economy that could serve the nation's economic and military needs. The scope and scale of his economic plan made it easy to overlook the effect his policies might have on local communities. Sending scores of women and children into factories that "ransacked" rather than cultivated the earth had unintended consequences. Over the course of decades, the development of manufacturing accomplished what Hamilton hoped it would, create a prosperous nation that was capable of defending itself. However, it also began to encourage a penchant for hustling and pretense that would eventually envelop the political culture.[30] He was, in this instance, as much the commercial liberal as in any other facet of his politics or thinking. In politics he saw the need for natural aristocrats who possessed the magnanimity to rise above mere self-interest. In economics, the spirit of enterprise seemed sufficient to serve the public good. That this spirit needed to be tempered by something higher seems not to have occurred to Hamilton.

That the Congress had the constitutional authority to encourage and develop manufacturing Hamilton had no doubt. The general welfare clause, he declared, signified "more than was expressed" and left it to the Congress to decide what constituted the substance of the general welfare. What limited Congress's power under the clause was the scope of its action; the purpose for which money is appropriated must be "*General* and not *local*; its operation extending in fact, or by possibility, throughout the Union, and not being confined to a particular spot." Hamilton clarified that the general welfare clause did not give Congress implied power to do absolutely anything it deemed consistent with the general welfare. "A power to appropriate money with this latitude which is granted too in *express terms* would not carry a power to do any other thing, not authorized in the constitution, either expressly or by fair implication." In other words, the general welfare clause does not give Congress power that it does not already have under a specific grant of power in some other part of the Constitution. Article I, Section 8 enumerates Congress's spending powers. The general welfare clause directs Congress to use its taxing and spending powers for the public good as opposed to the particular benefit of a group or region. Consequently, he believed, the clause limited power rather than expanding it. That said, Hamilton was certain that "whatever concerns the general Interests of *learning*, of *Agriculture*, of *Manufactures*, and of *Commerce*, are within the sphere of the national Councils *as far as regards an application of Money.*"[31]

The National Bank

Hamilton submitted his report on banking to Congress in December 1790; Congress chartered a national bank a few months later, but a debate over its constitutionality ensued that divided the Washington administration and left the president pondering whether he should sign or veto the bank bill. Secretary of State Jefferson and Attorney General Edmund Randolph opposed the bill on constitutional grounds. Madison, who had opposed it in the House of Representatives, continued to provide arguments against its constitutionality, including directly to Washington. This debate illuminates one of the earliest controversies involving the two competing theories of constitutional interpretation that have carried through American history to the present. One, so called loose constructionism, is attributed to Hamilton, and the other, so called strict constructionism, is considered the intellectual progeny of Jefferson. Had Jefferson and Madison not opposed the bank on policy grounds, it is unlikely that they would have devised a constitutional argument regarding it. The same can be said for Hamilton in his support of it. What is of interest is the extent to which each interpretation shares theoretical ground with each side's deeper philosophical foundations, apart from pure policy considerations. Is there, for example, something about Jeffersonian political theory that lends itself to constitutional fundamentalism? Likewise, is there something in Hamilton's political theory that requires a liberal reading of the Constitution?[32]

Hamilton's national bank was modeled after the Bank of England. Both were quasi-public banks that influenced economic development through control of credit markets. They also provided a reliable source of credit for government, enabling it to run the deficits that Hamilton believed were necessary for building infrastructure and, when necessary, fighting wars. Five of the twenty-five bank directors were appointed by the government, giving it some influence over bank policies. The bank was required to issue notes that were redeemable in coin. Such provisions were intended to check self-interest and balance public good and private good. Hamilton's dualistic view of human nature runs throughout his political and economic theories, and the national bank was no exception. Miller summarizes Hamilton's understanding of self-interest and human nature as they relate to the bank.

> Despite his good opinion of the workings of self-interest, Hamilton was careful not to give private bankers a wholly free hand in regulating the country's economy. For they, too, were men and therefore subject, in more or less degree, to all the passions that actuated mankind. Every denomination of men, no matter how respectable or affluent, he believed to be under the constant temptation to sacrifice the public good to private interest. Even in a bland and imperturbable banker, Hamilton knew, the Old Adam might sometimes peep through. The only way of keeping this enemy out of the national economy, he argued, was to give the government a check upon the private bankers.[33]

Included among the checks on the national bank was the authority of the treasury secretary to examine the bank's books and Congress's power to recharter the bank. The bank was also prohibited from incurring debts in excess of its capital stock.

Defense of the Funding System

Hamilton's *Defense of the Funding System,* submitted in January 1795, begins with the reminder that the war, not the funding system, created the debt. He repeated his adage that paying the debt was a moral and political obligation, and he deepened its theoretical defense: Both security and liberty depended on it; in fact, "national happiness" depended on paying the debt. Hamilton was careful not to portray the funding system as a panacea. In typical fashion, he characterized the situation in the light of human nature. Just as economic prosperity "nourishes and begets opulence, resource, and strength," it also begets "a sentiment of superiority, pride ambition insolence." These vices, temptations of the human condition, lead to war. The point was not, as a twentieth-century prohibitionist might say regarding alcohol, to forego good because it comes with evil. The context for politics is what Plato and Aristotle called the metaxy, the in-between of existence. Given the tension between good and evil in human nature, pure good is not possible in this world. Accepting the human condition for what it is means tolerating a degree of evil in order to accomplish a good. Did the funding system make such a compromise? Of course, all governmental policies must accommodate human nature. Those who try to avoid this reality, like the Jacobins,[34] end up doing far more evil than good. Progress does not come without regression; wealth, for example, is the parent of extravagance and other unintended consequences. That the critics of the funding system could identify vices and imperfections among the consequences of its implementation was of little concern to Hamilton. The issue in assessing its contribution to happiness was the balance between its virtues and vices.

> What good in fine shall we retain? Tis the portion of man assigned to him by the eternal allotment of Providence that every good he enjoys, shall be alloyed with ills, that every source of his bliss shall be a source of his affliction—except Virtue alone, the only unmixed good which is permitted to his temporal Condition.[35]

Hamilton's political economy contained elements of economic nationalism that were connected to mercantilism. Economic policy was directed to the creation of wealth and the growth of the nation. A more prosperous nation would be capable of defending itself against European empires and domestic insurrections.

Having a diversified economy and greater economic self-sufficiency was intended to insulate the nation from the machinations of European politics. The success of republican government depended on greater economic independence.

Economic nationalism was not the whole of Hamilton's political economy. Promoting domestic order and prosperity formed an equal focus, and that purpose also would require the development of manufacturing and the liberty for entrepreneurs to create more efficient ways of producing goods and services. Taxes were necessary but should be kept moderate, so as not to restrict the expansion of production and wealth. Hamilton's tax system did not preclude using taxes to ameliorate unvirtuous human behavior, as was the case with the whiskey tax, which raised revenue and decreased uncivil behavior. Improving the nation's credit rating would necessitate the consolidation of state and national debt incurred during the War for Independence. As with taxes, debt should be moderate. Excessive debt would cripple government, because too much of the budget would be devoted to debt payment, and additional debt would be more difficult to secure. If debt was too low, the nation would lack sufficient money supply to feed the development of manufacturing and economic development generally. In short, Hamilton favored relatively free markets that were guided by government to serve the national interest and the public good. As in other public affairs, he searched for the point where self-interest and the public good intersected, and he rarely failed to consider the importance of honor in the pursuit of these objectives.

CHAPTER 7

HAMILTON AND JEFFERSON

Where Hamilton looked at the world through a dark filter and
had a better sense of human limitations, Jefferson viewed the
world through a rose-colored prism and had a better sense of
human potentialities. Both Hamilton and Jefferson believed in
democracy, but Hamilton tended to be more suspicious of the
governed and Jefferson of the governors.
                            —Ron Chernow, *Alexander Hamilton*

HAMILTONIAN VERSUS JEFFERSONIAN
CONSTITUTIONALISM

It is rare to find books or articles on Hamilton that do not in
some way make comparisons between him and Thomas Jefferson. Their political rivalry was induced by both personal and
theoretical differences that shaped the development of early
American politics, including its political parties, policies, and
legal precedents. The historian John Fiske exaggerated the relevance of the divide when he wrote that, "all American history
has since run along the lines marked out by the antagonism of
Jefferson and Hamilton," and that the significance of the contest extends to "the history of all countries."[1] Claude G. Bowers
added that the "struggle of these two giants surpasses in importance any other waged in America because it related to elemental
differences that reach back into the ages, and will continue to
divide mankind far into the future." In Bowers's assessment, the
struggle was about the kind of republic Americans would develop, a democratic republic or an aristocratic republic.[2]

Because of such characterizations of the political and ideological differences between Hamilton and Jefferson, their respective political theories have been expanded into ideologies, Hamiltonianism and Jeffersonianism, that extend beyond their particular historical and political circumstances. Their differences are considered central to, if not defining of, the meaning of America, its revolution, and of republican government and democracy. At the core of their differences are two irreconcilable conceptions of politics that are based on irreconcilable views of human nature. Jefferson's faith in progress and the goodness of human beings accounts for a politics that tended to disparage the need for government-imposed order and promoted a romantic understanding of natural rights, especially the right to rebel. Hamilton, by contrast, was neither a progressive nor enamored with natural rights theory. His political theory stemmed from beliefs about human nature and the constant tension between order and disorder that defined its existential, social, and political manifestations.

Henry Cabot Lodge did much to propagate the understanding of American identity as the consequence of Hamilton's differences with Jefferson. He began the preface to his 1904 *Works of Alexander Hamilton* by stating:

> Two schools of political thought have existed in the United States, and their struggle for supremacy has made the history of the country. One was the national school, the other was the school of States'-rights. One believed in a liberal construction of the Constitution, and in a strong and energetic federal government, wielding all its powers to their full extent. The other believed in a strict construction of the Constitution, in a simple and restrained federal government, exercising in a limited way only such powers as were absolutely needful. One was founded by Alexander Hamilton, the other by Thomas Jefferson.[3]

In this portrayal of competing theories of American constitutionalism, Jefferson is cast as a constitutional fundamentalist who was suspicious of government power and consequently insistent that only as much government as is necessary to protect natural rights should be instituted. Indeed, he believed that rights are endangered by an overbearing government and that a constitution is primarily about limiting government by enumerating its powers on parchment. In considering the problem of protecting rights from ambitious government, he wrote, "Our peculiar security is in possession of a written Constitution." Jefferson recognized that changing circumstances would create demands on government that were unanticipated by the Constitution's framers. Constitutional change was necessary, but he cautioned, "Let us go on then perfecting it [the Constitution], by adding, by way of amendment to the Constitution, those powers which time & trial show are still wanting."[4] For Jefferson, the integration of the rule of law with social contract theory meant that the people ceded to government specific powers that were enumerated in the Constitution when they gave their consent to be governed. Implied powers (i.e., those powers without which enumerated powers cannot be exercised), except in a very restricted sense, were not part of his understanding of constitutions and the scope of government power. He considered the Tenth Amendment to be the foundation of the Constitution, because it clarified what was implicit in the body of the Constitution: that the national government could exercise only those powers specifically written into the Constitution and that all other powers were reserved to the people and the states. When it was necessary for government to reach beyond the limits of enumerated powers, Jefferson insisted, the people were to be the judge of its prerogative. Because there was no way for the federal judiciary to receive popular approval, it did not possess prerogative power.[5]

Introducing Hamilton's conception of implied powers into the American constitutional equation, thought Jefferson, would destroy the integrity of constitutional limits intended to protect liberty by confining government to specific powers. Loosely construing the meaning of the Constitution would allow government to exceed the limits of its power and sovereignty by making legal boundaries flexible and popular control of government difficult. At an extreme, loose construction and implied powers would destroy the very foundation of limited government. In his "Opinion on the Constitutionality of a National Bank," Jefferson argued that, "[t]o take a single step beyond the boundaries thus specially drawn around the powers of Congress, is to take possession of a boundless field of power, no longer susceptible of any definition."[6]

Jefferson's rejection of implied powers is derivative of his democratic political theory, which shares common ground with Jean-Jacques Rousseau and Thomas Paine. In short, the people could be trusted with liberty, but elites could not be trusted with power. Because the people were by nature mostly good, only a small and very limited government was needed to tend to the protection of rights and minor problems of order. From this premise Jefferson opposed almost all of Hamilton's policies: the national bank, the assumption of states' war debt, a standing army, suppression of insurrection and rebellions like the Whiskey Rebellion, and encouragement of manufacturing.

Jefferson's position on constitutional powers did not stem from a conservative yearning to preserve the wisdom of the ages. His opposition to loose constructions of the Constitution was not because he thought that fidelity to the document was necessary to maintaining continuity between the current generation and its inherited wisdom. Jefferson's constitutionalism was a mix of populism and legal fundamentalism. Ideally, he believed, constitutions would be completely reconstructed every generation so that one generation could not impose its wishes and values on another generation. In fact, Jefferson considered the best constitution one that was made by a generation that had no social or political connection to its ancestors or its descendents.[7] To conjure up such a situation, he imagined that every person in a generation was born on the same day and that every member of the preceding generation died on that same day. This unrealistic and ahistorical conception of generational birth and death would ensure that the constitution of the passing generation would have no influence on the rising generation. Constitutional fidelity was important within a generation to ensure that the will of the people was followed, but intergenerational continuity was unnecessary for good government. Government should strictly follow the people's will as expressed in law. Jefferson thought that Hamiltonian discretion in interpreting and exercising political power invited public officials to rule in their own or their social and economic class's interest, not in accordance with the public good.

Often characterized as an advocate of a loose reading of the Constitution, Hamilton is commonly juxtaposed to Thomas Jefferson and the latter's strict and narrow reading of the Constitution.[8] Hamilton's theory of constitutional interpretation has been connected to his efforts to transform the constitutional system in a way that would make it less federal and more unitary. Lance Banning, for example, refers to Hamilton's "lax attitude toward constitutional constraints," which supported the shifting of power from the states to the national government and from the Congress to the president. Banning claims that Hamilton's "broad construction of the Constitution" was used to justify these objectives and to move the political system in a less democratic direction.[9]

Hamilton's theory of constitutional interpretation is in need of fresh analysis and perspective. Like the characterization of Hamilton as a nationalist, classifying him as a loose constructionist obscures his judicial philosophy. As has been noted, he is often cited as the father of modern judicial activism and loose constructionism, yet his judicial theory has little in common with modern judicial activism, because it remained largely consistent with the original meaning of the Constitution whereas modern judicial activism breaks radically from it. Hamilton thought it was necessary for public officials to have a reasonable degree of discretion in both interpreting and exercising their constitutional powers. Because he was more trusting of political elites, he believed that such discretion would be used in a way that was consistent with the public good. It may be that his experience as an attorney made him acutely aware of the limits of law. Law approximates what justice requires, but it can never capture the exact dictates of justice, because circumstances have a bearing on what is just in any situation. Discretion was therefore unavoidable in practice, but it should be limited by republican virtue.

While Hamilton and Jefferson were both republicans, they advocated significantly different and irreconcilable types of republican government. Stated in terms of democratic theory, Jefferson preferred democracy that was more direct and plebiscitary. He is, in some respects, the intellectual father of American populism.[10] While Jefferson was not always consistent in his thinking and politics, there is a strong populist element to his political theory that is at times contradicted by his expression of opposite sentiments. He wrote to fellow statesman and Virginian Edward Carrington that the people "may be led astray for a moment, but will soon correct themselves." They are "the only censors of their governors: and even their errors will tend to keep these to the true principles of their institution." The people are "the only safeguard of the public liberty."[11] By "the people" Jefferson meant the living generation, not the multigenerational community of dead, living, and yet to be born of Burke's *Reflections*.[12]

Hamilton, by contrast, was wedded to a constitutional democracy implemented by natural aristocrats who provided judicious restraints against the momentary popular will.[13] Richard Hofstadter exaggerates the point when he claims that Hamilton "candidly disdained the people."[14] Hofstadter likely had in mind Hamilton's comment from the Constitutional Convention when he wrote that criticism. Robert Yates's notes from the Convention report that Hamilton said: "The voice of the people has been said to be the voice of God; and however generally this maxim has been quoted and believed, it is not true in fact. The people are turbulent and changing; they seldom judge or determine right."[15] Hamilton was equally disdainful of mobs[16] and tyrants; they were immoderate forms of popular will and political leadership, respectively.

He also could see the virtues of the people and of rulers. If he had been truly disdainful of the people, he never would have devoted so much time and effort to public argument and writing, something from which Jefferson tended to shy away. Jefferson often encouraged others, like Madison and Philip Freneau, to take on Hamilton in the public papers, leaving his own views publicly ambiguous. His most candid statements tend to be expressed in his private correspondence, as opposed to Hamilton, who was usually as frank in his public writings as he was in his private letters. Hamilton was as effusive a public figure as America has known,[17] while Jefferson was one of the nation's most guarded and deceptive. Few, if any, American Founders can match Hamilton's prolificness in writing to newspapers or his penchant for public debates. Moreover, Hamilton never wavered in his insistence that governmental power should always be used to promote the public good and that the public good should serve as the telos for political conduct. Because he did not flatter the demos by asserting its virtues and promoting its rights, he has tended to be regarded as an elitist who held the people in open contempt and secretly desired a monarchy. Unlike Jefferson and Paine, he did not consider the rise of republican government in America to be the beginning of a global ideological revolution that would rest power from traditional elites and place it in the hands of the people. Hamilton's political theory was not animated by progressive historicism; it was grounded in a perception of the human condition that explains his constant attention to the problem of civic order and his skeptical view of democracy.

HAMILTON AND JEFFERSON ON REBELLION AND REVOLUTION

The theoretical differences between Hamilton and Jefferson are especially apparent in a comparison of their reactions to instances of anarchy and rebellion like Shays's Rebellion, the French Revolution, and the Whiskey Rebellion. Their respective views of the Alien and Sedition Acts and the Virginia and Kentucky Resolutions also illuminate their contrasting political theories. While Jefferson was silent on Fries's Rebellion, Hamilton's comments and conduct demonstrate his political theory and fit consistently with his opinion of rebellion and insurrection generally.

At a time when Hamilton and the Federalists were creating a new constitution because they were certain that the weakness of the national government under the Articles of Confederation would lead to the ruin of the nation, Jefferson famously stated, in response to Shays's Rebellion and the formation of the American Constitution, "I own I am not a friend to a very energetic government. It is always oppressive . . . it is my principle that the will of the majority should always prevail."[18] Again in the context of Shays's Rebellion, he anticipated Hegel when writing in support of the dictum "Malo periculosam libertatem quam *quietam servitutem* [Rather a dangerous liberty than a peaceful servitude]. Even this evil is productive of good. It prevents the degeneracy of government, and nourishes a general attention to the public affairs."[19] To Jefferson's way of thinking, rebellion was a sign of health; it meant that the people would not tolerate undue restrictions on their liberty. Popular complaisance and inertia were signs that the people had lost their will to be free and self-governing. Where Hamilton wanted energy in government in order to control the demos, Jefferson desired an energetic citizenry and a skeletal government that would bow to the people's will.

While it would be an oversimplification to classify Jefferson as a populist, he undoubtedly advocated a much more direct and participatory form of democracy than did Hamilton. In reaction to Shays's Rebellion, Jefferson stated that "no country should be so long without one [a rebellion]"[20] and that "a little rebellion now and then is a good thing, and as necessary in the political world as storms in the physical."[21] He professed himself "convinced that those societies (as the Indians) which live without government enjoy in their general mass an infinitely greater degree of happiness than those who live under the European governments. Among the former, public opinion is in the place of law, & restrains morals as powerfully as laws ever did anywhere."[22] Jefferson saw a natural goodness to human beings that blossomed in an enlightened society, made heavy-handed government unnecessary, and rendered external authority of any type (e.g., political, religious, economic) repressive.

Jefferson agreed with Thomas Paine's *The Rights of Man*, a polemic written to refute Burke's *Reflections on the Revolution in France*. When secretary of state, he let it be known that he sided with Paine against Vice President Adams's criticism of *The Rights of Man*, although he apologized to Adams when a great public debate followed in the wake of his comment. He had not intended for his criticism to be published.[23] An enthusiastic supporter of the French Revolution,[24] he wished that "the glorious example" of France would "be but the beginning of the history of European liberty."[25] As he was inclined to do, Jefferson attached universal significance to the French Revolution and seemed incapable of accepting that there were reasonable boundaries and limits to revolutionary violence. A few years after the French Revolution, he reflected: "The liberty of the whole earth was depending on the issue of the contest, and was ever such a prize won with so little innocent blood? My own affections have been deeply wounded by some of the martyrs to this cause, but rather than it should have failed, I would have seen half the earth desolated. Were there but an Adam and an Eve left in every country, & left free, it would be better than as it now is."[26] Revealing his progressive historicism, he wrote to John Adams near the end of their lives, decades after the French Revolution, that "to recover the right of self-government . . . rivers of blood must yet flow, and years of desolation pass over. Yet the object is worth rivers of blood, and years of desolation."[27]

Having left the Washington administration at the time of the Whiskey Rebellion, Jefferson criticized with contempt the deployment of troops to enforce a law he considered "an infernal one" that would be "the instrument of dismembering the Union." He also criticized Washington's speech to Congress regarding the Whiskey Rebellion. Implying that Hamilton had a hand in the president's remarks, Jefferson paid special attention to the administration's attack on Jacobin and Republican societies. "The denunciation of the democratic societies is one of the extrao[r]dinary acts of boldness of which we have seen so many from the fraction [*sic*] of monocrats. It is wonderful [i.e., surprising] indeed, that the President should have permitted himself to be the organ of such an attack on the freedom of discussion, the freedom of writing, printing & publishing." He noted the irony in the fact that Federalists like Washington and Hamilton were members of the Society of the Cincinnati, an organization that had "carved out for itself hereditary distinction," met and corresponded in secret, while "accumulating a capital in their separate treasury." These were "the very persons denouncing the democrats." He accused the Federalists of wishing to confine the freedoms in question to "the few" while denying them to the many. Jefferson defended the whiskey rebels' and Democratic Societies' liberty to meet and consider separation from the union. "[T]o consult on a question does not amount to a determination of that question in the affirmative."[28] Jefferson tended to ignore the violent actions that surrounded such meetings and expression of those ideas. The whiskey tax was high, roughly 25 percent. It was intended not only as a source of revenue but also as a sin tax. Like the carriage and snuff taxes, the whiskey tax fell disproportionately on a region of the country that felt it was being singled out—the south. Jefferson thought that such taxes would divide the nation, because some states and regions would consider the tax punishment for opposition to Hamilton's fiscal system.

While Jefferson's inclination was to see the virtue in rebellion and to excuse rebels' excessive enthusiasm for liberty, Hamilton tended to regard rebellion as extreme disorder that could lead to anarchy and mob violence. In *Federalist* 21 he speculated that Shays's Rebellion could have been worse if it had been led by a power-crazed tyrant. "Who can determine what might have been the issue of her [Massachusetts's] late convulsions, if the malcontents had been headed by a Caesar or by a Cromwell? Who can predict what effect a despotism, established in Massachusetts, would have upon the liberties of New Hampshire or Rhode Island; of Connecticut or New York?" Included in *Federalist* 21 is a discussion of the Articles of Confederation's "capital imperfections," one of which is the absence of a guarantee from the national government to intervene in states that experience seditious rebellion. "Toward the prevention of calamities of this kind," Hamilton averred, "too many checks cannot be provided." In *Federalist* 9 Hamilton quoted Montesquieu at length to support the point that a "confederate republic," the union of smaller states into one state, would provide a security against popular insurrections, because the national government would have greater capacity to quell such rebellions.

The French Revolution

The French Revolution contributed to growing party strife in American politics, in part because, as Ron Chernow explains, it "forced Americans to ponder the meaning of their own revolution, and followers of Hamilton and Jefferson drew diametrically opposite conclusions."[29] Chernow adds, "No American was to expend more prophetic verbiage in denouncing the French Revolution than Alexander Hamilton."[30] Hamilton was as close to being America's version of Edmund Burke as there was, and he worried that Jacobin ideas would infect sound republican thinking in his homeland. As Jefferson and Paine came to the Jacobins' defense, believing that the French Revolution was part of the same global democratic movement begun in America, Hamilton observed the incompatibility of the two revolutions and the need for the United States to distance itself from France. Writing as "Pacificus," he defended Washington's neutrality proclamation and counseled the president and the American public to place their nation's interests above residual feelings of sympathy they might have for France as a consequence of her support in the American Revolution.[31] He regarded the dethroning of Louis XVI as the end of the revolutionary government's legality, and he became increasingly critical of the revolution and its leaders.[32] He was especially disturbed by the Reign of Terror, as he was by all mob violence, for it struck at the very foundation of order and destroyed the social ethos in which liberty flourished. Even during the American Revolution he was sensitive to the problem of anarchy and mob violence, as is evidenced by his reaction to Sears's Raid, which he criticized as "evil" and dangerous.

In his "Americanus" essays, he noted the "atrocious depravity in the most influential leaders of the [French] Revolution," and he called Marat and Robespierre "assassins still reeking with the blood of murdered fellow Citizens, monsters who outdo the fabled enormities of a *Busiris* and a *Procrustes.*"[33] Like Burke, Hamilton predicted that, as a result of the inhumanity of the revolution, France might "find herself at length the slave of some victorious Scylla or Marius or Caesar."[34] Again like Burke, he starkly compared the American and French revolutions and drew particular attention to the Americans, who, unlike the French, had been "at all times . . . content to govern ourselves; unmeddling in the Governments or Affairs of other Nations."[35] France's insistence that its revolution be a universal event, spreading its ideology and regime throughout Europe and the world, made it repugnant to genuine republicans and a threat to American security. In "The Warning," he condemned France's "rapacious and vindictive policy," calling it "a general plan of domination and plunder."[36]

His opposition to the French Revolution went beyond concerns about the efficacy of American foreign policy. Hamilton saw in that revolution a general danger to tradition, order, and political stability. A faction ignited by unrealistic expectations is apt to turn violent, undermine the conventional order, and destroy a nation's cultural moorings. Hamilton was also disturbed, as was Burke, by the Jacobin attack on traditional religion. The current era had witnessed the advance of ideas that "threaten the foundations of Religion, Morality and Society," declared Hamilton. In particular he noted the depreciation of Christian revelation and the substitution of "natural Religion," which "discarded [the Gospel] as a gross imposture." As the Jacobin movement progressed, the existence of God was questioned in France, "[t]he duty of piety . . . ridiculed," and earthly life declared the end of human existence. "Irreligion, no longer confined to the closets of conceiled sophists, nor to the haunts of wealthy riot, has more or less displayed its hideous front among all classes."[37] The companions of irreligion, Hamilton pointed out, were corresponding notions of politics and government that threatened the foundations of free institutions. In a statement that is contrary to liberal principles that relegate religion to private life, he argued that, like the premises that Christian revelation, the Gospel, the existence of God, and the duty of piety were unnecessary, it was "a favorite tenet of the [Jacobin] sect that religious opinion of any sort is unnecessary to society; that the maxims of a genuine morality and the authority of the magistracy and the laws are a sufficient and ought to be the only security for civil rights and private happiness."[38]

Counted among the pernicious ideas of the French revolutionary zeitgeist promoted by the Jacobins is that government can be confined to minimal power because enlightened plans of government will "ameliorate" human nature; "government itself will become useless, and Society will subsist and flourish free from its shackles." Opposing progressive historicism in Burkean fashion, Hamilton unleashed his deep disdain for the French Revolution by noting its destruction of tradition.

> The practical development of this pernicious system has been seen in France. It has served as an engine to subvert all her ancient institutions civil and religious, with all the checks that served to mitigate the rigor of authority; it has hurried her headlong through a rapid succession of dreadful revolutions, which have laid waste

property, made havoc among the arts, overthrow[n] cities, desolated provinces, unpeopled regions, crimsoned her soil with blood
and deluged it in crime[,] poverty[,] and wretchedness; and all
this as yet for no better purpose than to erect on the ruins of former things a despotism unlimited and uncontrolled; leaving to a
deluded, an abused, a plundered, a scourged and an oppressed
people not even the shadow of liberty, to console them for a long
train of substantial misfortunes, of bitter suffering.[39]

It is difficult to imagine a deeper philosophical and political divide than the one that separates Hamilton's and Jefferson's opinions on the French Revolution.

The Whiskey Rebellion

Hamilton's reaction to the Whiskey Rebellion parallels his response to Shays's Rebellion and the French Revolution. He had
sympathy for Shays's rebels because they were, to an extent, victims of the poor administration of government, including the
absence of a debt system to spread the burden of the states'
Revolutionary War debts more evenly among the states. His
sympathy was mitigated by his fear that local disorder and sedition would spread into surrounding communities and states and
undermine the larger political and social order. The failure of
western Pennsylvanians to pay the excise tax that included whiskey, was a different matter Massachusetts farmers who were burdened by excessive taxes that were the consequence of a crushing war debt. The whiskey tax was part of Hamilton's funding
system to bring order and stability to the financial chaos that
created the conditions for Shays's Rebellion. The whiskey rebels
had no legitimate grounds for their unlawful behavior, which
involved not only failure to pay the tax but also the abuse and
terrorizing of federal tax collectors by such acts as shunning, tarring and feathering, whipping, destroying their property, rob-
bing the mail, and kidnapping.[40]

From Hamilton's perspective, the whiskey rebels were inspired by the same disregard for law and order that characterized
the French revolutionaries; their difference was in large part one
of scale. Behind their anarchic behavior was an affinity for a
Rousseaustic belief in the goodness of man and a desire to be

liberated from religious, moral, and political constraints. Political and social anarchy were caused by ethical anarchy, Hamilton believed. This attitude was evident in his insistence that the troops who marched to put down the Whiskey Rebellion not take the law into their own hands. Before Washington and Hamilton joined the troops in Carlisle, they were informed that some of the soldiers were making lists of rebels they intended to kill and that they considered any whiskey drinker a rebel. Hamilton responded to these vigilante sentiments by stating, "It is a very precious & important idea, that those who are called out in support & defense of the Laws, should not give occasion, or even pretext to impute to them infractions of the laws."[41] Once he was with the troops, Hamilton instituted strict discipline, and even on one occasion issued an apology for his overzealous interrogation of a suspected rebel.

Alien and Sedition Acts and Virginia and Kentucky Resolutions

Hamilton was somewhat ambivalent about the Alien and Sedition Acts. They were passed by Congress and signed by President Adams at a time when, Chernow claims, "Hamilton increasingly mistook dissent for treason and engaged in hyperbole."[42] As the eighteenth century came to a close, Hamilton became more polemical and more politically partisan. Adams, who would suffer politically because of them, blamed Hamilton for the Alien and Sedition Acts, yet Hamilton was not the one who initiated or promoted them, although he was concerned about immigrants who were sympathetic to Jacobinism. Hamilton objected to provisions in the Sedition Act that he believed would divide the nation and incite civil war. He applauded a provision in the Sedition Act that allowed truth to be a defense in libel cases. In the end, however, he supported the infamous acts, and he hoped that they would quell the Republican assault on his character in the press that included mockery for his extramarital affair with Maria Reynolds and repeated charges of financial malfeasance.

When it came to questions of order versus liberty, Jefferson's prejudice was to believe that the people should be trusted with liberty. In his view, increasing government power throws the balance between order and liberty in the direction of coercion and tyranny and pushes freedom-loving people toward rebellion and revolution. Jefferson, who authored the Kentucky Resolution to nullify the Alien and Sedition Acts, wrote that they and other such laws might "drive these states into revolution and blood."[43] He was so disgusted by the Alien and Sedition Acts that he left Philadelphia for several months to avoid presiding over the Senate that passed them. He was, however, confident that the people would recognize the error of Federalist ways and at some future point would vote the Republicans into power.

Hamilton, by contrast, favoring order as the way to protect liberty, feared that the Virginia and Kentucky Resolutions would undermine the national union by encouraging tension and rivalry between the states and the national government. It was in this context that he privately proposed a constitutional amendment to break large states into smaller ones in order to lessen the ability of large states to challenge the authority of the national government. In the cases of the Whiskey Rebellion and Fries's Rebellion, Hamilton believed that the national government should proceed with overwhelming force. He wrote to Secretary of War James McHenry, "Whenever the Government appears in arms it ought to appear like a *Hercules*, and inspire respect by the display of strength."[44]

Something was different, however, about the circumstances surrounding the Virginia and Kentucky Resolutions, and caused Hamilton to council caution. For one thing, unlike the locales of Shays's rebels, the whiskey rebels, or Fries's rebels, Virginia and Kentucky were states with sovereign governments and citizens very loyal to them. In addition, Virginia and Kentucky were not trying to avoid paying taxes but were objecting to a policy about which Hamilton himself had reservations. In short, the dispute was not as clear cut as the Whiskey and Fries's Rebellions and it was potentially far more threatening to the stability of the union. To invite a showdown between federal troops and state militias in Virginia and Kentucky was to risk nothing short of civil war. The last thing the nation needed while it was struggling with the Quasi-War with France was an internal rebellion that would both depreciate the nation's defenses and, more importantly, divide the nation on a domestic issue along the same fault line that separated Federalists and Republicans on foreign policy.

Hamilton's caution is telling. It indicates that he was unsure that the federal government could appear as Hercules in opposition to Virginia and Kentucky. From the early part of the revolution, when he began to consider the efficacy of American government, he worried that the states were a threat to unifying the nation and consolidating power sufficiently to provide for national security. In 1799 he knew that large states like Virginia were capable of challenging the authority of the national government. The doctrines of interposition and nullification annunciated or implied in the Virginia and Kentucky Resolutions represented just such a challenge. Hamilton's response to the challenge was not to meet it with military force but to organize political opposition to it and find a way to use the Constitution to weaken powerful states, perhaps by dividing them into smaller parts. In this instance, Hamilton recognized that discretion was the better part of valor. As much as he could be headstrong and aggressive to the point of being impetuous, he was also capable of shrewd diplomacy and prudential restraint.

His reaction to the Virginia and Kentucky Resolutions invites consideration of his consistency and support for federalism. Writing in *The Federalist* upon winning ratification of the Constitution in New York, Hamilton appears far more receptive to the idea that the American republic is a compound entity, in which sovereignty is divided between the national government and the states. In *Federalist* 28, for example, he had reassured the opponents of ratification that if the national government violated the rights of the people, they could turn to their state governments for protection. In *Federalist* 26 he had touted the state legislatures as "guardians of the rights of the citizens, against encroachments from the federal government." Not only would they "sound the alarm to the people" if the national government infringed on the people's liberties, but "if necessary" they would act as "the ARM of their discontent."[45] In the circumstances of the Virginia and Kentucky Resolutions, however, Hamilton seemed unable to imagine what he had insisted in *Federalist* 26 and 28 was a great virtue of federalism. He had no trouble imagining cases of the reverse circumstances, in which the national government would protect the people from tyranny by the state governments. Shays's Rebellion was fresh in his mind when he wrote his *Federalist* papers, and the Whiskey Rebellion and Fries's Rebellion refreshed his memory and reinforced his prejudices. But dividing large powerful states into pieces would destroy the ability of states to protect their citizens from national tyranny and thus destroy federalism itself.

Karl-Friedrich Walling is correct in arguing that, contrary to Richard Kohn's assertion that Hamilton was a militarist, Hamilton showed restraint and moderation in his response to the Virginia and Kentucky Resolutions.[46] But, in defending Hamilton from what is a dubious criticism, Walling diverts attention from Hamilton's tepid support for federalism. It is difficult to reconcile Hamilton's statements in *Federalist* 26 and 28 with his reaction to the Virginia and Kentucky Resolutions, and especially with his proposal to divide large states. His insistence, in *Federalist* 28, that the state governments would serve as a check on the national government if the latter violated the rights of the people[47] left his readers with the impression that, under the Constitution, the national government and the states would be roughly equal partners that would exist in a healthy tension similar to that among the branches of the national government. If Hamilton's wish was granted and large states like Virginia were divided into smaller states, would states be powerful enough to check tyranny in the national government? Or would the national government always be Hercules? While in theory Hamilton could envisage the need for states to interpose themselves to protect individuals and communities, in the practice of public policy and the actual conduct of government, Hamilton seemed far less capable of recognizing the capacity of the national government to abuse power and the corresponding need for states to shield their citizens from national tyranny. The fact that Jefferson and Madison were often the lead representatives of the states' rights position and most vocal critics of the national government made it difficult for Hamilton to see beyond the politics of his day. Yet, it is precisely that kind of vision that he demonstrated when he used historical experience to broaden the horizon of possible responses to the political crises of the early republic. He saw in imperial France and England national governments prone to tyranny, but while he and his Federalist allies held the reins of American government, he maintained a confidence in centralized power that was difficult to justify by the historical experience he considered the standard for measuring political ideas and conduct.

Fries's Rebellion

As Hamilton worried about open rebellion to the Alien and Sedition Acts in Virginia and Kentucky, a property tax revolt developed in eastern Pennsylvania that was the consequence of Federalist policies related to the Quasi-War with France. The Adams administration had raised taxes and created a direct tax on property in 1798 to finance war mobilization, including a standing army, an unpopular policy in the counties surrounding Philadelphia. Jeffersonians galvanized around opposition to the Alien and Sedition Acts, the direct tax, and on what they considered excessive spending on war preparations. John Fries, a Revolutionary War veteran, led four hundred armed militiamen in a march on the Bethlehem, Pennsylvania, jail to free more than a dozen tax protesters who had been imprisoned by a federal marshal for failing to pay their property taxes and protesting new assessments that would raise their taxes. No one had been killed in the rebellion. In March 1799, President Adams issued an order to the federal army to subdue the rebellion. The responsibility for planning and leading the army's attack fell, in part, on Hamilton, who decided to combine state and federal troops to oppose the rebels.[48] With overwhelming force, the army took sixty prisoners and quashed the rebellion. Fries and other leaders were charged with treason, but they were pardoned by Adams. It was in this context that Hamilton made his remark to Secretary of War McHenry about the national government's need to appear like Hercules.

Historian Paul Douglas Newman insists that, unlike Shays's Rebellion and the Whiskey Rebellion, Fries's Rebellion was merely a rebellion not an insurrection. The Shays's and whiskey rebels were more radical; the former attempted to change the state's constitution and the latter to secede from the United States. As

Newman notes, Fries's rebels "never intended to make war against the governments of the state or the nation." They wanted "to expand the role of the people within the political system, as they understood it, rather than attacking it from the outside."[49] Such a distinction was lost on Hamilton, who tended to see armed resistance to government and the rule of law as pernicious and subversive to the established order. If citizens desired a more democratic political system, they could exercise their constitutional right to petition their representatives to amend the Constitution. Taking up arms and using force to undermine existing laws and policies, was moving toward anarchy, regardless of the rebels' political intentions. And if Fries's rebels were intent on further democratizing the American political system, that would only have added to Hamilton's suspicions about them and their tactics. He was convinced that democrats and populists were unruly and in some cases unwilling to be governed by law. Using armed force to interfere with the process of criminal justice in the name of democracy was likely to reinforce Hamilton's prejudice against rebellion. While Jefferson did not comment on Fries's Rebellion, refusing years later to respond to a prompt by John Adams to do so, his responses to Shays's Rebellion, the French Revolution, and the Whiskey Rebellion lead one to believe that he would have excused or encouraged the behavior of the rebels by placing blame for the conflict on policies that unnecessarily burdened the common people and would have cast the rebellion in the light of patriotic resistance to overly energetic government.

Newman describes Fries's rebels as part of a democratic revolution that saw the American Revolution as the beginning of a wider and deeper revolutionary movement. The Revolution of 1776 was less about independence, for them, and more about "a political, economic, and social process of expanding popular sovereignty." The revolution must continually be redefined, "always in a democratic direction."[50] Their aim was to make American government not just more participatory but more direct. If Newman is correct in his characterization of these revolutionaries' conception of the American Revolution, then it is apparent that they shared some ideological ground with Jefferson but little, if any, with Hamilton. The latter did not perceive the American Revolution as on ongoing project that would move the nation toward direct democracy. His philosophy of human nature and politics would never have allowed him to believe that human beings could routinely take up arms outside the boundaries of law and that this was an acceptable way to impart justice. He was far more likely to have seen such efforts as typical cases of lower passion and narrow self-interest getting the best of individuals who were willing to stir the passions of a mob, form into a faction, and incite violence against the conventional order. He would have seen it as dressing anarchic behavior in the pretense of populism and democratic morality, and it would have verified his opinion that the greatest threat to republican government in America was Jacobinism.

HAMILTON AND JEFFERSON ON SLAVERY

One aspect of Hamilton's political theory that has not commonly been compared to Jefferson's is his attitude toward slavery. Jefferson was ambiguous about slavery but is considered by some to be a champion of equality. His more democratic political theory and attachment to rights theory, especially in drafting the Declaration of Independence, has earned him a reputation he may not deserve. Hamilton, by contrast, is portrayed by many as an advocate of aristocracy if not monarchy. Without doubt he was an advocate of natural aristocracy. His reservations about the virtue of the people and direct democracy, lead many to believe that he opposed racial equality and that his political theory, contrary to Jefferson's, would not foster arguments against slavery.

Yet it was Hamilton who consistently opposed slavery and who provided a sound argument for racial equality. While he lacked Jefferson's flare for romantic populist prose, Hamilton was committed to racial equality in a way that was ahead of his time and consistent with the whole of his political theory. Jefferson could never quite get past what he perceived as the natural inequality between the white and black races. While he, at times, seemed resigned to the evils of slavery, he equivocated. In

Notes on the State of Virginia he was sober about the consequences of slavery.

> I tremble for my country when I reflect that God is just: that his justice cannot sleep forever: that considering numbers, nature and natural means only, a revolution of the wheel of fortune, an exchange of situation, is among possible events: that it may become probable by supernatural interference! The Almighty has no attribute which can take side with us in such a contest.—But it is impossible to be temperate and to pursue this subject through the various considerations of policy, of morals, of history natural and civil. We must be contented to hope they will force their way into every one's mind. I think a change already perceptible, since the origin of the present revolution. The spirit of the master is abating, that of the slave rising from the dust, his condition mollifying, the way I hope preparing, under the auspices of heaven, for a total emancipation, and that this is disposed, in the order of events, to be with the consent of the masters, rather than by their extirpation.[51]

Elsewhere, however, he questioned the very humanity of the black race. He asserted the superior beauty of the white race and offered as partial proof "the preference of the Oranootan for the black women over those of his own species."[52]

Hamilton did not write a great deal on slavery or race, but his experience was extensive and his comments were unambiguous. In his childhood, he was exposed to slavery in the Caribbean. His mother owned slaves and he witnessed the inhumanity of the slave trade. He knew about slave revolts in the West Indies. His in-laws, the Schuylers, owned a few slaves, as did his brother-in-law John Church. Scholars have speculated that he and Eliza Hamilton may have owed a few house slaves, but the evidence is unclear.

He did not support every effort to extinguish slavery, for example, those at the Constitutional Convention in 1787 or in the Quaker petitions in 1790. In such instances, he either realized that such reforms were politically unworkable and/or he was focused on other objectives that would have been jeopardized if abolitionist proposals were given priority. Most of his efforts to impede the institution of slavery were in state politics and not national in scope. Two exceptions to this general characterization were his support for John Laurens's plan to allow conscription of slaves into the patriot army with subsequent emancipation and his benign neglect of Article 7 of the Paris Peace Treaty, which required the British to refrain from taking Negroes with them when they left the North American continent. Slaveholders insisted that their property be returned after the war, but the British largely refused to comply. When the Jay Treaty was negotiated, it was hoped by many southerners that this unresolved matter would be settled. It was not; but Hamilton, like Jay, ignored the pleas of slaveholders and argued that international law justified letting the issue drop. Hamilton acknowledged that the laws of war allowed the British to claim American slaves as booty and either use them as slaves or set them free. If the slaves were set free, then the act was "irrevocable" and "restitution was impossible," because "[n]othing in the laws of Nations or in those of Great Britain will authorise the resumption of liberty once granted to a human being." Hamilton further submitted that "things *odious* or *immoral* are not to be presumed" in interpreting the meaning of treaties. That slaves freed by the British would be returned to bondage was "as *odious* and *immoral* a thing as can be conceived." Consequently, the claims of slaveholders with regard to Article 7 should be ignored, not only because the British were sure to deny them but because the "general interests of humanity" required it.[53]

Efforts by southern slaveholders to regain their slaves resulted in disputes in northern states, including New York, where Hamilton lived. Desperate masters and their slave hunters attempted to round up any black person they could get their hands on, free or not. In response, Hamilton joined the New York Society for the Manumission of Slaves. The organization protected free blacks from being kidnapped and enslaved, started the African Free School to teach blacks skills and morals, and petitioned the New York legislature to end slavery in the state. Chernow notes that the society's minutes "make clear that Hamilton was more than just a celebrity lending his prestige to a worthy cause. An activist by nature, he scorned timid measures and wanted to make a bold, unequivocal statement." His efforts to put New York and the New York Manumission Society on clearly defined courses toward abolition ultimately failed, but Hamilton then worked with the society to petition the state legislature to at least end New York's involvement in the slave trade.[54]

In the case of John Laurens's plan regarding the army, Hamilton's motives were mixed. At a time when the Continental Army was desperate for troops, Laurens made his proposal that slaves be permitted to join the army and, after serving, be freed. Here was a typical instance of Hamilton seeing a marriage of prudence, interest, and virtue. He knew how useful the enlistment of black soldiers would be, and he worried that if the Americans did not seize the opportunity, the enemy would. Black soldiers would demonstrate the equality of the races and the error of the "contempt we have been taught to entertain for the blacks." Contrary to the prevailing American view of black people, Hamilton suggested, "their natural faculties are probably as good as ours." The attitudes that supported slavery were contrary to reason and experience, he believed, and they would be recognized as such if blacks were given the opportunity to distinguish themselves in battle. He added that "the dictates of humanity" combined with the prudence of the policy compelled support for Laurens's plan.[55]

In general, then, Hamilton objected to Jefferson's vision for America because it was too democratic politically and in economics too one-dimensional and insular. Behind these fundamental differences lies the core of their respective theoretical assumptions about the human condition. For Jefferson, man was a rational being capable of self-government with little help from a ruling class. Hamilton, by contrast, assumed that humans were fallen creatures by nature and incapable of self-government without the existence of a class of natural aristocrats who were uncommon in their talents and republican virtue. For Jefferson, politics was a means to transform not only the nation, but also the world. The American and French Revolutions were world-changing events that promised a new world order inspired by the rise of democracy, equality, and universal rights. He rarely met a revolution, rebellion, or insurrection he did not like.[56] Such popular upheavals indicated that the people were not complaisant about liberty; they were willing to risk their lives to prevent tyranny. For Hamilton, politics could improve the quality of life but never change the order of being itself. His sober realism cast politics as the art of the possible and rendered the quest for justice and political order never ending. There was, however, a dignity and honor to politics that could ennoble the individual and the nation. While Hamilton supported American independence from Britain, he rarely met a revolution, rebellion, or insurrection that he did like. Order was the primary concern of government, and it was always in a precarious state. Fissures in the public order would lead to greater divisions and to popular unrest if not nipped in the bud. What Jefferson saw as a sign of the people's commitment to liberty Hamilton considered the beginning of social and political chaos that would destroy the very stability on which order depended. As so many commentators have suggested, the tension between Hamilton and Jefferson has done much to define two competing tendencies in the American tradition that are based on two fundamentally different views of human nature and society.

CONCLUSION

HAMILTON'S LEGACY

FEW WOULD DISPUTE that Alexander Hamilton influenced the development of American economic and political institutions and public policies in the early republic. His place in the development of American political thought, however, is not as clear. Because he was a practical statesman who often disparaged theory and because he did not produce a work of political theory that encapsulates his central political ideas, Hamilton is generally not considered to be among the leading American political theorists. He is known for his politics, personality, and policies but not for his political philosophy.

Hamilton's place as an American political thinker deserves reconsideration. Not only did he provide the early republic with firm and bold leadership, but in justifying and explaining his political actions he articulated a theory of politics that has served as the foundation for one of the two central varieties of American constitutionalism. His greatest contribution to American political thought may be his conception of constitutional government. Hamilton's *Federalist* essays and other writings and speeches encompass a theory of politics that is grounded in the moral realism of ancient and Christian political thought, the skepticism of David Hume, and the common sense philosophy of modern thinkers like James Steuart. His realism is evident in every facet of his political thinking. In foreign affairs, he combined an appreciation for power, interest, and circumstance with the virtue of honor and a concern for national character. He was an early opponent of American exceptionalism and provided a theoretical foundation for opposition to meddlesome foreign policies born of it. He recognized the dangers of Jacobinism to American republicanism and in his cautions against it provided one of the first arguments against a mass ideological movement. In doing so, his political theory shares its pedigree with that of Edmund Burke.

The similarities between the political theories of Burke and Hamilton have not been given due attention. In their books about Hamilton, Robert Hendrickson[1] and Clinton Rossiter[2] make passing references to particular theoretical commonalities in the writings of Burke and Hamilton, and other commentators have noted similarities, but a more systematic analysis is needed and would identify specific continuities in their political theories. There are several significant points of contact between the two thinkers. Both Burke and Hamilton used historical experience as the standard for judging the validity of ideas and policies. They rejected appeals to ahistorical abstraction, disparaging metaphysical and theoretical speculation. Historical circumstances were paramount in their prudential judgment. Consequently, they avoided ideological rigidity in their thinking because they understood that a priori rationalism could not account for the particular circumstances in which statesmen had to navigate the ship of state. In a similar vein, they recognized that radical change was antithetical to preserving order. They vehemently opposed the French Revolution and its Jacobin ideology because they believed ancient institutions to be essential guides in the search for a just political and social order. Yet both Burke and Hamilton were reformers. Their affinity for established ways of life did not mean that they opposed change; rather, they thought that change should be moderate and should avoid tearing up established institutions root and branch. They both abhorred slavery, and they both admired the British Constitution. Hamilton was significantly more sanguine about the benefits of manufacturing and economic development than was Burke, but they both favored free economies and recognized the occasional necessity of sacrificing economic efficiency for important national objectives.

In his political economy, Hamilton synthesized ideas from not only Hume and Steuart but Adam Smith and Jacques Necker. From Steuart he developed a prejudice against economic systems, and he treated economics as a human science that required prudence in the navigation of changing circumstances. He generally opposed tariffs and favored bounties. He believed that a diversified economy engaged in agriculture, commerce, and manufacturing was more likely to protect the nation than the one-dimensional agrarian economy advocated by Jefferson and Madison. Sensing that economic life was in transition, he regarded economic self-sufficiency, touted by the Republicans as the path to happiness, as a romantic illusion. A modern economy, Hamilton believed, required financial institutions like banks and a means for regulating currency. The United States needed to pay down its debt and increase the flow of investment capital if it was going to generate enough wealth to fund future debt, a military, and the infrastructure on which the economy depended. His tax system was among the more unpopular parts of his economic plan, but it provided a source of revenue that was lacking during the War for Independence and under the Articles of Confederation, and he asserted that taxes should be modest, so as not to choke off the production of wealth from which tax revenue was generated. While he advocated the use of debt as a source of capital and economic stimulation, he insisted that the debt remain small and responsible, which would ensure the nation a credit rating equal to those of the great states of Europe.

Hamilton's theory of constitutional government is the hallmark of his political theory. Explaining that human nature invites political institutions that can restrain the propensity toward greed and power, he adamantly supported the separation of powers and a system of checks and balances. Contrary to the prevarications propagated by Jefferson and others, Hamilton did not advocate monarchy; he favored a mixed constitutional government and he described his preferences for the American government in such terms; the executive should have the energy and independence of a monarch but be constrained by a legislature that combines democratic and aristocratic influences. Hamilton's least appreciated contribution to American political philosophy may be his understanding of judicial power. He was an early, if not original, advocate of judicial review, and he anticipated important Supreme Court decisions made by the Marshall court and others. He felt acutely that the rule of law was bolstered by a judiciary insulated from both popular control and the interference of legislative and executive manipulation.

Hamilton did not trust the momentary popular will, and his conception of executive power, as well as the role of the Senate, includes the notion that a permanent will should be present in the government to counteract and check the inclination of the people and of the House of Representatives to democratic impulse. The executive can provide this sense of permanence if it is indirectly elected and, if Hamilton had his way, serves for life. The same can be said of the members of the federal judiciary. The president needs independence and insulation from the popular will in order to promote the national interest, especially in regard to defense, and federal judges are more likely to uphold the Constitution if they are beyond the control of the momentary passions of the people. Hamilton presumed that a well-functioning constitutional system would be animated by individuals who possessed republican virtue. Without their judgment and leadership, the Constitution would be a dead letter. What happens in instances when these political elites fail to conduct themselves in accordance with republican virtue? In such cases, political institutions would provide checks to restrain will and appetite. Judges who replace the will of the people embodied in the Constitution with their own ideological preferences should be impeached. Hamilton's constitutionalism saw to it that for each part of the constitutional system there was a way to address poor or corrupt leadership.

Hamilton argued for and conducted his political affairs with great energy. His insistence on strong, energetic government seems antithetical to the aim of other American Framers to create a government that was restrained by its inefficiency. Jeffersonians have argued that Hamilton's political theory is contrary to the American revolutionary principles that oppose strength in the government. No doubt, significant theoretical differences divide Hamilton's constitutionalism from Jefferson's, but Hamilton's argument for strong, energetic government is by no means inconsistent with the American idea of making government inefficient in order to protect against tyranny. As a thoroughgoing constitutionalist, he believed that the separated powers and checks and balances within the government create a useful tension and inefficiency in government. But once the process of designing a government had come to a conclusion, when a constitutional consensus had been reached, the task of administering the laws and policies would begin, and the administration of government, in Hamilton's view, requires an energy and efficiency that the executive branch is most suited to provide. The creation of the Constitution illustrates Hamilton's belief in this divide: The delegates to the Constitutional Convention debated, argued, synthesized, and compromised; they did what the constitutional process compels statesmen to do, consider the interests of various groups and try to reach a compromise that promotes the public good. No one group got everything it wanted. Hamilton signed a document with which he was not in full agreement, but afterward, no one worked harder than he for its ratification or to give it life by creating institutions and policies that helped realize the objectives of the Preamble.

In areas where government is granted power, Hamilton argued that the Constitution gave it the full range of means to carry out its duties. He has been credited by some and vilified by others for developing the doctrine of loose constructionism. He advocated a looser reading of the Constitution than did Jefferson, but his theory of constitutional interpretation did not reach the more radical extents of twentieth-century progressive judicial activism. His critics charge that he led a counter-revolution that used this judicial theory to undermine what the American Revolution had established. Hamilton's judicial theory, however, has been poorly understood. Sound constructions of the Constitution account for the exigencies of politics, but Hamilton never advocated a brand of constitutional interpretation that gave judges license to rewrite the nation's fundamental law. He was a firm advocate of the rule of law and did not look favorably on those who would bend the law to meet their self-interest. Statesmen, Hamilton believed, required a degree of discretion that gave them the latitude to adjust to changing circumstances. His variety of discretion was of a different pedigree than later theories of the "living constitution." When clear lines of constitutional demarcation are not provided, "a reasonable latitude of judgment must be allowed."[3] Hamiltonian discretion is not animated by metastatic faith, the desire to change the order of being. His underlying philosophical anthropology was a constant ground that kept his political theory from straying into the idealistic realm of progressive historicism.

Hamilton's theory of constitutional interpretation is open to question in regard to the confidence he placed in government's ability to serve the public good by pushing its constitutional powers to or beyond their pinnacle. When Hamilton defended the creation of the national bank, his critics charged that he construed the "necessary and proper" clause in a way that left little room for limiting Congress's power. What he implied but never made explicit was the idea that, in conjunction with the written understanding of constitutional power, which remains to some degree vague, statesmen must exercise the virtue of prudence. Hamilton's political theory depends on the existence of talented public officers, with the discretion to construe the powers of government broadly. When power is vested in the hands of a ruler like Washington, who was a model of republican virtue, the outcome might be different from when discretion rested in the hands of persons with little regard for historical precedents and who believed they had the ability to use political power to transform human nature.

One of Hamilton's theoretical blind spots, especially evident when he was in power, guiding Washington's administration, was the potential for broad interpretation of the law by men like Aaron Burr, who were unprincipled, or like George Clinton, who were motivated by parochial interests. Hamilton was an excellent judge of character and recognized a personality type that was dangerous to the constitutional order when he saw one. He went to great lengths in the press to alert the public to such individuals, and in doing so took on the responsibility of policing the ruling class. He was not so quick to recognize how broad constructionism could be justified in face of the likelihood that individuals of intemperate mind, sinister design, and idyllic dreams would inevitably occupy the offices held by Washington, Marshall, and himself. It may be true that interpretative discretion is simply a necessity of constitutional government, given the dynamics of changing circumstances and the limits of written legal sanctions and boundaries. Nonetheless, good political theory accounts for a broad range of circumstances and character types. Hamilton, who was skeptical about the wisdom of the people, seemed surprised at times that the people were willing to vote men like Burr, Clinton, Jefferson, and even John Adams into high office.

Some of Hamilton's biographers have attributed his strained relationship with Adams to jealousy. They claim that Hamilton considered himself a more worthy protégé of Washington. Whatever the case may be, Hamilton could have been more explicit, as Madison was in *Federalist* 10, about what to expect when enlightened statesmen are not at the helm. Moreover, Hamilton could have given more attention, as Jefferson did, to the education of political leaders and citizens. Hamilton seems to have assumed that the supply of natural aristocrats would continue to be as sufficient as it was in the founding period. Incorporating greater historical scope into his political theory would have alerted him to a potential problem with loose constructionism. This criticism does not diminish the validity of a theory of constitutionalism that relies on the discretion of political leaders, but it suggests that more must be done to bring to light the potential dangers of such an approach and to conceive of ways that those dangers might be mitigated. Hamilton's answer to the problem of judicial encroachments on legislative power, articulated in *Federalist* 81, has proven insufficient. Impeachment is not a prudent check on judges who construe the power of judicial review so broadly that it depreciates or violates the separation of powers and the rule of law. Hamilton's simple solution to judicial tyranny places members of Congress in the difficult position of removing from office judges who have decided a case on grounds other than the law. The inclination, if not the temptation, would be to remove judges from the bench when they decided cases in a way that did not meet the political or ideological preferences of Congress or the people. This would, no doubt, destroy the independence of the court and encourage overreaction to what is now merely the common practice of ideological politics.

On the whole, Hamilton's contribution to American political thought is significant. He ranks as an equal to those, like Jefferson, Franklin, Madison, and Adams, who have received more sympathetic treatment from historians and political theorists.

His political theory is especially interesting because it grapples with what were in the eighteenth century and continue today to be enduring questions of political order. How much power should government have? How should constitutions be interpreted? What is the relationship between the national government and constituent states? What kind of character is necessary for constitutional government to promote the ends of politics? Hamilton's answers to these questions were not always as theoretically penetrating as they might have been if he had been more detached from the immediate struggles of politics. Yet, his consideration of important political and theoretical problems was marked by a clarity and earnestness often absent from political thinking.

Perhaps Hamilton's greatest contribution was his morally realistic philosophical anthropology, which served as the foundation for his theory of constitutionalism, his theory of political administration, his political economy, and his theory of international relations. Hamilton brought the sobriety of moral realism to every aspect of his political conduct and thinking. He avoided utopian and romantic conceptions of politics at a time when Jacobinism and the American Revolution were inciting pernicious idealism. Especially when buttressed by the ever-steady influence of George Washington, Hamilton's imagination led him to conceive of constitutional politics in a way that was concrete and historically rich. He did much to give American constitutionalism its sound theoretical footing.

Where Hamilton tended to be at his theoretical and political weakest was in regard to one aspect of federalism and the cultural supports for constitutionalism. He was somewhat blind to the dangers of a national government that was too strong to be checked by the states. Although he was not in favor of an interventionist foreign policy, the national government that he helped build would, once in the hands of more progressive leaders, minimize the power of the states to the point that, in both foreign and domestic affairs, the national government could exceed its constitutional limits without much resistance. The point of this observation is not to blame Hamilton for the constitutional indiscretions of subsequent generations of American leaders but to identify a weakness in his political theory that failed to recognize the full implications of centralizing power.

What is most striking about Hamilton's political theory is the
relationship between his general philosophical anthropology and
his specific views of government and economy. His underlying
conception of human nature is dualistic. Human beings possess
mixed inclinations of good and evil; human motives are a blending of higher and lower desires. Consequently, one finds a common thread running through Hamilton's political ideas: that the
mixture of good and evil in human nature requires mixed political and economic institutions. American constitutional government should not be a pure regime. It needs to be a mixture
of monarchy, aristocracy, and democracy. The republic is a mixture of national and state sovereignty, and within each of those
sovereign entities power is separated among branches and levels
of government that exist in tension with one another, in order
to create restraints on power. In economics, Hamilton advocated the mixing of private and public influences and the mixing
of agriculture, manufacturing, trade, and commerce. The idea of
giving one monolithic interest or industry anything akin to a
monopoly was anathema to Hamilton's quest for moderation
and balance. The mixing and balancing of power and interest
was not intended to give higher and lower inclinations equal
chances for success; it was expected that individuals of extraordinary character would tip the scales in favor of what was more
permanent and less ephemeral and what served the public good.

While Hamilton's sober reading of human nature and politics
has been interpreted by some as dark and pessimistic, it provides
a realistic assessment of politics and of the challenges that government faces, and in so doing marks the great achievement of
American constitutionalism: civilization depends on a realistic
understanding of the human condition and the quality of character that makes constitutional government possible. It is one of
Alexander Hamilton's achievements that he managed to articulate this central insight during the throes of war, constitutional
formation, and the challenges of the early republic. One is hard-
pressed to find in the founding generation a statesman or thinker
who surpassed Hamilton in realism and constitutional insights.
For this reason alone, he should be considered one of the leading figures in American political thought.

NOTES

Throughout these notes, the following sources are cited using abbreviations: *The Papers of Alexander Hamilton*, ed. Harold C. Syrett and Jacob E. Cooke (27 vols., New York: Columbia University Press, 1961–1987) are cited as *PAH*, followed by volume and page numbers. *The Federalist* is cited by article number and page number from the Liberty Fund's "Gideon Edition," edited by George W. Carey and James Mc-Clellan (Indianapolis: Liberty Fund, 2001). The collection of works by Thomas Jefferson titled *Writings*, edited by Merrill D. Peterson (New York: Library of America, 1984) is cited as TJ, *Writings*. In shortened titles, Alexander Hamilton's name is sometimes abbreviated as *AH*.

Introduction. Hamilton's Significance

1. A concise summary of trends in Hamilton scholarship is provided by Jacob E. Cooke in *Alexander Hamilton: A Profile* (New York: Hill & Wang, 1967), vii–xxiii. A book-length review of scholarly and popular views of Hamilton is provided by Stephen F. Knott, *Alexander Hamilton and the Persistence of Myth* (Lawrence: University Press of Kansas, 2002).

2. John Steele Gordon, *Hamilton's Blessing: The Extraordinary Life and Times of Our National Debt* (New York: Penguin Books, 1997). Thomas J. DiLorenzo, *Hamilton's Curse: How Jefferson's Archenemy Betrayed the American Revolution—and What It Means for America Today* (New York: Crown Forum, 2008). DiLorenzo's book is a good example of an analysis that lacks critical distance, not to mention professional standards. It is full of quotes taken out of context, improper citations, and distortions of Hamilton's ideas and policies. It replaces well-supported scholarly judgment with ideological distortion.

3. Ira C. Lupu calculated in 1998 that Hamilton's *Federalist* 78 is the second most frequently cited *Federalist* paper in Supreme Court opinions (thirty times). His *Federalist* 81 has been cited twenty-seven times (third most frequent) and *Federalist* 32 twenty-five times (fifth). See Ira C. Lupu, "The Most-cited *Federalist Papers*," *Constitutional Commentary* 15 (Fall 1998).

4. A useful chart indicating the frequency of citation of the *Federalist* in U.S. Supreme Court decisions is provided by Dan T. Coenen, *The Story of* The Federalist*: How Hamilton and Madison Reconceived America* (New York: Twelve Tables Press, 2007), 213.

5. Kelo v. City of New London, Connecticut, 545 U.S. 469, 125 S. Ct. 2655 (2005).

6. Hamdi v. Rumsfeld, 542 U.S. 507, 124 S. Ct. 2633 (2004).

7. The legal precedent for the sole organ theory was *U.S. v. Curtiss-Wright Corporation* (1936). It can be traced back to Hamilton's argument in *Federalist* 74, as noted by Justice Thomas, as well as his defense of Washington's neutrality proclamation.

8. U.S. v. Lopez, 514 U.S. 549 (1995).

9. American Insurance Association v. Garamendi, 539 U.S. 396 (2003).

10. See, for example, William M. Wiecek, *Liberty under Law: The Supreme Court in American Life* (Baltimore: Johns Hopkins University Press, 1988), 48–49; Kent Newmyer, *John Marshall and the Heroic Age of the Supreme Court* (Baton Rouge: Louisiana State University Press, 2001), passim; and Samuel J. Konefsky, *John Marshall and Alexander Hamilton: Architects of the American Constitution* (New York: Macmillan, 1964).

11. On the bicentennial of Hamilton's death, the New-York Historical Society launched an extensive exhibit on Hamilton, called "Alexander Hamilton: The Man Who Made Modern America." A web version of the exhibit is available at www.alexanderhamiltonexhibition.org/index.html.

12. Hamilton's support for meritocracy is a central part of Richard Brookhiser's *Alexander Hamilton: American* (New York: Free Press, 1999). Robert Hendrickson notes Hamilton's rise from obscurity and poverty and finds it noteworthy that "the author of the Horatio Alger stories chose Hamilton as one of his pen names." Hendrickson, *Hamilton I, 1757–1789* (New York: Mason/Charter, 1976), xii.

13. Clinton Rossiter, *Alexander Hamilton and the Constitution* (New York: Harcourt, Brace & World, 1964), 12, 58.

14. The term "second reality" was used by Eric Voegelin and others use it to denote theoretical conceptions that misconceive reality by claiming partial truths to be whole realities and thus obscure rather than illuminate reality.

15. This is not to say that Hamilton did not share any theoretical ground with Jefferson, Paine, Franklin, or Madison. Felix Gilbert's *To the Farewell Address: Ideas of Early American Foreign Policy* (Princeton: Princeton University Press, 1961) is one example of a scholarly work that connects Paine's *Common Sense* to Hamilton's contributions to Washington's Farewell Address.

16. See Irving Babbitt, *Democracy and Leadership* (1924; Indianapolis: Liberty Fund, 1979) and Claes G. Ryn, *Democracy and the Ethical Life: A Philosophy of Politics and Community* (1978; Washington, D.C.: Catholic University of America Press, 1990).

17. Works of political theory cannot avoid using technical theoretical terms that can have different meanings depending on the context of their use and the intention of the author. While clear definition is essential to the clarity of the analysis and argument, rather than define terms like "moral realism" and "imagination" here, I will explain them in context as the analysis develops.

18. For the theoretical differences and similarities between Hamilton and Madison see Richard K. Matthews, *The Radical Politics of Thomas Jefferson: A Revisionist View* (Lawrence: University Press of Kansas, 1984), 97–118; Matthews, *If Men Were Angels: James Madison and the Heartless Empire of Reason* (Lawrence: University Press of Kansas, 1995), chapter 6; and James H. Read, *Power versus Liberty: Madison, Hamilton, Wilson, and Jefferson* (Charlottesville: University of Virginia, 2000).

19. *PAH*, 22: 192.

20. *PAH*, 4: 425.

21. *PAH*, 21: 106.

22. *PAH*, 25: 321.

23. For analysis of Woodrow Wilson's humanitarian politics see Thomas Fleming, *The Illusion of Victory* (New York: Basic Books, 2003); and Richard M. Gamble, *The War for Righteousness* (Wilmington, Del.: ISI Books, 2003).

24. *PAH*, 19: 59.

25. For the distinction between the things of God, Caesar, and Apollo, see Claes G. Ryn, "The Things of Caesar: Toward the Delimitation of Politics," in *Essays on Christianity and Political Philosophy*, ed. George W. Carey and James V. Schall (Lanham, Md.: University Press of America, 1984), 107–33. Hamilton wrote poetry as a child and young man, but once engaged in the life of a statesman, he rarely did so.

26. *Federalist* 1: 1.

27. For Locke's view of executive prerogative see John Locke, *Second Treatise of Government*, ed. C. B. Macpherson (1690; Indianapolis: Hackett, 1980), 83–88.

28. Hamilton's view of democratic anarchy's degeneration into tyranny is similar to Plato's view as expressed in *Republic*, Book VIII.

29. Ron Chernow, *Alexander Hamilton* (New York: Penguin Books, 2004), 64.

30. Years later, in 1780, Hamilton corresponded with Sears and showed no ill will or animosity toward him (*PAH*, 2: 472–73).

31. The connection between the political theory of Hamilton and that of Burke is implied by Claude G. Bowers in *Jefferson and Hamilton: The Struggle for Democracy in America* (London: Constable, 1925) and noted by Frederick Scott Oliver in *Alexander Hamilton: An Essay on American Union* (New York: G. P. Putnam's Sons, 1928), 5–6. Neither Bowers nor Oliver, however, makes more than superficial references to similarities in the works of Burke and Hamilton.

32. *PAH*, 1: 176–78.

33. Chernow, *AH*, 137.

34. Ibid., 110.

35. Benjamin Franklin, *Writings* (New York: Library of America, 1987), 1140.

36. *PAH*, 4: 253, or Max Farrand, ed., *The Records of the Federal Convention of 1787*, (1911; New Haven: Yale University Press, 1966), 2: 645–46.

37. Chernow, *AH*, 110, 187.

38. Ibid., 564.

39. Thomas Jefferson, *The Papers of Thomas Jefferson*, vol. 28, ed. John Catanzariti (Princeton: Princeton University Press, 1995), 28: 475, letter to James Madison, September 21, 1795; or *The Papers of James Madison*, ed. J. C. A. Stagg (Charlottesville: University Press of Virginia, 1989), 16: 88.

40. Forrest McDonald, *Alexander Hamilton: A Biography* (New York: W. W. Norton, 1979), 274–75.

41. *Papers of Thomas Jefferson*, 26: 444, letter to James Madison, July 7, 1793.

42. *PAH*, 4: 216–17, or Farrand, *Records of the Federal Convention*, 1: 381.

43. Convention debates for June 22, Farrand, *Records of the Federal Convention* 1: 289–93.

44. For detailed analyses of Hamilton's pseudonyms, see Douglass Adair, *Fame and the Founding Fathers: Essays by Douglass Adair* (Indianapolis: Liberty Fund, 1974), 385–405; and McDonald, *AH: A Biography*, 85–86.

45. *PAH*, 20: 494.

Chapter 1. The Personal Background of a Political Theorist

Epigraph. Ron Chernow, *Alexander Hamilton* (New York: Penguin Books, 2004), 4.

1. *PAH*, 1: 4.

2. Chernow, *AH*, 26.

3. Louis M. Hacker, *Alexander Hamilton in the American Tradition* (New York: McGraw-Hill, 1957), 31.

4. Forrest McDonald, *Alexander Hamilton: A Biography* (New York: W. W. Norton, 1979), 10.

5. Broadus Mitchell, *Alexander Hamilton: A Concise Biography* (1976; New York: Barnes & Noble, 2007), 23–25.

6. Chernow, *AH*, 115.

7. John C. Miller, *Alexander Hamilton and the Growth of the New Nation* (1959; New Brunswick, N.J.: Transaction Publishers, 2004), 440.

8. Chernow, *AH*, 337.

9. Miller, *AH and Growth of the Nation*, 141.

10. Henry Cabot Lodge, *Alexander Hamilton* (Boston: Houghton Mifflin, 1898; Elibron Classics Replica Edition, 2005), 272.

11. *PAH*, 25: 186, 190.

12. *PAH*, 25: 319.

13. On Hamilton's character see Miller, *AH and Growth of the Nation*, 226–27; John Marshall, *The Life of Washington* (Indianapolis: Liberty Fund, 2000), 336–37.

14. Miller, *AH and Growth of the Nation*, 347.

15. Ibid., 31.

16. *PAH*, 1: 156.

17. *PAH*, 1: 277.

18. *PAH*, 11: 589.

19. *PAH*, 3: 495.

20. *PAH*, 7: 84.

21. Richard Brookhiser, *Alexander Hamilton, American* (New York: Free Press, 1999), 3.

22. Gilbert L. Lycan, *Alexander Hamilton and American Foreign Policy: A Design for Greatness* (Norman: University of Oklahoma Press, 1970), 57.

23. Thomas Fleming, *Duel: Alexander Hamilton, Aaron Burr, and the Future of America* (New York: Basic Books, 1999), 323–31. For reactions to Hamilton's death, see Stephen F. Knott, *Alexander Hamilton and the Persistence of Myth* (Lawrence: University Press of Kansas, 2002), 13–26.

24. *PAH*, 1: 37.

25. Joseph J. Ellis, *Founding Brothers: The Revolutionary Generation* (New York: Vintage Books, 2002), 248.

26. TJ, *Writings*, 1515.

27. Ibid., 1516.

28. Ellis, *Founding Brothers*, 248.

29. Knott, *AH and Persistence of Myth*, 6.

30. See, Irving Babbitt, *Democracy and Leadership* (1924; Indianapolis: Liberty Fund, 1979).

31. "Metastatic faith" is a neologism used by political scientist Eric Voegelin to denote belief that the structure of reality can be trans-

formed by political action. Voegelin employs the term to describe the prophet Isaiah's belief in the politically and ontologically transforming power of spiritual faith. Voegelin applies the term to modern ideological movements like Marxism and progressivism that are premised on a reordering of being that removes the tensions of human existence between good and evil, justice and injustice, etc.

32. On the idealism of Jefferson see Babbitt, *Democracy and Leadership*, 268–79; and Claes G. Ryn, *Democracy and the Ethical Life: A Philosophy of Politics and Community* (1978; Washington, D.C.: Catholic University of America Press, 1990), 183–87.

33. See Bower Aly, *The Rhetoric of Alexander Hamilton* (New York: Russell & Russell, 1965).

34. Chernow, *AH*, 189.

35. McDonald, *AH: A Biography*, 314.

36. *PAH*, 25: 188.

37. The theoretical similarity between Hamilton and Adams is called into question by Forrest McDonald in *Alexander Hamilton: A Biography* (330–31).

38. For more detailed analysis of Hamilton's intellectual life as a boy see Chernow, *AH*, 24.

39. *PAH*, 25: 324.

40. *PAH*, 12: 504–5.

41. Miller, *AH and Growth of the Nation*, 28.

42. Clinton Rossiter, *Alexander Hamilton and the Constitution* (New York: Harcourt, Brace & World, 1964), 118–19.

43. David J. Bederman, *The Classical Foundations of the American Constitution: Prevailing Wisdom* (Cambridge: Cambridge University Press, 2008), 6.

44. Chernow, *AH*, 206.

45. For a partial list of the contents of Hamilton's library, see Allan McLane Hamilton, *The Intimate Life of Alexander Hamilton* (New York: Charles Scribner's Sons, 1910), 74–75. A recently compiled list of the contents of Hamilton's library has been published by Jeremy Dibbell and can be found on the web at www.librarything.com/catalog/AlexanderHamiltonI.

46. Chernow, *AH*, 52–53.

47. *PAH*, 20: 280.

48. *PAH*, 1: 35–37.

49. *PAH*, 19: 461, 464; 1: 122.

50. *PAH*, 21: 365.

51. *PAH*, 20: 545.

52. Miller, *AH and Growth of the Nation*, 457.

53. Douglass Adair, *Fame and the Founding Fathers: Essays by Douglass Adair* (Indianapolis: Liberty Fund, 1974), 200–226.

54. Chernow, *AH*, 664.

55. Ibid., 659–60.

56. McDonald, *AH: A Biography*, 356.

Chapter 2. Hamilton's Philosophical Anthropology

Epigraph. Clinton Rossiter, *Alexander Hamilton and the Constitution* (New York: Harcourt, Brace & World, 1964), 114.

1. *Federalist* 6: 21.

2. Max Farrand, ed., *The Records of the Federal Convention of 1787* (1911; New Haven: Yale University Press, 1966), 1: 376, 378.

3. *PAH*, 25: 605.

4. *PAH*, 25: 381.

5. *PAH*, 19: 59–60. In *Federalist* 76, Hamilton connects this mixed view of human nature to constitutional government when he argues, "The supposition of universal venality in human nature, is little less an error in political reasoning, than that of universal rectitude. The institution of delegated power implies, that there is a portion of virtue and honour among mankind, which may be a reasonable foundation of confidence: and experience justifies the theory."

6. *PAH*, 2: 651.

7. *PAH*, 19: 59–60.

8. *PAH*, 5: 41.

9. Benjamin F. Wright, for example, asserts that Hamilton was in favor of "benevolent despotism" and "hereditary monarchy." See his "*The Federalist* on the Nature of Political Man," *Ethics* 59 (January 1949): 6, 13.

10. For detailed analysis on Hamilton and slavery see, Harvey Flaumenhaft, *The Effective Republic: Administration and Constitution in the Thought of Alexander Hamilton* (Durham: Duke University Press, 1992), 36–37; John Patrick Diggins, "Alexander Hamilton, Abraham Lincoln, and the Spirit of Capitalism" (271–73) and Daniel G. Lang, "Hamilton in Haiti" (232–38), both in *The Many Faces of Alexander Hamilton*, ed. Douglas Ambrose and Robert W. T. Martin (New York: New York University Press, 2006), 232–38; Ron Chernow, *Alexander Hamilton* (New York: Penguin Books, 2004), 210–16; Michael D. Chan, "Alexander Hamilton on Slavery," *Review of Politics* 66 (Spring 2004): 207–31; and Chan, *Aristotle and Hamilton on Commerce and Statesmanship* (Columbia: University of Missouri Press, 2006): 197–207.

11. Chernow, *AH*, 312.

12. James B. Staab, *The Political Thought of Justice Antonin Scalia: A Hamiltonian on the Supreme Court* (Lanham, Md.: Rowman & Littlefield, 2006), xxii.

13. Louis M. Hacker, *Alexander Hamilton in the American Tradition* (New York: McGraw-Hill, 1957), 7.

14. Gerald Stourzh, *Alexander Hamilton and the Idea of Republican Government* (Stanford: Stanford University Press, 1970), 173.

15. Darren Staloff, *Hamilton, Adams, Jefferson: The Politics of Enlightenment and the American Founding* (New York: Hill & Wang, 2005), 50, 56.

16. Henry F. May, *The Enlightenment in America* (Oxford: Oxford University Press, 1979).

17. *PAH*, 13: 470.

18. Michael Rosano adheres to the tenets of Leo Strauss. Other Straussian commentators on Hamilton include Gerald Stourzh, Martin Diamond, Walter Berns, Harvey Flaumenhaft, Paul A. Rahe, and Karl-Friedrich Walling.

19. Michael J. Rosano, "Liberty, Nobility, Philanthropy, and Power in Alexander Hamilton's Conception of Human Nature," *American Journal of Political Science* 47 (January 2003), 61–63.

20. Ibid., 66.

21. On the consistency of Machiavelli with the older tradition see Claes G. Ryn, "The Ethical Problem of Democratic Statecraft," in *Power, Principles, and Interests: A Reader in World Politics*, ed. Jeffrey Salmon, James P. O'Leary, and Richard Shultz (Lexington, Mass.: Ginn Press, 1985), 109–24; and Sebastian de Grazia, *Machiavelli in Hell* (New York: Vintage Books, 1994).

22. Russell Kirk, *The Conservative Mind: From Burke to Eliot* (Washington, D.C.: Regnery Publishing, 1995), 74.

23. Lyman Bryson, Foreword to Bower Aly, *The Rhetoric of Alexander Hamilton* (1941; New York: Russell & Russell, 1965), v.

24. Rossiter, *AH and the Constitution*, 182.

25. John Lamberton Harper, *American Machiavelli: Alexander Hamilton and the Origins of U.S. Foreign Policy* (Cambridge: Cambridge University Press, 2004), 5.

26. Lance Banning, *Conceived in Liberty: The Struggle to Define the New Republic, 1789–1793* (Lanham, Md.: Rowman & Littlefield, 2004), 4.

27. Vernon Louis Parrington, *Main Currents in American Thought: The Colonial Mind, 1620–1800* (Norman: University of Oklahoma Press, 1927), 292, 296, 301. For a detailed argument on the Hobbesian foundations of Hamilton's political thought, see Stourzh, *AH and Republican Government*.

28. *PAH*, 1: 51; also Pacificus, "Self preservation is the first duty of a

Nation" (*PAH*, 15: 66). That Hamilton identified self-preservation as a component of human nature does not in itself classify him as Hobbesian. Cicero acknowledged the importance of self-preservation in human motives (*On Duties*, ed. M. T. Griffin and E. M. Atkins [Cambridge: Cambridge University Press, 1991], 6). The issue in assessing the proximity of Hamilton's political theory to Hobbes's is whether the former, like Hobbes's theory, reduces humans to little more than selfish beings or, like Cicero's, includes a higher purpose (*summum bonum*) in political life beyond self-preservation.

29. *PAH*, 1: 87.

30. *PAH*, 1: 87.

31. For Vattel's definition of natural law see *The Law of Nations*, ed. Bela Kapossy and Richard Whatmore (Indianapolis: Liberty Fund, 2008), 69–70n.

32. *PAH*, 1: 87.

33. Cicero, *On the Commonwealth and On the Laws*, ed. James E. G. Zetzel (Cambridge: Cambridge University Press, 2002), 71; Richard Hooker, as in this quotation from *The Works of that Learned and Judicious Divine Mr. Richard Hooker with an Account of His Life and Death by Isaac Walton, 3 vols.*, arranged by the Rev. John Keble MA; 7th edition revised by the Very Rev. R. W. Church and the Rev. F. Paget (Oxford: Clarendon Press, 1888), vol. 1 (par. 673):

> Howbeit laws do not take their constraining force from the quality of such as devise them, but from that power which doth give them the strength of laws. That which we spake before concerning the power of government must here be applied unto the power of making laws whereby to govern; which power God hath over all: and by the natural law, whereunto he hath made all subject, the lawful power of making laws to command whole politic societies of men belongeth so properly unto the same entire societies, that for any prince or potentate of what kind soever upon earth to exercise the same of himself, and not either by express commission immediately and personally received from God, or else by authority derived at the first from their consent upon whose persons they impose laws, it is no better than mere tyranny.

34. For another analysis connecting Hamilton and Hobbes see Stourzh, *AH and Republican Government*, 108–11.

35. Locke, of course, cites Hooker in the *Second Treatise of Government*. The point is not that Hamilton and Locke have no points of overlap with regard to the meaning of natural law but that, on a continuum, Hamilton is closer to Cicero and Hooker than to Locke.

36. [Alexander Hamilton and James Madison], *The Pacificus-Helvidius Debates of 1793–1794*, ed. Morton J. Frisch (Indianapolis: Liberty Fund, 2007), 32.

37. *Federalist* 28.

38. I disagree with Max Skidmore's contention that Hamilton "leaned toward the doctrines of Hobbes" (Max J. Skidmore, *American Political Thought* [New York: St. Martin's Press, 1978], 75).

39. *Federalist* 15: 73.

40. *PAH*, 2: 617–18.

41. *PAH*, 2: 635.

42. *PAH*, 18: 102. See also Hamilton's *Report on the Public Credit*, 1795, in which he states that "*progressive accumulation of Debt . . . must ultimately endanger* all Government" (quoting President Washington in part from his sixth annual message to Congress on November 19, 1794; emphasis in original) (*PAH*, 18: 59), and Hamilton's *Report on Manufacturing*, communicated to the House of Representatives, December 5, 1791:

> . . . it interests the public Councils to estimate every object as it truly is; to appreciate how far the good in any measure is compensated by the ill; or the ill by the good, Either of them is seldom unmixed.
>
> Neither will it follow, that an accumulation of debt is desirable, because a certain degree of it operates as capital. There may be a plethora in the political, as in the Natural body; There may be a state of things in which any such artificial capital is unnecessary. The debt too may be swelled to such a size, as that the greatest part of it may cease to be useful as a Capital, serving only to pamper the dissipation of idle and dissolute individuals: as that the sums required to pay the Interest upon it may become oppressive, and beyond the means, which a government can employ, consistently with its tranquility, to raise them; as that the resources of taxation, to face the debt, may have been strained too far to admit of extensions adequate to exigencies, which regard the public safety. (*PAH*, 10: 282)

43. *PAH*, 7: 331.

44. Aristotle's best regime, the polity, is a mixture of two corrupted forms of government and it intends to check and balance partisan influence. It also relies on leaders of high character and experience, the magnanimous man and the *spoudaios* (mature man), to lift the community above mere self-interest.

45. Chernow, *AH*, 18–19.

46. Ibid., 60, 177.

47. *PAH*, 1: 126.

48. Chernow, *AH*, 23.

49. Thomas Hobbes, *Leviathan* (New York: Penguin, 1968), 160.

50. John C. Miller, *Alexander Hamilton and the Growth of the New Nation* (1959; New Brunswick, N.J.: Transaction Publishers, 2004), 106, 437.

51. Chernow, *AH*, 3.

52. On the distinction between nationalism and patriotism, see, John Lukacs, *Democracy and Populism: Fear and Hatred* (New Haven: Yale University Press, 2005), 71–73.

53. *Federalist* 6: 21, 23–24.

54. On the role of autonomous groups in the creation of order and liberty, see Robert Nisbet, *The Quest for Community: A Study in the Ethics of Order and Freedom* (San Francisco: ICS Press, 1990).

Chapter 3. Theoretical Foundations of Constitutionalism

Epigraph. John C. Miller, *Alexander Hamilton and the Growth of the New Nation* (1959; New Brunswick, N.J.: Transaction Publishers, 2004), 198.

1. The thesis provided here runs counter to that in Barry Alan Shain, "Understanding the Confusing Role of Virtue in *The Federalist*: The Rhetorical Demands of Two Audiences," in *The Many Faces of Alexander Hamilton*, ed. Douglas Ambrose and Robert W. T. Martin (New York: New York University Press, 2006). Shain's thesis is based strictly on *The Federalist* and treats Hamilton, Madison, and Jay as a uniform author who promotes "a new politics of interest that made political virtue unnecessary" (142). Shain draws on Thomas Pangle's *Spirit of Modern Republicanism: The Moral Vision of the American Founders and the Philosophy of Locke* (Chicago: University of Chicago Press, 1988).

2. Miller, *AH and Growth of the Nation*, 319.

3. *PAH*, 19: 40, 59.

4. *PAH*, 20: 113.

5. Gerald Stourzh argues that Hamilton was not disinterested but motivated by ambition for glory. "He did not subordinate his personal interests to those of his country; he subordinated his pecuniary interests to his life's ruling passion, the quest for glory." *Alexander Hamilton and the Idea of Republican Government* (Stanford: Stanford University Press, 1970), 106. In my view, Hamilton was motivated not by glory as much as by a classical sense of honor that required subordination of self-interest to the republic.

6. *PAH*, 5: 42.

7. *PAH*, 5: 85.

8. *PAH*, 25: 276; 20: 386.

9. *Federalist* 71: 370; 84: 446.

10. David Hume, *A Treatise of Human Nature*, ed. L. A. Selby-Bigge and P. H. Nidditch (Oxford: Clarendon Press, 1985), 415.

11. For Paine's view of popular will and democracy see Michael P. Federici, *The Challenge of Populism: The Rise of Right-Wing Democratism in Postwar America* (New York: Praeger, 1991), 9–13. For Jefferson's view of popular will and democracy see ibid., 16–21.

12. *Federalist* 71: 370.

13. *Federalist* 10: 43.

14. *PAH*, 19: 89. (The editors of *The Papers of Alexander Hamilton* used angle brackets to enclose scholarly guesses at words or parts of words that are illegible or missing because of physical damage in the original document.)

15. *PAH*, 3: 485.

16. *Federalist* 6: 23.

17. *PAH*, 3: 486, 496.

18. *PAH*, 20: 541.

19. Historically based legal norms are something distinct from the trans-historical natural rights or natural laws of Jefferson's Declaration of Independence.

20. See Hamilton to Washington, September 15, 1790, *PAH*, 7: 36–57.

21. *PAH*, 24: 350.

22. *PAH*, 19: 59.

23. David Hume, "Idea of a Perfect Commonwealth," in *Essays Moral, Political, and Literary*, ed. Eugene F. Miller (Indianapolis: Liberty Fund, 1987), 514.

24. David Hume, *Enquiries Concerning the Human Understanding and Concerning the Principles of Morals*, ed. L. A. Selby-Bigge and P. H. Nidditch (Oxford: Clarendon Press, 1975), 44–45.

25. *PAH*, 26: 740.

26. *PAH*, 12: 361.

27. *PAH*, 5: 38–39.

28. The mixed nature of the American Constitution has been debated for some time. Martin Diamond has argued that the American political system is not in any way mixed but is a mitigated democracy ("Democracy and *The Federalist*: A Reconsideration of the Framers' Intent," in *As Far as Republican Principles Will Admit: Essays by Martin Diamond*, ed. William A. Schambra [Washington, D.C.: AEI Press, 1992], 17–36). Paul Eidelberg (*The Philosophy of the American Constitution: A Reinter-*

pretation of the Intentions of the Founding Fathers) disagrees and concludes that the American Constitution creates a mixed regime. Gary Wills (*Explaining America*) tends to agree with Diamond because he claims that the Framers created a "pure republic." Carl Richard sides with Eidelberg when he argues that "the classics supplied mixed government theory, the principal basis for the U.S. Constitution" (*The Founders and the Classics: Greece, Rome, and the American Enlightenment* [Cambridge: Harvard University Press, 1994], 8). See Richard's chapter "Mixed Government and Classical Pastoralism," and M. N. S. Sellers, *American Republicanism: Roman Ideology in the United States Constitution* (New York: New York University Press, 1994), 221–23, 236–37.

29. *PAH*, 5: 150.

30. For a summary of the classical understanding of mixed constitutions, see David J. Bederman, *The Classical Foundations of the American Constitution: Prevailing Wisdom* (Cambridge: Cambridge University Press, 2008), 59–85.

31. Felix Morley, *Freedom and Federalism* (1959; Indianapolis: Liberty Fund, 1981), 63–65.

32. Hamilton's career in public office is perhaps the best example of what he meant by energy, a word he used in describing good government. He was not hesitant to exercise power and was often bold in its use, creating for the United States the assumption plan, a national banking system, a system of taxation, and a mint. During Adams's presidency, Hamilton was especially critical of Secretary of War McHenry, who was, he thought, plagued by an inertia that hampered efforts to build up the military in preparation for a possible war with France.

33. *PAH*, 4: 186, 193.

34. *PAH*, 4: 200, or Max Farrand, ed., *The Records of the Federal Convention of 1787*, (1911; New Haven: Yale University Press, 1966), 1: 299; see also 1: 291–92.

35. Morley, *Freedom and Federalism*, 64.

36. *PAH*, 4: 192, or Farrand, *Records of the Federal Convention*, 1: 288.

37. Miller, *AH and Growth of the Nation*, 388.

38. *PAH*, 20: 128, letter to Oliver Wolcott, April 20, 1796.

39. Cecelia M. Kenyon, "Alexander Hamilton: Rousseau of the Right," *Political Science Quarterly* 73 (June 1958): 161.

40. Ibid., 166.

41. Ron Chernow, *Alexander Hamilton* (New York: Penguin Books, 2004), 231–35.

42. Nathaniel Hawthorne, "Alexander Hamilton," *The American Magazine* II (May 1836), 356.

43. Thomas Jefferson, *The Anas*, vol. 1, par. 240, in TJ, *Writings*, 670.

Stephen F. Knott's, *Alexander Hamilton and the Persistence of Myth* (Lawrence: University Press of Kansas, 2002) traces the "monarchist myth" through the ages, connecting it to Hamilton's contemporaries, Jefferson for example, and later thinkers, such as Martin Van Buren, Nathaniel Hawthorne, James Fenimore Cooper, and Washington Irving.

44. Chernow, *AH*, 228.

45. Thomas Jefferson, *The Writings of Thomas Jefferson*, vol. 15, ed. Andrew A. Lipscomb (Washington, D.C.: Thomas Jefferson Memorial Association, 1903), 15: 18–20.

46. Political scientist Jeremy D. Bailey has suggested that Jefferson's conception of executive power incorporates stronger executive energy than most scholars recognize. Yet, even assuming that Bailey's analysis is correct, it does not account for a key difference in the conceptions of executive power of Jefferson and Hamilton. While Jefferson was willing to grant presidents great latitude in exercising prerogative powers, the standard for judging a president's legitimacy was the popular will. Similar views of the democratic presidency were expressed by Woodrow Wilson and Franklin Roosevelt; it was FDR who laid the cornerstone for and dedicated the Jefferson Memorial as well as put Jefferson on the nickel. Hamilton would never have accepted an understanding of executive power that rested on the foundation of popular will alone, because he considered it fickle and, by itself, outside the framework of deliberative constitutional government. In fact, Jefferson's vision of a democratic president who could justify going outside the Constitution and the law, as long as the people approved, fits neatly into Hamilton's belief that Jefferson was himself hungry for power and was willing to use the people to satisfy his will to power. See Hamilton's arguments against Jefferson in *PAH*, 12: 252, 504–6. For Bailey's argument see his *Thomas Jefferson and Executive Power* (Cambridge: Cambridge University Press, 2007).

47. Miller, *AH and Growth of the Nation*, 29, 367; *PAH*, 11: 439 and 1: 510. See also Darren Staloff, *Hamilton, Adams, Jefferson: The Politics of Enlightenment and the American Founding* (New York: Hill & Wang, 2005), 103.

48. It is interesting that Samuel Chase was appointed to the Supreme Court by Washington in 1796, after Hamilton had left his post as secretary of the treasury. Washington sought Hamilton's advice after he left office, including asking him for suggestions to fill cabinet positions. See, for example, *PAH*, 19: 395–97. There is no record, however, of either Washington's asking for Hamilton's advice about Chase's appointment to the Court or Hamilton's objecting to it.

49. *PAH*, 1: 563.

50. *PAH*, 1: 581–82.

51. *PAH*, 3: 495.

52. Cicero, *On Duties*, ed. M. T. Griffin and E. M. Atkins (Cambridge: Cambridge University Press, 1991), 7.

53. Ibid., 23.

54. Ibid., 113, 116. The theoretical roots of Hamiltonian nationalism can be identified in Cicero's understanding of the relationship between the individual and the republic.

55. *PAH*, 1: 440–41.

56. Niccolò Machiavelli, *The Prince*, trans. and ed. David Wootton (Indianapolis: Hackett, 1995), 55.

57. *PAH*, 1: 441. See, also, Chernow, *AH*, 109.

58. Chernow, *AH*, 164.

59. Ibid., 142–44.

60. *PAH*, 2: 465–68.

61. Chernow, *AH*, 73, 189.

62. For the influence of ancient and Christian political theory on the formation of the American constitutional order see Richard, *The Founders and the Classics*; Carl J. Richard, *Greeks and Romans Bearing Gifts: How the Ancients Inspired the Founding Fathers* (Lanham, Md.: Rowman & Littlefield, 2009); Sellers, *American Republicanism*; Russell Kirk, *The Roots of American Order* (Wilmington, Del.: ISI Books, 2003); James McClellan, *Liberty, Order, and Justice: An Introduction to the Constitutional Principles of American Government* (Indianapolis: Liberty Fund, 2000); Bederman, *Classical Foundations of the Constitution*; Forrest McDonald, *Novus Ordo Seclorum: The Intellectual Origins of the Constitution* (Lawrence: University Press of Kansas, 1985); Douglas W. Kmiec and Stephen B. Presser, *The History, Philosophy, and Structure of the American Constitution* (Cincinnati: Anderson Publishing, 1998).

63. Gordon S. Wood, *Empire of Liberty: A History of the Early Republic, 1789–1815* (Oxford: Oxford University Press, 2009), 104.

64. *PAH*, 8: 531.

65. This aspect of Hamilton's political theory shares common ground with Thomas Aquinas's principle of double effect.

66. *PAH*, 2: 18.

67. *PAH*, 5: 42.

68. *PAH*, 5: 96.

69. *PAH*, 18: 94.

70. *PAH*, 7: 331.

71. *PAH*, 1: 126.

72. *PAH*, 18: 95.

73. *PAH*, 19: 59.

74. *PAH*, 12: 252.
75. *PAH*, 19: 43.
76. Chernow, *AH*, 600.
77. *PAH*, 23: 604.
78. *PAH*, 19: 23.
79. *PAH*, 23: 604.
80. See *PAH*, 25: 557, and 4: 193.
81. *PAH*, 23: 600.
82. Julius Goebel, Jr., ed. *The Law Practice of Alexander Hamilton: Documents and Commentary*, vol. 1 (New York: Columbia University Press, 1964), 352.
83. Miller, *AH and Growth of the Nation*, 109–10.
84. *PAH*, 3: 135, emphasis in original.
85. *PAH*, 4: 11–12.
86. *PAH*, 19: 40–41.
87. *Federalist* 28: 138–39.
88. *Federalist* 28: 136.

Chapter 4. Hamilton and American Constitutional Formation

Epigraph. William Bennett Munro, *The Makers of the Unwritten Constitution* (New York: Macmillan, 1930), 27.
1. *PAH*, 22: 404.
2. Ron Chernow, *Alexander Hamilton* (New York: Penguin Books, 2004), 248–50.
3. Plutarch, *Plutarch's Lives*, trans. John Dryden (New York: Modern Library, 2001), 1: 129–46.
4. John Fiske, *Essays Historical and Literary*, vol. 1: *Scenes and Characters in American History* (New York: Macmillan, 1902), 118.
5. See *Federalist* 17.
6. *PAH*, 5: 102.
7. John C. Miller, *Alexander Hamilton and the Growth of the New Nation* (New Brunswick, N.J.: Transaction Publishers, 2004), 161.
8. *Federalist* 23: 115.
9. Forrest McDonald, *States' Rights and the Union:* Imperium in Imperio, *1776–1876* (Lawrence: University Press of Kansas, 2002), 109.
10. *Federalist* 23: 116.
11. *Federalist* 15: 70.
12. See *PAH*, 1: 99, 164; 3: 489; 21: 439.
13. *PAH*, 21: 439.
14. *Federalist* 15: 71.
15. *Federalist* 22: 105.

16. *Federalist* 22: 105–6.

17. *PAH*, 1: 99.

18. McDonald, *States' Rights and the Union*, 4.

19. Ibid., 4.

20. Jeffrey Tulis has suggested that in Hamilton's conception the president initiates policy, uses veto power to shape policy, and serves to unify the policy-making branches of government. See Jeffrey K. Tulis, *The Rhetorical Presidency* (Princeton: Princeton University Press, 1987), 7–8.

21. Frank Chodorov, "Imperium in Imperio," *Analysis* IV (June 1950).

22. *Federalist* 39: 199.

23. *Federalist* 9: 41.

24. *Federalist* 32: 154.

25. *Federalist* 22: 111.

26. *Federalist* 32: 157.

27. Bernard Bailyn, ed., *The Debate on the Constitution: Federalist and Anti-Federalist Speeches, Articles, and Letters during the Struggle over Ratification*, (New York: Library of America, 1993), part 1: 232, emphasis in original.

28. Brutus, "Essay XII," in *The Anti-Federalist Papers and the Constitutional Convention Debates*, ed. Ralph Ketcham (New York: New American Library, 1986), 300.

29. Ibid., 298.

30. Brutus, "Essay XV," in ibid., 307.

31. *Federalist* 81: 420; 78: 402.

32. *PAH*, 3: 550.

33. *PAH*, 3: 304.

34. *PAH*, 7: 84.

35. Thomas Paine, *Common Sense and Other Political Writings*, ed. Nelson F. Adkins (New York: Bobbs-Merrill, 1953), 51.

36. *PAH*, 13: 470. On the impossibility of utopian and idealistic constructions of politics, Hamilton shared theoretical ground with John Adams, who, in his *Defense of the Constitutions* (vol. 3), wrote: "The passions and appetites are parts of human nature, as well as reason and the moral sense. In the institution of government, it must be remembered that, although reason ought always to govern individuals, it certainly never did since the Fall, and never will, till the Millennium; and human nature must be taken as it is, as it has been, and will be." *The Political Writings of John Adams*, ed. George W. Carey (Washington, D.C.: Regnery, 2000), 251.

37. *Federalist* 71: 370–71.

38. *Federalist* 71: 371.

39. Hamilton used the phrase "purely republican" in *Federalist* 71 and

73. He also used it in a letter to Timothy Pickering (September 18, 1803) defending his plan for presenting a new constitution at the Constitutional Convention.

40. Hamilton is clearly at odds with Locke and Rousseau, who advocated legislative supremacy.

41. *PAH*, 4: 202; or Max Farrand, ed., *The Records of the Federal Convention of 1787* (1911; New Haven: Yale University Press, 1966), 1: 301.

42. Farrand, *Records of the Federal Convention*, 1: 288. In Yates's and King's notes and in Hamilton's outline for his speech, Hamilton's comment appears to be less definitive than Madison's notes suggest. Yates's version does not include the notion that the British system should be applied to the U.S. but records Hamilton's saying that it was "the best model the world ever produced" (299). King's record of the comment reads: "I think the British Govt. is the only proper one for such an extensive Country. . . we are not in a situation to receive it. . . I am however sensible that it can't be established by consent, and we ought not to think of other means" (303–4). Hamilton's outline states: "Here I shall give my sentiments of the best form of government—not as a thing attainable by us, but as a model which we ought to approach as near as possible" (308).

43. TJ, *Writings*, 1320, letter to Dr. Walter Jones, January 2, 1814.

44. TJ, *Writings*, 1235–36.

45. *PAH*, 26:324.

46. Chernow, *AH*, 398.

47. Julian Boyd and Douglass Adair quoted in Thomas P. Govan, "Alexander Hamilton and Julius Caesar: A Note on the Use of Historical Evidence," *William and Mary Quarterly* 32 (July 1975): 475–80. See also Carl J. Richard, *The Founders and the Classics: Greece, Rome, and the American Enlightenment* (Cambridge: Harvard University Press, 1995), 92–93.

48. Douglass Adair, *Fame and the Founding Fathers* (Indianapolis: Liberty Fund, 1974), 402–3.

49. Pocock's analysis relies exclusively on secondary sources and fails to consult Hamilton's work, which is absent from his citations and bibliography (*The Machiavellian Moment: Florentine Political Thought and the Atlantic Republican Tradition* [Princeton: Princeton University Press, 1975]).

50. Gerald Stourzh, *Alexander Hamilton and the Idea of Republican Government* (Stanford: Stanford University Press, 1970), 239 (n. 85).

51. Jefferson, "Letter to George Washington, May 23, 1792," in TJ, *Writings*, 987.

52. *PAH*, 12: 252.

53. For a description of the context of Hamilton's quote, see Forrest McDonald, *Alexander Hamilton: A Biography* (New York: W. W. Norton, 1979), 251–53; and James H. Read, "Alexander Hamilton's View of Thomas Jefferson's Ideology and Character," in *The Many Faces of Alexander Hamilton*," ed. Douglas Ambrose and Robert W. T. Martin (New York: New York University Press, 2006), 82–101. Like Pocock, Read interprets the quoted passage as a reference to Burr. He makes a persuasive case but ignores Hamilton's "Catullus" essays, written at roughly the same time. If these essays are taken into account, it would seem that Hamilton had both Jefferson and Burr in mind. His reference to Caesar in Essay III of "Catullus" is clearly aimed at Jefferson, not Burr.

54. See, for example, *Federalist* 1: "[A] dangerous ambition more often lurks behind the specious mask of zeal for the rights of the people, than under the forbidding appearances of zeal for the firmness and efficiency of government. History will teach us, that the former has been found a much more certain road to the introduction of despotism, than the latter, and that of those men who have overturned the liberties of republics, the greatest number have begun their career, by paying an obsequious court to the people . . . commencing demagogues, and ending tyrants" (3).

55. *PAH*, 12: 504–6.

56. Pocock, *The Machiavellian Moment*, 529.

57. Among the scholars whose view of Hamilton's monarchism contradicts that of Pocock are John C. Miller and Stephen Knott.

58. See Jefferson's letter to Madison, September 6, 1789, in TJ, *Writings*, 959–64.

59. Stourzh, *AH and Republican Government*, 108–9.

60. Miller, *AH and Growth of the Nation*, 317.

61. Farrand, *Records of the Federal Convention*, 1: 289.

62. *Federalist* 71: 371.

63. *Federalist* 71: 372.

64. *PAH*, 4: 207–11, 253–74.

65. *PAH*, 25: 557.

66. *PAH*, 4: 193–94.

67. *PAH*, 4: 195.

68. *Federalist* 69.

69. Jefferson's view of executive power is a complex topic covered in detail by Jeremy D. Bailey, who argues that Jefferson's view evolved to the point that he embraced executive energy as long as it was democratically accountable. The difference between Jefferson's view and Hamilton's is that the former connected the legitimacy of executive power to popular consent and the latter did not. See, Bailey, *Thomas*

Jefferson and Executive Power (Cambridge: Cambridge University Press, 2007). In this instance I am referring to the part of Jefferson's thought that favored term limits for the president, opposed standing armies, and expressly rejected energetic government, including its creation of a national banking system and quelling of Shays's Rebellion and the Whiskey Rebellion.

70. *Federalist* 70: 362.

71. *Federalist* 70: 363.

72. *Federalist* 70: 363.

73. *Federalist* 74: 385.

74. *Federalist* 70: 367.

75. De Lolme quoted in *Federalist* 70: 368. See also Jean Louis de Lolme's, *The Constitution of England; Or an Account of the English Government* (1817; Indianapolis: Liberty Fund, 2007).

76. *Federalist* 70: 368.

77. TJ, *Writings*, 913, Jefferson to John Adams, November 1787.

78. *Federalist* 71: 370.

79. In Rousseau's *The Social Contract*, the assembly must raise two propositions at the beginning of its meetings "which can never be suppressed": "Does it please the sovereign to preserve the present form of government?" and "Does it please the people to leave its administration to those who are now in charge of it?" (*Jean-Jacques Rousseau: The Basic Political Writings*, trans. and ed. Donald A. Cress [Indianapolis: Hackett, 1987], 203).

80. *Federalist* 71, 371.

81. In the *Second Treatise of Government*, Locke argued that "there can be but *one supreme power*, which is *the legislative*, to which all the rest are and must be subordinate . . ." If the legislature betrays the trust of the people, by creating laws contrary to their will, the executive is not institutionally equipped to veto the laws. Rather, the people exercise their "*supreme power to remove or alter the legislative* . . ." Locke does provide the executive with prerogative power that can be used to "act according to discretion" when enforcing law, but this power is something different from the American Framers' power of executive veto. John Locke, *Second Treatise of Government*, ed. C. B. Macpherson (1690; Indianapolis: Hackett, 1980), 77–78, 84.

82. *Federalist* 73: 379.

83. *Federalist* 73: 381.

84. *Federalist* 73: 381.

85. *Federalist* 84: 444.

86. *Federalist* 84: 445.

87. About a decade after Hamilton wrote *Federalist* 84, the Alien and

Sedition Acts were passed by Congress and signed into law by President Adams, even with the First Amendment in place. Rather than being punished at the polls, the Federalists gained three seats in the House of Representatives in the ensuing 1798 congressional elections, reaching the zenith of their power and popularity. While Virginia and Kentucky passed resolutions declaring the Alien and Seditions Laws to be invalid, seven states responded to Kentucky and Virginia by claiming that they were necessary and that states had no power to nullify federal laws. By the election of 1800, the fortunes of the Federalists had dramatically changed, and they lost twenty-two seats in the House of Representatives, control of the Senate, and the presidency. Once in office, Jefferson and the Republicans were not eager to revoke the Alien and Sedition Acts. One act had expired before the 1800 election, another would shortly thereafter. A third was repealed in 1802, and the fourth is still in existence. Hamilton's point that the limits of civil liberties are determined by the zeitgeist is borne out by not only this example but numerous others. As any good course on constitutional law reveals, both the American people and the courts in the United States have treated the boundaries of speech and press as adaptable to changing circumstances. For Jefferson and the Alien and Sedition Laws, see Leonard W. Levy, *Jefferson and Civil Liberties: The Darker Side* (Chicago: Ivan R. Dee, 1989), 46, 50, 56–57, 59, 163.

88. *Federalist* 84: 445–46.

89. For a discussion of Hamilton's view of freedom of the press, see Robert W. T. Martin, "Reforming Republicanism: Alexander Hamilton's Theory of Republican Citizenship and Press Liberty," in *The Many Faces of Alexander Hamilton*," ed. Douglas Ambrose and Robert W. T. Martin (New York: New York University Press, 2006), 109–33.

90. Julius Goebel, Jr., ed., *The Law Practice of Alexander Hamilton: Documents and Commentary* (New York: Columbia University Press, 1964), 1: 809–10.

91. Richard B. Morris, ed., *Alexander Hamilton and the Founding of the Nation* (New York: Dial Press, 1957), xii.

92. See Herbert Croly, *The Promise of American Life* (Boston: Northeastern University Press, 1989); and Peter McNamara, "Hamilton, Croly, and American Public Philosophy," in *The Many Faces of Alexander Hamilton*," ed. Douglas Ambrose and Robert W. T. Martin (New York: New York University Press, 2006), 247–66.

93. *PAH*, 8: 98.

94. *Federalist* 33: 160.

95. *PAH*, 3: 486–87.

96. [Alexander Hamilton and James Madison], *The Pacificus-Helvid-*

ius Debates of 1793–1794, ed. Morton J. Frisch (Indianapolis: Liberty Fund, 2007), 27.

97. *PAH*, 8: 106, 107, 103, 111 (emphasis original).

98. For a discussion of Hamilton's "textualism" and its contrast to the modern concept of living constitutionalism, see James B. Staab, *The Political Thought of Justice Antonin Scalia: A Hamiltonian on the Supreme Court* (Lanham, Md.: Rowman & Littlefield, 2006), 187–200.

99. *Federalist* 22: 110.

100. Croly, *Promise of American Life*, 400.

Chapter 5. Hamilton's Foreign Policy

Epigraph. *PAH*, 15: 82–86; also in [Alexander Hamilton and James Madison], *The Pacificus-Helvidius Debates of 1793–1794*, ed. Morton J. Frisch (Indianapolis: Liberty Fund, 2007), 33.

1. *The Collected Works of Eric Voegelin*, ed. Ellis Sandoz, vol. 22, *Renaissance and Reformation* (Columbia: University of Missouri Press, 1998), 4.

2. Ron Chernow, *Alexander Hamilton* (New York: Penguin Books, 2004), 627.

3. *PAH*, 2: 660.

4. *PAH*, 20: 433.

5. Federalists like Hamilton and Washington were not the only ones to argue that the United States should stay out of European affairs. Thomas Paine, for example, in *Common Sense* made a similar argument. Felix Gilbert traces the connections between Paine's view of American interests and the views of Hamilton and Washington in *To the Farewell Address: Ideas of Early American Foreign Policy* (Princeton: Princeton University Press, 1961).

6. John Lamberton Harper provides a balanced and cogent analysis of Hamilton's "Grand Plan" and various interpretations of its meaning. See his *American Machiavelli: Alexander Hamilton and the Origins of U.S. Foreign Policy* (Cambridge: Cambridge University Press, 2004), 205–36.

7. Gilbert L. Lycan, *Alexander Hamilton and American Foreign Policy: A Design for Greatness* (Norman: University of Oklahoma Press, 1970), 84–88.

8. Ibid., 373–409.

9. *PAH*, 23: 227.

10. Richard K. Matthews, *The Radical Politics of Thomas Jefferson: A Revisionist View* (Lawrence: University Press of Kansas, 1984), 115, 113.

11. James F. Pontuso, "Political Passions and the Creation of the American National Community: The Case of Alexander Hamilton," *Perspectives on Political Science* 22 (Spring 1993): 79.

12. In a speech to the New York legislature in 1787, Hamilton suggested that "several" of the states were "large empires in themselves" (*PAH*, 4: 81).

13. Hamilton, letter to James Duane, September 3, 1780, *PAH*, 2: 403.

14. *PAH*, 18: 498, Camillus II.

15. *PAH*, 21: 382, 383, 412; 22: 441.

16. *PAH*, 26: 72.

17. *PAH*, 1: 178.

18. *Federalist* 6: 23.

19. *Federalist* 11: 51.

20. Lycan, *AH and Foreign Policy*, 68.

21. *PAH*, 20: 284–85.

22. For Hamilton's defense of standing armies see *Federalist* 29.

23. For a lucid and insightful analysis of Hamilton and the Vermont crisis, see Karl-Friedrich Walling, *Republican Empire: Alexander Hamilton on War and Free Government* (Lawrence: University Press of Kansas, 1999), 83–92. Walling does draw too stark a distinction between ancient and modern political ideas. He states that, "the spirit of the modern age was . . . incompatible with that of the ancients" (85–86). No doubt, aspects of ancient political thought were inapplicable to the circumstances of "modern" America. Yet, Hamilton and the Framers borrowed generously from the ancients. For the compatibility of ancient and American constitutionalism see, Russell Kirk, *The Roots of American Order* (Wilmington, Del.: ISI Press, 2003), chapters 3 and 4; and Kirk, "What Did Americans Inherit from the Ancients," appendix to *America's British Culture* (New Brunswick, N.J.: Transaction, 1993); David J. Bederman, *The Classical Foundations of the American Constitution: Prevailing Wisdom* (Cambridge: Cambridge University Press, 2008), Carl J. Richard, *The Founders and the Classics: Greece, Rome, and the American Enlightenment* (Cambridge: Harvard University Press, 1995); and Richard, *Greeks and Romans Bearing Gifts: How the Ancients Inspired the Founding Fathers* (Lanham, Md.: Rowman & Littlefield, 2009).

24. *PAH*, 4: 128.

25. *PAH*, 4: 135.

26. *PAH*, 4: 140.

27. *Federalist* 11: 54.

28. Karl-Friedrich Walling contrasts the views of Hamilton and the anti-Federalists in *Republican Empire*, 101–5.

29. *Federalist* 11: 51.

30. Lycan, *AH and Foreign Policy*, 100–102.

31. See Walter A. McDougall, *Promised Land, Crusader State: The American Encounter with the World since 1776* (Boston: Houghton Mifflin, 1997), 15–56.

32. Forrest McDonald, *Alexander Hamilton: A Biography* (New York: W. W. Norton, 1979), 265.

33. *Pacificus-Helvidius Debates*, 10–16.

34. Ibid., 11, 13–14, 16.

35. Ibid., 27–28.

36. *PAH*, 20: 494.

37. *Pacificus-Helvidius Debates*, 33–36.

38. Ibid., 46.

39. John C. Miller, *Alexander Hamilton and the Growth of the New Nation* (New Brunswick, N.J.: Transaction Publishers, 2004), 373–78.

40. Ibid.

41. Hamilton's two "Americanus" essays were intended to be his final contributions to the Pacificus-Helvidius debates.

42. *Pacificus-Helvidius Debates*, 101.

43. Ibid., 108.

44. Ibid., 114.

45. See Richard Price, "Observations on the Importance of the American Revolution," in *Colonies to Nation: A Documentary History of the American Revolution*, ed. Jack P. Greene (New York: W. W. Norton, 1975), 422–25.

46. For a detailed description of Hamilton's stoning and duel challenges see, Joanne B. Freeman, *Affairs of Honor: National Politics in the New Republic* (New Haven: Yale University Press, 2001), xiii–xxiv.

47. *PAH*, 19: 74.

48. *PAH*, 18: 480.

49. *PAH*, 18: 483.

50. *PAH*, 18: 495.

51. *Federalist* 23: 113.

52. *PAH*, 19: 107.

53. *PAH*, 19: 137.

54. *PAH*, 21: 37, April 10, 1797 letter from Hamilton to William Loughton Smith.

55. *PAH*, 19: 91–92.

56. Miller, *AH and Growth of the Nation*, 422.

57. *PAH*, 21: 522.

58. *PAH*, 21: 495, letter from Hamilton to Timothy Pickering, June 7, 1798.

59. *PAH*, 22: 453, letter from Hamilton to Theodore Sedgwick, February 2, 1799.

60. Julius Goebel, Jr., ed., *The Law Practice of Alexander Hamilton: Documents and Commentary* (New York: Columbia University Press, 1964), 1: 829.

61. McDonald, *AH: A Biography*, 358.

62. For analysis of Hamilton's position on the Alien Law and of related topics, see James Morton Smith, "Alexander Hamilton, the Alien Law, and Seditious Libels," *Review of Politics* 16 (July 1954): 305–33; and Robert W. T. Martin, "Reforming Republicanism: Alexander Hamilton's Theory of Republican Citizenship and Press Liberty," in *The Many Faces of Alexander Hamilton*, ed. Douglas Ambrose and Robert W. T. Martin (New York: New York University Press, 2006), 109–33.

63. *PAH*, 23: 604.

64. Chernow, *AH*, 575–77; and Miller, *AH and Growth of the Nation*, 486–88.

65. McDonald, *AH: A Biography*, 357–58.

66. Miller, *AH and Growth of the Nation*, 560–63.

67. See McDougall, *Promised Land, Crusader State*.

68. *PAH*, 3: 557.

69. *PAH*, 20: 284.

70. W. B. Allen, ed., *George Washington, A Collection* (Indianapolis: Liberty Fund, 1988), 523.

71. Ibid., 522–23.

72. Noemie Emery exaggerates Hamilton's affinity for the nation when she writes, "It was not only his country, but his religion, his home and his family as well" (*Alexander Hamilton: An Intimate Portrait* [New York: G. P. Putnam's Sons, 1982], 26).

73. John Lukacs, *Democracy and Populism: Fear and Hatred* (New Haven: Yale University Press, 2005), 31, 36.

Chapter 6. Hamilton's Political Economy

Epigraph. Andrew C. McLaughlin, *A Constitutional History of the United States* (New York: D. Appleton-Century, 1935), 225.

1. *PAH*, 3: 321.

2. For specific connections between the political economy of Hamilton and Adam Smith, see Edward G. Bourne, "Alexander Hamilton and Adam Smith," *Quarterly Journal of Economics* 8 (April 1894): 328–44.

3. Ron Chernow, *Alexander Hamilton* (New York: Penguin Books, 2004), 170.

4. *PAH*, 3: 78–79.

5. Drew R. McCoy, *The Elusive Republic: Political Economy in Jeffersonian America* (New York: W. W. Norton, 1980), 146–47.

6. *PAH*, 4: 189, or Max Farrand, ed., *The Records of the Federal Convention of 1787* (New Haven: Yale University Press, 1966), 1: 285.

7. *PAH*, 2: 242.

8. Peter McNamara, *Political Economy and Statesmanship: Smith, Hamilton, and the Foundation of the Commercial Republic* (DeKalb: Northern Illinois University Press, 1998), 97.

9. For Jacques Necker's influence on Hamilton's political economy, see Donald F. Swanson and Andrew P. Trout, "Alexander Hamilton, 'the Celebrated Mr. Necker,' and Public Credit," *William and Mary Quarterly* 47 (July 1990): 422–30.

10. James Steuart, *An Inquiry into the Principles of Political Economy* (London: A. Millar & T. Cadell, 1767; e-book 2008), Book 1, preface.

11. John C. Miller, *Alexander Hamilton and the Growth of the New Nation* (New Brunswick, N.J.: Transaction Publishers, 2004), 47.

12. Michael D. Chan, *Aristotle and Hamilton on Commerce and Statesmanship* (Columbia: University of Missouri Press, 2006), 57, 217.

13. Edmund Burke, *Reflections on the Revolution in France*, ed. J. G. A. Pocock (1790; Indianapolis: Hackett, 1987), 54.

14. *PAH*, 8: 132.

15. Burke, *Revolution in France*, 53.

16. Ibid., 7.

17. Forrest McDonald, "The Constitution and Hamiltonian Capitalism," in *How Capitalistic Is the Constitution*, ed. Robert A. Goldwin and William A. Schambra (Washington, D.C.: American Enterprise Institute, 1982), 68.

18. Chernow, *AH*, 110–11.

19. Article VI of the Constitution provides that, "All debts contracted and engagements entered into, before the adoption of this Constitution, shall be as valid against the United States under this Constitution, as under the Confederation."

20. Forrest McDonald, *Alexander Hamilton: A Biography* (New York: W. W. Norton, 1979), 157.

21. See Gordon S. Wood, *Empire of Liberty: A History of the Early Republic, 1789–1815* (Oxford: Oxford University Press, 2009), 292–93 and chapter 17.

22. McLaughlin, *Constitutional History of the United States*, 225.

23. McDonald, "The Constitution and Hamiltonian Capitalism," 69.

24. Miller, *AH and Growth of the Nation*, 258.

25. *PAH*, 18: 46–148.

26. *PAH*, 19: 53.

27. Karl-Friedrich Walling, *Republican Empire: Alexander Hamilton on War and Free Government* (Lawrence: University Press of Kansas, 1999), 194.

28. Miller, *AH and Growth of the Nation*, 253–54.

29. *PAH*, 10: 253, 256, 260.

30. For the development of American hustling and pretense, see Walter A. McDougall, *Throes of Democracy: The American Civil War Era, 1829–1877* (New York: HarperCollins, 2008).

31. *PAH*, 10: 303–4.

32. These questions are taken up in chapter 7.

33. Miller, *AH and Growth of the Nation*, 261.

34. Hamilton asked, "Shall we put in practice the horrid system of the detestable Robespierre?" *PAH*, 19: 52.

35. *PAH*, 19: 52.

Chapter 7. Hamilton and Jefferson

Epigraph. Ron Chernow, *Alexander Hamilton* (New York: Penguin Books, 2004), 267.

1. John Fiske, *Essays Historical and Literary*, vol. 1, *Scenes and Characters in American History* (New York: Macmillan, 1902), 170.

2. Claude G. Bowers, *Jefferson and Hamilton: The Struggle for Democracy in America* (London: Constable, 1925), v.

3. Henry Cabot Lodge, ed., *The Works of Alexander Hamilton*, 2nd ed. (New York: G. P. Putnam's Sons, 1904), 1: ix.

4. Thomas Jefferson, "Letter to Wilson Cary Nicholas, September 7, 1803," in TJ, *Writings*, 1140.

5. For Jefferson's view of prerogative power and democratic consent, see Jeremy D. Bailey, *Thomas Jefferson and Executive Power* (Cambridge: Cambridge University Press, 2007).

6. Thomas Jefferson, "Opinion on the Constitutionality of a National Bank," in TJ, *Writings*, 416.

7. Jefferson, "Letter to James Madison, September 6, 1789," in TJ, *Writings*, 959–64.

8. See, for example, William J. Quirk and R. Randall Bridwell, *Judicial Dictatorship* (New Brunswick, N.J.: Transaction Publishers, 1995).

9. Lance Banning, *Conceived in Liberty: The Struggle to Define the New Republic, 1789–1793* (Lanham, Md.: Rowman & Littlefield, 2004), 12.

10. For Jefferson's influence on American populism, see, Michael P. Federici, *The Challenge of Populism: The Rise of Right-Wing Democratism in Postwar America* (New York: Praeger, 1991).

11. Jefferson, "Letter to Edward Carrington, January 16, 1787," in TJ, *Writings*, 880.

12. Edmund Burke, *Reflections on the Revolution in France*, ed. J. G. A. Pocock (1790; Indianapolis: Hackett, 1987), 85.

13. For more detailed analysis of the differences between plebiscitary and constitutional democracy, see Claes G. Ryn, *Democracy and the Ethical Life* (1978; Washington, D.C.: Catholic University of America Press, 1990); and Irving Babbitt, *Democracy and Leadership* (1924; Indianapolis: Liberty Fund, 1979).

14. Richard Hofstadter, *The American Political Tradition and the Men Who Made It* (New York: Alfred A. Knopf, 1949), 5.

15. *PAH*, 4: 200, or Max Farrand, ed., *The Records of the Federal Convention of 1787* (1911; New Haven: Yale University Press, 1966), 1: 299.

16. It is interesting to note that Madison's view of democracy in the *The Federalist* tends to be much closer to Hamilton's than to Jefferson's. In *Federalist 55* (288) Madison comments, "Had every Athenian citizen been a Socrates, every Athenian assembly would still have been a mob."

17. For a contrary view of Hamilton to the one presented here, see Roger G. Kennedy, *Burr, Hamilton, and Jefferson: A Study in Character* (Oxford: Oxford University Press, 1999).

18. Jefferson, "Letter to James Madison, December 20, 1787," in TJ, *Writings*, 917–18.

19. "Letter to Madison, January 30, 1787," in TJ, *Writings*, 882.

20. TJ, *Writings*, 918.

21. Jefferson, "Letter to James Madison, January 30, 1787," in TJ, *Writings*, 882.

22. Jefferson, "Letter to Edward Carrington, January 16, 1787," in TJ, *Writings*, 880.

23. *The Papers of Thomas Jefferson*, vol. 20, ed. Julian P. Boyd (Princeton: Princeton University Press, 1982), 20: 302–3, letter to Adams, July 17, 1791.

24. For Jefferson's unwavering commitment to the French Revolution, see Conor Cruise O'Brien, *The Long Affair: Thomas Jefferson and the French Revolution, 1785–1800* (Chicago: University of Chicago Press, 1996).

25. Jefferson, "Letter to Madame d'Enville, April 2, 1790," in TJ, *Writings*, 965–66. See Susan Dunn, *Sister Revolutions: French Lightning, American Light* (New York: Faber & Faber, 1999), 13.

26. Jefferson, "Letter to William Short, January 3, 1793," in TJ, *Writings*, 1004.

27. Jefferson, "Letter to John Adams, September 4, 1823," in TJ, *Writings*, 1478.

28. Jefferson, "Letter to James Madison, December 28, 1794," in TJ, *Writings*, 1015–16.

29. Chernow, *AH*, 431. Chernow provides an extensive and detailed analysis of Hamilton's response to the French Revolution in chapter 25.

30. Ibid., 434.

31. For Hamilton's comments on France's selfish motives during the American Revolution, see Hamilton, "The Answer," in *PAH*, 20: 432–34.

32. Gilbert L. Lycan, *Alexander Hamilton and American Foreign Policy: A Design for Greatness* (Norman: University of Oklahoma Press, 1970), 140.

33. [Alexander Hamilton and James Madison], *The Pacificus-Helvidius Debates of 1793–1794*, ed. Morton J. Frisch (Indianapolis: Liberty Fund, 2007), 100–101. *PAH*, 15: 671.

34. *Pacificus-Helvidius Debates*, 101. *PAH*, 15: 671.

35. *Pacificus-Helvidius Debates*, 114. *PAH*, 16: 19.

36. *PAH*, 20: 518–19.

37. *PAH*, 26: 738–39.

38. *PAH*, 26: 738–39.

39. *PAH*, 26: 740.

40. For details of the whiskey rebels and Hamilton's response, see, Chernow, *AH*, 468–78; Hamilton's letter to Washington, August 5, 1794, "Report on Opposition to Internal Duties," *PAH*, 17: 24–58; and Hamilton's "Tully" letters, *PAH*, 17: 132–35, 148–50, 159–61, 175–80. Paul Douglas Newman's analysis of Fries's Rebellion includes comparisons to both Shays's Rebellion and the Whiskey Rebellion. Newman characterizes the whiskey rebels as far more violent and politically radical than the Fries's rebels. See, Paul Douglas Newman, *Fries's Rebellion: The Enduring Struggle for the American Revolution* (Philadelphia: University of Pennsylvania Press, 2004), 55–60.

41. *PAH*, 17: 317.

42. Chernow, *AH*, 569.

43. Thomas Jefferson, "Draft of the Kentucky Resolution," in *Liberty and Order: The First American Party Struggle*, ed. Lance Banning (Indianapolis: Liberty Fund, 2004), 235.

44. *PAH*, 22: 552–53.

45. *Federalist* 26: 130.

46. See Karl-Friedrich Walling, *Republican Empire: Alexander Hamilton on War and Free Government* (Lawrence: University Press of Kansas, 1999), 248–75.

47. *Federalist* 28: 138–39.

48. Chernow, *AH*, 578.

49. Newman, *Fries's Rebellion*, ix–x.

50. Ibid., xii.

51. Thomas Jefferson, *Notes on the State of Virginia: Query XVIII* (New York: Library of America, 1984), 289. For a more detailed analysis of Jefferson's views of slavery, see Joseph Ellis, *American Sphinx: The*

Character of Thomas Jefferson (New York: Vintage Books, 1998), 210–13, 312–16, 512–14.

52. Jefferson, *Notes on the State of Virginia: Query XIV*, 265.

53. *PAH*, 18: 518–19.

54. Chernow, *AH*, 210–16.

55. *PAH*, 2: 18.

56. For exceptions to Jefferson's general support for revolution and insurrection, see Bailey, *Thomas Jefferson and Executive Power*, 53–55.

Conclusion. Hamilton's Legacy

1. Robert Hendrickson, *Hamilton I, 1757–1789* (New York: Mason/ Charter, 1976), 78.

2. Clinton Rossiter, *Alexander Hamilton and the Constitution* (New York: Harcourt, Brace & World, 1964), 150, 180–82.

3. *PAH*, 8: 107.

RECOMMENDED READING

A few notable books on Hamilton's political thought provide the intellectual foundation for the analysis provided here, which sometimes borrows from and builds on them and sometimes deviates from them. Clinton Rossiter's *Alexander Hamilton and the Constitution*, Karl-Friedrich Walling's *Republican Empire: Alexander Hamilton on War and Free Government*, Harvey Flaumenhaft's *The Effective Republic: Administration and Constitution in the Thought of Alexander Hamilton*, and Gerald Stourzh's *Alexander Hamilton and the Idea of Republican Government* are works of political theory that cover particular aspects of Hamilton's political philosophy. There is, however, no extensive and comprehensive study of Hamilton's political theory. Forrest McDonald's *Alexander Hamilton: A Biography* is useful in describing Hamilton's basic political and economic ideas. Ron Chernow's *Alexander Hamilton* provides a wealth of material on Hamilton's life, allowing connection of his character and experience to his political ideas and actions. John C. Miller's *Alexander Hamilton and the Growth of the New Nation*, like Chernow's book, is a detailed biography that chronicles Hamilton's life. Darren Staloff's *Hamilton, Adams, Jefferson: The Politics of the Enlightenment and the American Founding* places Hamilton's political thought in the tradition of the Enlightenment with qualifications; and Charles Cerami's *Young Patriots* and Michael Meyerson's *Liberty's Blueprint: How Madison and Hamilton Wrote* The Federalist, *Defined the Constitution, and Made Democracy Safe for the World* both focus on Hamilton's collaboration with Madison in the period of constitutional formation. Gilbert L. Lycan's *Alexander Hamilton and American Foreign Policy*, Walling's *Republican Empire*, John Lamberton Harper's *American Machiavelli: Alexander Hamilton and the Origins of U.S. Foreign*

Policy, and Lawrence S. Kaplan's *Alexander Hamilton: Ambivalent Anglophile* are substantial studies of Hamilton's political ideas in the area of foreign affairs. There are a few books written on *The Federalist* that treat Hamilton's contribution as a significant theoretical work. They include, George Carey's *The Federalist: Design for a Constitutional Republic*, David F. Epstein's *The Political Theory of* The Federalist, Paul Eidelberg's *The Philosophy of the American Constitution*, Gottfried Dietze's *The Federalist: A Classic on Federalism and Free Government*, and Morton White's *Philosophy,* The Federalist, *and the Constitution*. Books on Hamilton's political economy and economic ideas include Louis M. Hacker's *Alexander Hamilton in the American Tradition*, Peter McNamara's *Political Economy and Statesmanship: Smith, Hamilton, and the Foundation of the Commercial Republic*, and Michael D. Chan's *Aristotle and Hamilton on Commerce and Statesmanship*. Stanley Elkins and Eric McKitrick's *The Age of Federalism: The Early American Republic, 1788–1800* covers the seminal events in Hamilton's tenure as treasury secretary.

Reviews of Hamiltonian literature include Stanley D. Rose, "Alexander Hamilton and the Historians" in the *Vanderbilt Law Review* (11 [1957–58]: 853–87), and Jacob E. Cooke, ed., *Alexander Hamilton: A Profile* ([New York: Hill and Wang, 1967]: vii–xxvi).

INDEX

Morris, Gouverneur, 53, 125
Morris, Richard B., 142–43
Morris, Robert, 30, 96
Morristown, New Jersey, 16, 32
Munro, William Bennett, 99

Napoleon, 126, 153, 178–79
Napoleonic Wars, 32
National bank, 18, 97, 152, 158, 196,
  198; AH's economic policies and,
  31, 62, 188, 192–93, 199, 202, 204,
  210–11; AH's loose constructionism and, 21, 143–46, 243; energetic
  government and, 259n32; Jefferson
  and Madison on, 23, 216–17,
  266n69; *McCulloch v. Maryland*
  and, 3; as a mixed good, 62
National debt, 1, 4, 62, 158, 190, 192,
  202–3, 206, 213
National defense, 40, 102, 188, 192,
  205
National Gazette, 35
National security, 3, 31, 100, 154, 169,
  172, 206, 229
Nationalism, 14–15, 21, 65–66, 68,
  182–86, 212–13, 257n52, 261n54
Natural aristocracy, 5, 24, 53–54, 70
Natural inequality, 54, 233
Naturalism, 29, 48
Natural law, 51, 60–61, 74, 97, 116,
  184, 255n31, 255n33, 255n35, 258n19
Natural rights, 12, 56, 60–61, 104–5,
  129, 196, 198, 215, 258n19
Necessary and proper clause, the,
  142, 144–45, 243
Necker, Jacques, 44, 194–95, 239,
  272n9
Neutrality, 18–19, 31–32, 155–56, 159–63,
  165–66, 169, 224
Neutrality proclamation, 18–19, 32,
  159–64, 166
Nevis, 26, 63
Newburgh conspiracy, 30
New Deal, 186, 191
New Hampshire, 101, 223
New Jersey Plan, 79, 122–23, 131

Newman, Paul Douglass, 231–32,
  275n40
New Orleans, 152, 178
Newton, Isaac, 39, 125
New York: AH as delegate from,
  31, 36; executive power in, 135,
  139–40; politics of, 96; ratification
  of Constitution by, 5, 31, 53, 70,
  76, 103, 229; Sears's Raid and,
  12–14; slavery and, 235; treatment
  of Loyalists in, 73, 83, 116, 156–57;
  Vermont crisis and, 157–58
New-Yorker Gazetteer, 12
New York Evening Post, 31
New-York Journal, 84
New York Society for the Manumis-
  sion of Slaves, 235
New York State Assembly, 31
North America, 16, 25, 27, 151, 155–56,
  165, 178, 181, 188, 235

"Opinion on the Constitutionality of
  a National Bank" (Jefferson), 216
Orwell, George, 184

"Pacificus," (AH pseudonym), 19,
  23, 32, 61, 145, 148, 160, 163–64,
  224, 254n28, 270n41
Paine, Thomas, political theory of,
  contrasted to AH's, 6–7, 14,
  39–40, 53, 56–57, 61, 72, 82, 100,
  118–19, 131, 154, 217, 220–21, 223,
  248n15, 258n11, 268n5
Parliament, British, 73, 104, 109, 159
Passions, the: Burke on, 196; democratic, 11, 72–73, 75–76, 87, 92,
  97, 116, 121, 133–34, 138, 173, 241;
  human nature and, 20, 51–53, 69,
  71–72, 154–55, 194, 211, 233, 263n36;
  Hume on, 71, 193; leadership and,
  84, 91, 182; revolutionary, 13, 72,
  181; subordination to reason, 35,
  62, 72, 160, 171, 180
Patriotism, 17, 45, 51, 72, 183–84,
  257n52
Patriots, American, 12, 14